Moreton Morrell Site

MARKET RESEARCH in PRACTICE

MARKET RESEARCH IN PRACTICE SERIES

Published in association with The Market Research Society
Consultant Editors: David Barr and Robin J Birn

Kogan Page has joined forces with The Market Research Society (MRS) to publish this unique series which is designed specifically to cover the latest developments in market research thinking and practice. Taking a practical, action-oriented approach, and focused on established 'need to know' subjects, the series will reflect the role of market research in the international business environment. This series will concentrate on developing practical texts on:

■ how to use, act on and follow up research;
■ research techniques and best practice.

Great effort has been made to ensure that each title is international in both content and approach and where appropriate, European, US and international case studies have been used comparatively to ensure that each title provides readers with models for research relevant to their own countries.

Overall the series will produce a body of work that will enhance international awareness of the MRS and improve knowledge of its Code of Conduct and guidelines on best practice in market research.

Other titles in the series:

The Effective Use of Market Research, Robin J Birn
Market Intelligence: How and Why Organizations Use Market Research, Martin
    Callingham

Forthcoming titles:

Questionnaire Design
Business to Business Market Research
Consumer Insight

To obtain further information, please contact the publisher at the address below:

Kogan Page Ltd
120 Pentonville Road
London N1 9JN
Tel: 020 7278 0433
www.kogan-page.co.uk

MARKET RESEARCH IN PRACTICE

MARKET RESEARCH in PRACTICE

A GUIDE TO THE BASICS

**PAUL HAGUE, NICK HAGUE
& CAROL-ANN MORGAN**

**KOGAN
PAGE**

London & Sterling, VA

Publisher's note

Every possible effort has been made to ensure that the information contained in this book is accurate at the time of going to press, and the publishers and authors cannot accept responsibility for any errors or omissions, however caused. No responsibility for loss or damage occasioned to any person acting, or refraining from action, as a result of the material in this publication can be accepted by the editor, the publisher or any of the authors.

First published in Great Britain and the United States in 2004 by Kogan Page Limited

Reprinted 2004

120 Pentonville Road
London N1 9JN
United Kingdom
www.kogan-page.co.uk

22883 Quicksilver Drive
Sterling VA 20166-2012
USA

© Paul Hague, Nick Hague and Carol-Ann Morgan, 2004

The right of Paul Hague, Nick Hague and Carol-Ann Morgan to be identified as the authors of this work has been asserted by them in accordance with the Copyright, Designs and Patents Act 1988.

ISBN 0 7494 4180 1

British Library Cataloguing-in-Publication Data

A CIP record for this book is available from the British Library.

Library of Congress Cataloging-in-Publication Data

Hague, Paul N.
  Market research in practice: a guide to the basics/Paul Hague, Nick Hague and Carol-Ann Morgan.
    p. cm.
  Includes bibliographical references and index.
  ISBN 0-7494-4180-1
  1. Marketing research. I. Hague, Nick, 1974- II. Morgan, Carol-Ann, 1958- III. Title.
  HF5415.2.H253 2004
  658.8'3--dc22

2004002449

Typeset by Datamatics Technologies Ltd, Mumbai, India
Printed and bound in Great Britain by Creative Print and Design (Wales), Ebbw Vale

Contents

The Market Research Society

With over 8,000 members in more than 50 countries, The Market Research Society (MRS) is the world's largest international membership organization for professional researchers and others engaged in (or interested in) market, social and opinion research.

It has a diverse membership of individual researchers within agencies, independent consultancies, client-side organisations, and the academic community – at all levels of seniority and in all job functions.

All MRS members agree to comply with the MRS Code of Conduct (see Appendix), which is supported by the Codeline advisory service and a range of specialist guidelines on best practice.

MRS offers various qualifications and membership grades, as well as training and professional development resources to support these. It is the official awarding body in the UK for vocational qualifications in market research.

MRS is a major supplier of publications and information services, conferences and seminars, and many other meeting and networking opportunities for researchers.

MRS is 'the voice of the profession' in its media relations and public affairs activities on behalf of professional research practitioners, and aims to achieve the most favourable climate of opinion and legislative environment for research.

The Market Research Society (Limited by Guarantee) Company Number 518685

Company Information: Registered office and business address:
15 Northburgh Street, London EC1V OJR
Telephone: 020 7490 4911
Fax: 020 7490 0608
e-mail: info@marketresearch.org.uk
Web site: www.mrs.org.uk

The editorial board

CONSULTANT EDITORS

David Barr has been Director General of The Market Research Society since July 1997. He previously spent over 25 years in business information services and publishing. He has held management positions with Xerox Publishing Group, the British Tourist Authority and Reed International plc. His experience of market research is therefore all on the client side, having commissioned many projects for NPD and M&A purposes. A graduate of Glasgow and Sheffield Universities, David Barr is a Member of the Chartered Management Institute and a Fellow of The Royal Society of Arts.

Robin J Birn has been a marketing and market research practitioner for over 25 years. In 1985 he set up Strategy, Research and Action Ltd, which is now the largest international market research company for the map, atlas and travel guide sector, and the book industry. He is a Fellow of The Market Research Society and is also the editor of *The International Handbook of Market Research Techniques*.

ADVISORY MEMBERS

Martin Callingham was formerly Group Market Research Director at Whitbread, where he ran the Market Research department for 20 years and was a non-executive director of the company's German restaurant chain for more than 10 years. Martin has also played his part in the market research world. Apart from being on many committees of the MRS, of which he is a Fellow, he was Chairman of the Association of Users of Research (AURA), has been a council member of ESOMAR, and has presented widely, winning the David Winton Award in 2001 at the MRS Conference.

Nigel Culkin is a Fellow of the Market Research Society and member of its Professional Development Advisory Board. He has been a full member since 1982. He has been in academia since 1991 and is currently Deputy Director, Commercial Development at the University of Hertfordshire, where he is responsible for activities that develop a culture of entrepreneurism and innovation among staff and students. He is Chair of the University's Film Industry Research Group (FiRG), supervisor to a number of research students and regular contributor to the media on the creative industries.

Professor Merlin Stone is Business Research Leader with IBM's Business Consulting Services, where he works on business research, consulting and marketing with IBM's clients, partners and universities. He runs the IBM Marketing Transformation Group, a network of clients, marketing agencies, consultancies and business partners, focusing on changing marketing. He is a director of QCi Ltd., an Ogilvy One company. Merlin is IBM Professor of Relationship Marketing at Bristol Business School. He has written many articles and 25 books on marketing and customer service, including *Up Close and Personal: CRM @ Work, Customer Relationship Marketing, Successful Customer Relationship Marketing, CRM in Financial Services* and *The Customer Management Scorecard,* all published by Kogan Page, and *The Definitive Guide to Direct and Interactive Marketing,* published by Financial Times-Pitman. He is a Founder Fellow of the Institute of Direct Marketing and a Fellow of the Chartered Institute of Marketing.

Paul Szwarc began his career as a market researcher at the Co-operative Wholesale Society (CWS) Ltd in Manchester in 1975. Since then he has worked at Burke Market Research (Canada), American Express Europe, IPSOS RSL, International Masters Publishers Ltd and PSI Global prior to joining the Network Research board as a director in October 2000.

Over the past few years Paul has specialized on the consumer financial sector, directing multi-country projects on customer loyalty and retention, new product/service development, and employee satisfaction in the UK, European and North American markets. Paul is a full member of The Market Research Society. He has presented papers at a number of MRS and ESOMAR seminars and training courses.

Preface

The world of market research is not getting any simpler. Surveys nowadays cover many countries and require researchers to accommodate different languages and cultures. Data are no longer presented simply and factually but are worked to death by statistical tools. Wherever possible they are squeezed into business models in an attempt to make more sense of the findings. The Web has 2 billion pages of facts, figures, and stuff and nonsense. Paradoxically this makes life more difficult as we seek the one nugget of information that eludes us. In this increasingly complex world, we need market research more than ever.

Our book is an introduction to market research. In one volume we offer the reader a taste of the whole process from planning a project, executing it, through to analysis and presenting the findings. It is aimed at students who need to understand the theory of the subject as well as people who want to carry out or manage their own surveys. Essentially it is a practical book, hence its title. In order to enliven the subject, the book is laced with examples of studies we have carried out over the last 30 years. This brings us to our first acknowledgement. Between us we have worked on a few thousand projects, each one paid for by a client. A typical project costs an amount equal in value to a new medium-sized saloon car. Commissioning market research is like buying a pig in a poke – the quality of the job is only evident when it is complete. We are ever grateful for these commissions. They are a supreme vote of confidence. They provide a livelihood. Not least they have enabled us to learn our craft.

One thing has remained the same over the years and that is the axiom: good market research is about asking the right question of the right person. In order to do this we need a field force. Market research interviewers use our questionnaires day in and day out. Sometimes these questionnaires are less than perfect – but the interviewers make them work for us. These people are not in the spotlight. When we present the findings and bathe in the spotlight of a successful conclusion (hopefully), these stalwarts have moved on and their heads are down on the next survey. The data processing staff, whose timetable was squeezed because the project was running late, do not have time to draw breath as they too are working on their next screamingly urgent deadline. These 'support' staff are the unsung heroines and heroes of market research, and we salute them. We especially thank Ann Kemp, a colleague who has recently retired for a well-earned rest after working for 30 years as a superb controller of our interviewing force.

Market research is almost always a team effort. Most projects involve a small battalion of people. Indeed, this book is an example of team work. For a start, we are three authors. We thank the steering team from The Market Research Society that gave birth to the idea of the book and our editor, Emily Steel of Kogan Page, for expertly and patiently keeping the timetable on track. We are also indebted to Natalie Marshall, a fellow research executive, who prepared the bibliography.

However, the real help as always comes from our patient families who have to suffer parents and partners who seldom come home early. Ray, Josh, Frankie and Christine – thank you for waiting for us.

Finally, our greatest debt goes to you, the reader, without which there would be no market for our scribblings. Our hope is that we stimulate you to want to learn more about this fascinating, frustrating and most rewarding subject that occupies our life.

1 Introduction

WHO NEEDS MARKET RESEARCH?

You are walking through a farmers market where the stalls are full of plump produce. The stallholders have their wares positioned so that they are displayed to best advantage. Some are shouting to catch your attention. There are price tickets clearly displaying the cost of each item. It is busy and very noisy. Business is brisk and sellers and buyers seem to be in perfect harmony — each understands the other. It is highly unlikely that any of the stallholders have ever read a market research textbook, designed a questionnaire or carried out a survey; but they certainly do carry out market research.

Customers comment on the produce and the stallholders listen and respond, adjusting the next day's or week's stock. Each looks at the others' prices and knows instantly if they are out of line. And if they are, a quick adjustment is made. The stallholders watch and listen to each other to see how effective they are at catching the attention of the crowd, and if someone has a good idea, others quickly copy it. The stallholders' antennae are constantly monitoring the market because if they were not, they would soon be out of business.

You are whisked off now to the offices of a global company in Philadelphia. The company has plants in 30 different countries and it employs 30,000 people. It sells directly to 5,000 customers and services hundreds of thousands of others through 500 distributors. How does the boss of this company stay in tune with its market?

First, he or she has internal sources. Managers of each territory make their reports. The functional heads compile data on sales, finance and production. And whenever time allows, the boss does his/her own tour. But the position is no way as clear as it is to the stallholder. There are conflicting views from staff. Cultural differences around the world blur the understanding. Customers are distanced by distributors and there are few opportunities for them to express their opinion. What is more, unlike the stallholder who can quickly make adjustments to changing conditions, it takes an army of people weeks and months to make changes in the global company. The cost of a wrong decision is a fall in sales and profitability, resulting in the loss of thousands of jobs and millions of dollars off the share price. This company cannot rely on its antennae to tell it what is going on, it needs a process.

NEW ROLES FOR MARKET RESEARCH

Market researchers have a tool kit made up of desk research, telephone interviews, face-to-face interviews, self-completion questionnaires, focus groups and observation. They employ special techniques for selecting samples and analysing the data. Much of this book is devoted to these subjects, explaining how each works and how to do your own market research. However, it is equally important to understand what market research is for — why it is carried out. It is helpful, therefore, before we get into the tool kit, to consider the role of market research in decision making as this provides a context for the later discussions of methods and techniques.

We should begin this contextual understanding by reflecting on how young is the subject of formal market research and how and why it started.

Formalized market research had its origins in the United States in the 1930s when the competition between large corporations required a closer fix on customers' needs and buying habits. There was distrust that direct questioning would produce dishonest answers and so the first commercial market research relied heavily on observation. The number of baked bean tins were counted on the shelves of supermarkets at the beginning and end of a period, and account was taken of the movement of the inventory. The audit was born. Famous market research companies such as Nielsen and Attwood in the United States and Audits of Great Britain (AGB) emerged. For the first time, managers had objective, accurate data on their sales, the size of the market, trends and their competitors' shares.

In the 1950s and 1960s business competition intensified and market researchers, building on the experience of social researchers, used sample surveys with questionnaires to obtain attitudinal data. The market research interview was accepted as the main vehicle for collecting information and survey companies blossomed. For the first time, managers had objective and systematically collected data to help them understand what people were doing with or thinking about their products.

In the 1970s and 1980s attitudinal research moved to a different level and surveys were developed to track customer satisfaction.

In the last few years computing power has become cheaper and more powerful and the emphasis has turned to 'squeezing' data for more insights using modelling such as factor and cluster analysis for segmentation, conjoint analysis for pricing decisions, data fusion to fill in gaps of missing data and geomapping to find best locations for retailing or distribution.

THE EFFECT OF REGIONAL CULTURE ON THE USE OF MARKET RESEARCH

Managers are always making decisions based on their experience, the facts known to them internally and their intuition. Perhaps the way forward is obvious, or the size of the decision does not merit a huge spend on fact finding. Maybe action is required today and there is no time for formalized research even though it would be welcome. There is nothing wrong with intuition and 'common' sense and it is a natural part of decision making in business. However, where the decisions require large financial resources and where the costs of failure are high, there is a need for decision making based on robust and reliable data. As we have already pointed out, companies operating in large and international markets that are changing apace cannot rely on anecdotal and intuitive approaches to decision making. The purpose of market research is to reduce business risk.

It is perhaps surprising that major investments and strategic decisions are still made without adequate information. The reasons for this may include some professional failures on the part of market research

3

practitioners such as an inability or unwillingness to be involved in decision making, as well as differences in corporate cultures. In the United States and northwest Europe, market research is almost standard practice as an aid to making large decisions. However in southern Europe, much of Asia and the developing world, market research is used less and there is more reliance on hunch and intuition. This is partly historical in that market research is less established and still finding its feet in these regions. It may also be because of cultural diffidence and suspicion about a methodology that people believe may not be a reliable means of getting to the heart of the matter.

THE USE OF MARKET RESEARCH IN BUSINESS MODELS AND FRAMEWORKS

Almost all the frameworks that help us understand our businesses and markets require data. Market research is therefore a vital component in many of the marketing paradigms. In Igor Ansoff's products and markets matrix there are four business situations depending on whether the market we are addressing is new or one that is known to us, and whether the product/service we are selling is new or in our existing portfolio (see Figure 1.1). Market research has a role in all four situations.

	Existing Markets	New Markets
New Products	Market research can show the likelihood of adoption of new products	Market research can show unmet needs and provide an understanding of unfamiliar markets
Existing Products	Market research can measure customer satisfaction to find out how to maintain a competitive edge	Market research can find new territories for products or services

Figure 1.1 *Ansoff and market research*

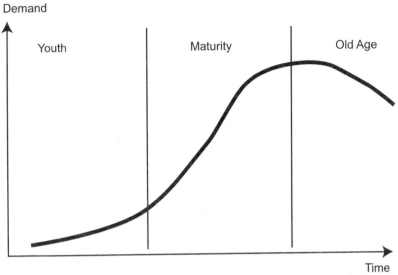

Demand

Youth

Maturity

Old Age

Time

Market research explores the unmet needs for the new product and helps estimate the likely demand. It could be used to set prices and shape the specification of the product

Market research shows how to build a brand and a competitive edge. Customer satisfaction studies point to strengths that can be built upon and weaknesses that can be rectified

Market research shows ways of rejuvenating the product, perhaps by incorporating new features or finding new markets

Figure 1.2 *Market research in the product/service life cycle*

In Theodore Levitt's life cycle, market research plays an important role at each of the stages (see Figure 1.2).

The four Ps (product, price, place and promotion) are the pillars of marketing. Each requires market research to help understand how these subjects work (see Figure 1.3).

In this book the emphasis is on market research for business decisions. However market research is also widely used in opinion polls (for political marketing), social issues and policy making and personnel management (for example, employee attitude surveys).

Product	Price
Market research can test attitudes to products by describing them or showing them in focus groups, hall tests, or placing them in the home and work place	Pricing research can vary from simple questions such as 'How likely or unlikely are you to buy at this price?' through to more sophisticated trade-off questions using conjoint analysis
Place This is the distribution part of the marketing equation and market research can help plan the most effective route to market	**Promotion** Market research can help in all aspects of promotion from developing ideas for the adverts through to testing which advert is most effective

Figure 1.3   *Market research in the four Ps*

CONSUMER AND BUSINESS-TO-BUSINESS MARKET RESEARCH

The most fundamental division of markets is between those involving members of the general public and people buying or specifying on behalf of another organization such as a business.

In consumer markets, the number of potential buyers of a product is often a significant proportion of a total population running into millions. Techniques used to research these markets include quantitative methods based on rigorous sampling as well as qualitative techniques that explore complex consumer perceptions and motivations. Consumer markets can be further subdivided between FMCGs (fast moving consumer goods — food and similar frequent purchases) and other markets — media, travel and leisure, financial, consumer durables and so on. Modern marketing concepts and market research largely grew up in FMCG markets and this sector remains the area where most commercial market research is carried out. Consumer markets — FMCGs in particular — are also retail markets, and anyone marketing through retail distribution needs to know as much about what is happening in the shops as amongst final consumers. What is happening at the store level is, therefore, a major concern and is the information output of some of the largest continuous market research programmes (for example, by organizations such as Nielsen).

Business-to-business market research employs the same techniques but in different ways. Many business-to-business markets are characterized by a much smaller population to survey, many times measured in hundreds or thousands rather than the consumer millions. What is more, the business-to-business markets are frequently very variable, made up of companies in different industries and with huge differences in size. A researcher may be looking at the market for office equipment and face a sample that could include General Motors and a 'Mom and Pop' organization providing some form of services to the local community.

Within the businesses there are often complex groups involved in influencing the buying decision (the DMU or decision making unit). The obvious groups, such as procurement, place the orders but technical and production departments may set a specification and financial departments impose budgets.

In these complex business-to-business markets with smaller and more varied populations and with tangled decision making units, we need different research methods. Sample sizes are smaller in number and the researcher may be leaning as much on judgement and interpretation as on the rigor of the method.

Markets (whether consumer or business-to-business) are not confined to single countries. Increasingly marketing is international with global brands and marketing programmes. International companies may require their market research to cover North America, Europe and Asia in the same survey. International research programmes are logistically more complex and commonly require access to more extensive resources than may be required for domestic-only research. However, as we discuss in Chapter 3, there are many sources of secondary data that can be readily accessed on international markets.

THE SCOPE OF MARKET RESEARCH INFORMATION

In consumer and business-to-business markets, the decisions that research is guiding tend to be similar. Whether the product is soap powder or servo motors, research could cover subjects such as the product specification and its relation to consumer needs and require-ments, branding, pricing, distribution methods, advertising support, market definition and segmentation, forecast sales levels and so on. Each of these decisions requires information from the market to reduce business risk. Common information requirements met through market research are listed below although this is by no means exhaustive and can of course be classified in different ways. Also no single research commission would cover all or even most areas; as argued later, research that is focused and restricted to what is really crucial to the decision, is more likely to be effective.

The applications for market research in Table 1.1 are not exhaustive. Market research can specifically be used to assess the competition, to determine employee satisfaction, to explore the values of a brand, to determine readership, examine sources of purchase — indeed it can be used to obtain a deeper understanding of the dozens of marketing-related decisions faced in business every day. Whether or not it is used depends on the financial implications of the decision and the speed with which a result is required. A decision linked to an investment of a small number of dollars and where the results are required tomorrow is less likely to be researched than one that has massive financial ram-ifications and where time is available to think about it.

Although information is potentially a requirement in all markets, the characteristics of specific markets mean that there is considerable variation in the detailed coverage sought in each case. Market segmen-tation, for example, means something rather different for FMCGs than for engineering components. Similarly, in industrial markets there is often a greater need for understanding the structure of suppliers and their organization, while in consumer markets branding issues may be of greater concern.

QUANTITATIVE AND QUALITATIVE RESEARCH

One important classification of market research information, regardless of the type of market, is between quantitative and qualitative. Quantitative research is concerned with the measurement of a market and can include the calculation of market size, the size of market seg-ments, brand shares, purchase frequencies, awareness measures of

Table 1.1 *Information that can be obtained through market research*

Market size and structure	Methods used to assess market size and structure
The value of the market in currency value and units sold each year	Published market research reports desk research
The historical trends in size of the market	Market surveys aimed at calculating consumption and brands purchased
The key consuming segments of the market	
The competition and its shares	
The route to market	
Use of and attitude to products	**Methods used to assess use and attitudes**
Awareness of suppliers	Quantitative surveys carried out by telephone, mail/Internet, face to face
Attitudes to suppliers	Focus groups
Attitudes to products	
Volume and frequency of purchases	
Customer satisfaction	**Methods used to assess customer satisfaction**
Ratings of customers (and sometimes potential customers) to show what they think is important in influencing their buying decision and how satisfied they are with their supplier on each issue	Quantitative surveys carried out by telephone, mail/Internet, face to face
Promotion effectiveness	**Methods used to assess promotion effectiveness**
Key messages for campaigns	Focus groups
Effectiveness of adverts and promotions	Face to face interviewing Pre and post quantitative surveys
Brand impact	**Methods used to assess brand impact**
Awareness of brands	Focus groups
Values attached to brands	Telephone interviewing

Table 1.1 *Continued*

The influence of brands in the purchasing decision	Face to face interviewing
Pricing effectiveness	**Methods used to assess pricing effectiveness**
Optimum prices	Market research in test markets
Price values attached to features of the offer	Trade-off analysis using conjoint techniques
Product tests/concepts	**Methods used to assess products**
Likelihood of purchasing different products	Hall tests
Attitudes to products	Focus groups
Attitudes to new concepts	Quantitative research
Unmet needs identification	
Segmentation	**Methods used to assess segmentation**
Opportunities for segmentation based on demographics, behaviour or needs	Quantitative surveys with factor and cluster analysis

brands, distribution levels and so on. Such quantitative data is required to some level of accuracy (though not in all cases to very high levels) and the methods used must be capable of achieving this. In consumer markets at least, quantitative information is almost always based on extrapolating from a sample to the general population or market, and the research design and particularly the sampling methods must be sufficiently rigorous to allow this.

Qualitative information is rather harder to define but the emphasis is on 'understanding' rather than simple measurement — advert A is recalled better than advert B (quantitative information), but how does A work as an advert and why is it more effective than B? Much qualitative research is concerned with empathizing with the consumer and establishing the meanings he or she attaches to products, brands and other marketing objects. Another focus is motivation. For example, why does one product rather than another meet consumer needs and what are these needs that are being met? Qualitative research is conducted amongst a sample, but in this case usually a small one, since there is no attempt to extrapolate to the total population. In the case of attitudes to brands, for example, qualitative research may determine that there is a specific view held about the brand, whereas quantitative research would tell us what proportion holds that view.

Quantitative and qualitative research are often complementary, and in a research design both may feature. The qualitative element frequently takes place at the front end of the study, exploring values that need measuring in the subsequent quantitative phase. The 'qual' research may offer a diagnostic understanding of what is wrong while the 'quant' research provides hard data across different respondent groups that can lead to specific recommendations with measures that can be used as controls to determine the effectiveness of actions.

THE MARKET RESEARCH PROCESS

The collection of any facts relevant to a marketing decision can be considered as market research. However, we are concerned in this book with something rather more than an occasional and haphazard use of snippets. We suggest a definition of market research to be as follows: *the systematic collection, analysis and interpretation of information relevant to marketing decisions.*

In our definition, the word 'systematic' does not necessarily imply that market research is a scientific discipline, as we often use procedures such as observation and focus group research that are long on interpretation and short on mathematics. In this respect market research is closer to the social sciences than those such as physics that can be more precise about the laws of nature.

Market research can be carried out as a one-off project to meet a specific requirement, in which case it is called ad hoc research, or it can involve continuous or regular tracking such as the monitoring of the market share held by a product or brand. The purposes for which ad hoc or for that matter continuous research are carried out are enormously diverse, but the process followed in virtually any ad hoc (and in principle most continuous) projects is as illustrated in Figure 1.4.

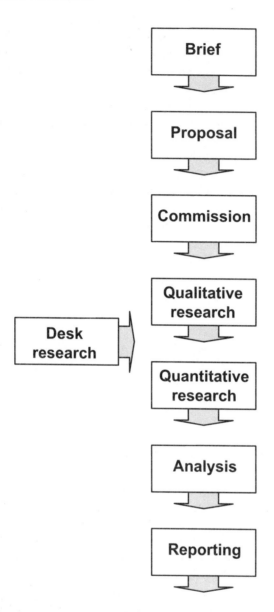

Figure 1.4   *The market research process*

The starting point of any market research project is to have a brief — a background to the problem or the opportunity, and statement of what information is required in order to make a decision. It is especially true in market research that a problem well defined is a problem half solved, as this leads naturally to the definition of the objectives of the survey — what the work is meant to achieve. If this is not done adequately — too often it is not — the effort put into the work will be wasted. Objectives are a statement of what the research will be used for and what specific items of information are being sought.

A plan of how this objective is to be met and how the information is to be obtained is then required. This is the proposal or research design, and it will cover the use of both qualitative and quantitative methods, detailing who will be interviewed, what number and whether this will be by face-to-face, telephone or self-completion. The resources needed (especially the money) and the timescale are also important at this planning stage. The planning of a market research project is the subject of Chapter 2.

Fieldwork or data collection is the visible part of market research. Fieldwork normally involves interviewing and completing a questionnaire for each individual or organization in the sample. This may be numbered in tens, hundreds or even thousands. The individual questionnaires and responses are usually of little or no interest; what is required is an aggregation of the whole sample or perhaps groupings within that sample. This larger picture is obtained by analysing the data using proprietary software that allows cross-cuts of the data.

Once an analysis and aggregation of the data has been produced it needs interpreting and presenting in a meaningful way so that the decision maker can act on the results. This is the reporting stage of the process, and may involve the researcher making recommendations. Data analysis is discussed in Chapter 13 and reporting is the subject of Chapter 14.

THE ORGANIZATION OF MARKET RESEARCH

There are limits to what can be achieved by a lone market researcher. The researcher can certainly carry out desk research, and it is arguable that someone working inside a client organization is the best person to do this (see Chapter 3). The insider will be able to interpret the data far better than an outsider. A market researcher on his or her own could also send out an e-based questionnaire to a sample of customers and analyse the returns (see Chapter 12). However, most market research requires fieldwork of some kind or another and logistics, budgets and the need to meet timetables requires some division of labour and a team approach. Fieldwork options are an important part of the market research process, and we devote a good deal of space to them in this book. They are discussed in detail in Chapters 4 (focus groups), 5 (depth interviews), 9 (face-to-face interviewing), 10 (telephone interviewing) and 11 (self-completion questionnaires).

The tasks covered in the outline of the market research process can be rather crudely divided between 'thinking 'and 'doing'. Thinking type tasks include planning the research, selecting an appropriate research design, developing questionnaires and similar tools, deciding how the data needs analysing and interpreting, and communicating the results. These tasks require professional level skills and a background in the body of theory underpinning market research.[1] However, unlike the doing parts of the process, a large team is not usually required for these parts of the process; in many projects the work can be well handled by one person.

The two main doing parts of research are data collection and data analysis. Some types of data collection (for instance, focus group moderation) are best carried out by professional-level staff, but in most cases this would be impractical or unduly expensive since quite sizeable teams are required for the data collection element of even average-sized projects. Consider, for example, a quantitative study of a consumer market in which it is decided that 1,000 face-to-face interviews are required with a nationally representative sample. It may well be decided to plan this as a programme of 50 interviews around 20 sampling points spread around the country. The costs and time of travel, points immediately to the need for a team of 20 interviewers (one per point). To keep the fieldwork within an acceptable timetable and to avoid interviewer fatigue it will be more common to use two to four interviewers per sampling point — 40 to 80 interviewers in total for an 'average' job. These interviewers need to be trained in gaining and carrying out interviews but there is no reason why they should also be proficient in other parts of the process. In practice this is how most market research fieldwork is successfully carried out — by teams of trained but not professional-level staff.

Data processing is the area of market research where information technology has had the longest-standing impact (IT is now also spreading to other parts of the process, including data collection). The data is often entered into computers at the time of the interview by the interviewers, who use laptops in face-to-face interviews (CAPI — computer aided personal interviewing) or desktops in telephone interviews (CATI — computer aided telephone interviewing). Not all data is entered directly as the interview is carried out, some is captured on paper questionnaires and transferred to computers at a later time by 'coding' and 'data entry' staff. Again, therefore, the professional researcher needs the assistance of a sizeable team in order to carry out the work effectively. Also, the IT aspect of data processing has brought in new specialists ('spec writers') into the market research industry and extended the team required for many types of project.

The complicated logistics required to carry out surveys means that this has to be outsourced to specialized agencies. In-house research staff act as interfaces with other departments in their organization, helping write the specifications for research and evaluating tenders and controlling the projects. In the mature economies of the western world there are hundreds of market research suppliers ranging from small firms offering specialist services of focus group moderation or statistical modelling through to the international giants with offices across the globe.

Possibly one consequence of the organizational split between market research suppliers (agencies) and clients (the companies making the marketing decisions) is that market research does not realize its full potential in contributing to decision making. The researcher, however experienced and skilled, is often remote and a stranger to those making decisions. He or she is also insulated from other factors which may need to be taken account of in decision making — production capabilities, finance, wider corporate goals and so on. In addition, rightly or wrongly, market researchers are often seen as backroom people; valuable in a narrow field but not capable of taking the broader view or contributing to long-term strategy. This is a role that is changing as researchers have the advantage of drawing on experience in the many markets they examine and because they now have access to a much more powerful arsenal of statistical tools that aid their interpretation.

SUMMARY

Market research is the systematic collection, analysis and interpretation of information relevant to marketing decisions. The industry was spawned in the United States in the 1930s and it has been widely embraced by large companies in most of North America and Europe. Companies that use business models and frameworks in their marketing planning almost always need market research.

The applications for market research have grown over the years, and increasingly market researchers use modelling to improve the relevance of their data. The most common applications for market research are to show the market size and shares of suppliers, to measure use and attitudes to products, to assess customer satisfaction and loyalty, to measure the effectiveness of promotions, to determine optimum pricing strategies, brand influence and to determine effective segmentation strategies.

There are two important schools in market research — qualitative and quantitative. Qualitative research is often used as a precursor to a larger study and it provides diagnostic data and insights using focus groups and depth interviews. Quantitative research is concerned with larger numbers of interviews, 200 at least and sometimes 1,000 to 2,000 or more. These numbers provide measures of behaviour and attitudes that represent the larger market from which the sample has been drawn.

The market research process begins with a definition of the problem — the brief. This is prepared by the sponsor of the research and it is converted into a proposal by the market researchers. The proposal shows the design of the study which often involves input from desk research, and fieldwork made up of qualitative and quantitative methods. Analysis and reporting concludes the project.

Most market research programmes involve a good deal of labour for the interviewing and analysis. For this reason, large surveys have to be carried out by specialist market research agencies organized to carry out the many tasks.

2 Market research design

HOW IDEAS ARISE FOR MARKET RESEARCH

How do ideas for market research arise? First of all, someone has to know something about the capabilities of market research before he or she can think of it as a possible solution. Most people know something about market research in a general sense. They know it can be used to find out how many people do something or think something. But do they fully appreciate that it can be used to work out how much people are prepared to pay for each feature of a product? Do they know that you can work out the importance of issues that influence customer satisfaction without asking the customer how important each issue is? If you don't know what something can do, it is fully understandable that it may not come to mind.

Furthermore, there are very few processes in business that say 'Before we make that decision, we must carry out market research'. The decision to do so is entirely judgemental. The manager faces a problem or has an idea and at some stage he or she may (or may not) think this is a candidate for market research.

Now it is significant that we have suggested that the person that has the idea for the research is a manager. After all, it is managers who make decisions, and remember that market research is there to reduce

Table 2.1 *The gestation period for a market research idea*

What happens	Idea	Internal debate	External debate	Information collection
Who generates it	From a manager about an idea or problem	Between the manager and his or her managing director, and between the manager and a market research manager	Manager or market research manager presents problem to agencies for their suggested solutions	Agency is selected and carries out the work
How long does it take	A few days and often a week or a month	A week and more often a few weeks	A week or two	Four to 12 weeks

business risk in decision making. This problem or idea usually gestates and develops before it is brought to the attention of the market research agency that is challenged with finding the information. On its way, the idea may well have been bounced between people, including an internal market research manager who helps scope the idea in a way that the agency can best deal with. The point is this, it may well be weeks and sometimes months before the idea or problem is finally put before the agency and what was reasonably urgent then, is desperately urgent now. Time may determine the research solution simply because there is not much of it and there is a limit to what can be done in the period. Therefore it is not surprising that the agencies at the end of the line are squeezed to work quickly.

MARKET RESEARCH SUPPLIERS

There is a limit to how much market research can be carried out by a company that has a need for information. Surveys usually involve a small army of people who design the questionnaire, ask the questions, enter the data on to computers, run the analysis and interpret the results. An industry has grown up to supply these services.

The market research industry is service-oriented and, like many service industries, it is fragmented, with dozens if not hundreds of suppliers. Some of these suppliers are specialists, offering fieldwork only. Others are specialists in certain types of work – such as qualitative research or studies of the chemical industry. Yet others are generalists that can handle a complete cross-section of work over a wide range of markets.

Ad hoc research is the mainstay of the large majority of agencies. Projects are carried out for individual clients and designed as one-offs to meet specific needs and objectives. Because the ad hoc research agencies work closely with clients, and involve themselves in the full background to the research requirement, their service shades into management consultancy.

Anyone new to market research always wants to know what ad hoc research costs. The costs could range extremely widely, depending on the number of interviews, who they are with, how they are carried out, and in which countries. However, as a rough indication, the starting level for complete projects is around the US $10,000 mark and can go up to six figures, though many are in the US $25,000 to US $80,000 range.

An excellent starting point for finding a market research agency is through one of the trade associations in each country that represents the market research industry (for example, the Market Research Society of the United Kingdom or the American Marketing Association, the Market Research Association or the American Association Of Public Opinion Research). The best source of market research companies from around the world can be found on the ESOMAR Web site (http://www.esomar.org/), which offers an up-to-date directory of 1,500 research organizations that can be searched, online.

THE MARKET RESEARCH BRIEF – A STATEMENT OF THE PROBLEM

A research brief is a statement from the sponsor setting out the objectives and background to the case in sufficient detail to enable the researcher to plan an appropriate study. As a general rule, a market research study is only as good as the brief. The brief is important to the researcher: it educates and influences the choice of method. It gives the objective to which the project is geared.

The brief is no less important for the researcher working in-house than for the agency. Research carried out by company personnel is frequently treated less stringently than when there is a price tag. The in-house researcher does, however, have the benefit of close and constant access to other internal staff able to fill in on background and product details. Though the brief is less formal, it may well be (and should be) as thorough as any delivered to an agency.

Some clients prefer to deliver their brief orally, developing points of detail during the initial discussion with the researcher. Alternatively the brief may be fully thought through and committed to paper. This can be especially important when a number of research agencies are invited to submit proposals. A written brief provides a standard which is the same for all contestants.

Whether written or oral, the research sponsor should pay regard to a number of subjects which constitute a good brief. It is at this stage that it would be useful to have a framework for scoping the issues. This framework can be thought of as a series of questions, the answers to which will constitute a very thorough brief.

1. *Why do this market research? – what action will be taken when the research is completed?*
   This is arguably the most important part of the brief as it will allow the researcher to work out all the other things that are required such as the specific information that will be useful (see item 5 below).

2. *What has caused this problem or led to this opportunity?*
   Here it is helpful to describe the history that has led up to the research. A description of the product/service is important and it would also be good to talk about the way that the market is changing.

3. *What is known about the area of research already?*
   It can be helpful to market researchers to be aware of what is already known, then they can build on it and not waste money or time reinventing it. Also, knowledge on the structure and behaviour of a market allows the researchers to be more precise in their proposals. For example, most sponsors of research have carried out some desk research or have internal reports that provide views of the market. This could be made available to the researchers

who are planning a research programme if they need a deeper understanding of the market.

4. *Target groups for the research.*

   Survey research has to be targeted at someone. The target for interviewees needs to be scoped precisely. If they are householders, should they be people who have bought a product or who are thinking of buying a product? Should they be buyers or specifiers? Should they be multiple purchasers or not? When the various target groups are listed there is a temptation to say 'Yes, all of these', but remember that the greater the scope of the project, the more it will cost and (usually) the longer it will take.

5. *What specific information is needed from the research (for example, market size, trends, buying behaviour, customer needs, segmentation)?*

   The person wanting the market research has almost certainly got some key information gaps that need filling. Listing them will help the professional market researchers work out if they are the right ones required for the decision and action that is planned. The professional market researchers can be expected to flesh out the information objectives with their own suggestions, as they know better than anyone what can and cannot be achieved by market research.

6. *What is the proposed budget?*

   Seldom are there unlimited funds for research, and more often there are very limited funds. In this case it is helpful to know what the budget is, for otherwise the researchers could design a full and comprehensive plan that delivers detail and accuracy to meet the action and information requirements, only to be sent back to the drawing board because there is only US $15,000 (or whatever).

7. *Are there any initial ideas for the research method?*

   A client who is sponsoring a research project may well have a method in mind. Now is also the time to say if there is distrust of telephone interviews and a preference for face-to-face or if focus groups would be well received.

8. *Are there any reporting requirements?*

   Increasingly the default method of reporting in the market research industry is a PowerPoint deck of slides which doubles as the presentation and the report. Researchers have no problem writing a narrative report but they would typically have to charge an extra three or four days of their time for its preparation – incurring a cost of a few thousand dollars.

The client may be eager to have access to some of the nitty-gritty of the research findings such as the tabulations and verbatim comments from open-ended questions. It is wise to specify this at the brief, for otherwise it may not be included in the research specification.

9. *When are the findings required?*
Most research has a demanding timetable and sometimes this can be punishing. The dates by which the research is required should be specified so that even if they are really difficult, the research supplier can try to be accommodating, perhaps with an interim debrief or regular reporting sessions.

The research brief should be a dialogue, and even the most thorough brief covering all the issues we have listed will generate some additional questions from the researchers. This is healthy and to be expected, as it indicates that the problem is being thought through and interest is being shown. Sometimes the written brief and a series of phone calls are sufficient for the agency to get on with their part of the process – the proposal – and sometimes there will be justification for a face-to-face meeting. Nearly, but not always, these briefing sessions are on the client's turf where it is easier to show the product, look at brochures and reports and meet with other people who may be able to contribute to the debate.

THE MARKET RESEARCH PROPOSAL – THE RETURN OF BRIEF (ROB)

Having received the brief the researcher, whether in-house or from an agency, must submit a written proposal to the sponsor which states an appreciation of the problem, the objectives, the research method and the timing. It is critical that the proposal is in writing as this is the offer of a contract which is likely to have a considerable financial value.

The nature of market research is such that it is seldom possible to pin every aspect of the contract down in detail. For a start, the questionnaire has not yet been developed and this is a key to the survey. The number and type of questions in the questionnaire will have a material influence on the quality of the work. Flexibility is going to be needed on many aspects of the work, and as the research progresses and information is uncovered, there may need to be some changes to

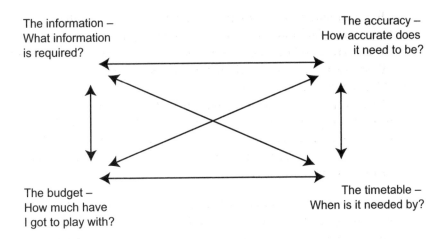

The information –
What information
is required?

The accuracy –
How accurate does
it need to be?

The budget –
How much have
I got to play with?

The timetable –
When is it needed by?

Figure 2.1 *The trade-off between cost, quality and time*

the objectives. For the most part, however, the research methods will remain the same, as this is the basis of the price. Armed with the brief, the researcher now knows what the client is looking for and must balance four factors in arriving at an appropriate design (see Figure 2.1).

THE INFORMATION REQUIRED

The information required may not have been presented in the most orderly fashion in the brief. A research sponsor knows what action will be taken if the outcome is positive, and will have a view on the type of information that will help in that decision. All this will be shared in the brief. The researcher must now offer some order to the decision outcomes, the research objectives and any specific questions that may be asked. Examples of these three levels are shown in Table 2.2.

The researcher must work out what can reasonably be included in the project as an objective as well as what may have to be left out. As the researcher is thinking about the objectives, inevitably there will be consideration of the methods by which these will be achieved.

Consider Table 2.2 and think about what methods you would use for this range of outcomes, objectives and questions. Actually the researcher has a choice, and could use a qualitative tool such as focus groups to get

Table 2.2 *Outcomes, objectives and questions*

Level 1 Outcome		Launch the product	
Level 2 Research objective	Product preferences	Trends in buying behaviour	Price elasticity
Level 3 Questions to be answered	Do they prefer the new product to the old one? Do they prefer the new product to the competition's? What would improve the preferences for the product	Are people buying more of the product? How is the market likely to change in the next five years? What factors are driving the changes in the market?	How much will people buy at different prices? What is the optimum price for the product?

a reasonable fix on the answers. However, even with a number of focus groups it would still be a qualitative finding. You would have a good feel and understanding of all the answers to the questions but that is what would be – a feel and understanding. If the research is being commissioned to make a decision on the launch of a new product, some quantification may be required. Here the choices are twofold: home placement tests, or mall/hall tests (where the respondent is recruited from the shopping mall and brought to a nearby hall to experience the product). The arguments in favour of one approach rather than another or mixing different approaches will be made in the proposal under the 'methods' section.

THE ACCURACY

When professional market researchers ask their clients how accurate any data should be, the answer is often such as 'very accurate' or 'as accurate as possible'. However accuracy, at least where fieldwork is involved, has a price and as a general rule, increases in accuracy not only cost more but cost disproportionately more.[1]

A high level of accuracy is not always needed to meet the overall research objective. If a company is entering a new market, where common sense and observation tells us the market is huge, there may be little point in spending lots of money closely measuring its size. An approximation will do and the money saved may be better spent on some other information need. For example, a company that considers sales of US $1 million per annum to be worthwhile might not care if the total market size was US $100 million or US $150 million (an accuracy of +/– 50 per cent). If, however, in an advertising research study, the objective was to measure the impact of a campaign on brand awareness through comparing before and after campaign measures, the accuracy must be at least commensurate with the anticipated increase in awareness.

The required accuracy must, therefore, be linked to how the resulting data will be used – the nature of the decisions the research will guide. Even if a precise definition of accuracy is not practically possible (as is often the case), some judgement should still be made on the reliability sought from the information. This may be as simple as a contrast between an attempt at measurement (quantitative research) compared with description and explanation (qualitative research). Both approaches can contribute to effective marketing decisions but it is important that neither is used for the wrong application. Like information coverage, accuracy levels need to be considered before deciding on appropriate research methods.

THE BUDGET

What budget should be made available for the research project? The methodologically pure researcher would argue that the budget should be whatever is needed to meet the research objectives, provide the information required and finance the methods needed to produce that information to the defined accuracy level. However, in practice, it is more a question of what funds are available or can be afforded for the project relative to other calls on business expenditure. Furthermore, even if cash is freely available, there are other considerations and especially the amount at risk in the decision which the research is to guide. If the decision entails capital expenditure of US $20 million, a research budget of US $50,000 may be well worth spending – if the research indicates that the planned expenditure is a poor investment, only the research cost will be lost rather than most or all of the US $20 million investment. (In writing this we are reminded of the many chemical plants that have been built around the world in anticipation of growth in demand that has never materialized. We suspect that many were commissioned without any solid market research studies.) However, if the business investment decision has low cost implications, the justification for carrying out the research will be less. Obviously there is no point in spending US $10,000 on research to decide whether to invest in a project entailing only this level of expenditure.

The only qualification we would make to this bland statement is regarding research that contributes to a series of future decisions. We recently carried out a research project examining the effectiveness of a planned promotional campaign for an industrial gas manufacturer. The cost of the research was US $30,000 and the campaign itself was only US $200,000. However, the gas manufacturer runs many such campaigns across its divisions and learning about what makes its advertising more effective sharpened all its campaigns and will do so for some years to come. The long time payback will be considerable.

THE TIMETABLE

A research plan needs a timetable. The two factors that determine the timetable are the deadline and how long the planned research activities will take to carry out. Resources determine the latter, and experience of the intended methods will enable realistic estimates to be made of how long each stage will take. On the other hand, the deadline is likely to be driven by external events and time frames. The research results may be needed to fit the lead time in installing plant, or for a business plan. A demanding deadline of two or three weeks for a research project may effectively limit it to a quick (and dirty?) design as there just is not enough time to do the job properly. Whether researchers should turn down such jobs is hardly worth debating since in this commercial world agencies will nearly always try to accommodate their clients' needs. To an extent it may be possible to speed up the research to fit such demands. Certainly good research can be carried out within a short timetable but beyond some point, quality will be compromised.

Most research agencies need around six weeks to carry out a project given the likelihood of the need for three or four sequential stages. Getting questionnaires designed is in theory only a day's work for a professional researcher. However, getting it approved and modified to the final version (often it is at version 5 before it is finally piloted) can take an age as it bounces around like a pinball between the different parties within the client company. The timetable given in Table 2.3 is probably realistic for a project involving four focus groups and 500 interviews with the general public.

WHAT TO EXPECT IN A PROPOSAL (RETURN OF BRIEF)

The proposal is one of the most important documents a researcher ever writes. (Indeed it is one of the few documents that researchers write, as reporting is nearly always in PowerPoint slides). The content, structure and quality of the proposal may account for well over 50 per cent of the decision to place the business with an agency. Within the client company the proposal will do the rounds, winning or losing approval with its many readers without the accompaniment of the human voice of the author. It is the most important weapon the agency can use to win business.

The proposal is more than just a research design with a price; it is a statement of the agency that has prepared it. Whereas the brief may be confused, limited in scope or lacking in detail, the proposal must bring clarity, add to the understanding and make an authoritative claim for the recommended research method. A spelling or grammatical error could be sufficient to cause the client to see this as a reflection of sloppy working standards and disregard the content of the rest of the proposal.

The introduction

The proposal may run to 10 pages or so in length. It deserves a title page and table of contents. In a lengthy proposal, the first section could be a summary, but more usually it is an introduction to the subject stating the background and circumstances that have led to the research project being considered. This background contains the first words that will be read in the document and they need to resonate. It may contain some

Table 2.3 *A typical market research timetable*

	Week 1	Week 2	Week 3	Week 4	Week 5	Week 6	Week 7	Week 8	Week 9	Week 10
Commissioning meeting	▓									
Focus group recruitment		▓								
Focus groups			▓							
Qualitative debrief				▓						
Questionnaire design					▓					
Sample composition					▓					
Fieldwork							▓			
Analysis									▓	
Presentation development									▓	
Presentation										▓

additional information to add to the story following a search on the Internet or the odd interview (also demonstrating keenness of interest in the subject). As the reader gets to the end of the first section, the proposal has done a good deal of its selling job.

The objectives

Next is the section on objectives. This is another important chapter to the client as it is a statement of what will be obtained for the money. Typically the research would be given an overall goal such as: *to assess the market for weather forecasting services amongst electricity generating, transmission and distribution (retail) companies in the United States.*

A more detailed listing of the many research objectives would then follow. A flavour of these can be gleaned from two or three objectives taken out of a list of what amounted to around 10 objectives in the actual proposal.

1. To gain an understanding of how weather affects business operations of energy companies in the three target markets and their key weather information needs (that is, the perceived importance of the weather to their business and business planning processes and the type of products/services they need).
2. To gain an understanding of the extent of weather information usage and the nature of that use (that is, what they use it for, how and why). This would include: where they get their existing weather information from, how it is delivered, the problems they encounter, how much they spend, and if they do not use weather information, why not.
3. To assess the perceived future demand for weather information products and services in the target energy markets (including, do respondents perceive they will use weather information more or less in the future?).

The methods

To the researcher, the methods section is probably the most important. If the researcher gets this wrong, the objectives will not be achieved. The client will clearly be interested in the methods but much will be taken on trust. If the researcher says that a particular method is appropriate, then it may go unquestioned.

In the section on methods the researcher may begin with a brief overview of the approach and the factors that have influenced the design. It is not unusual in a research programme to have an eclectic range of methods including some secondary research (desk research) to support the primary fieldwork. The fieldwork could have a qualitative phase and this could be a number of depth interviews or focus groups. If there is a quantitative stage it will be spelled out in detail arguing the reasons for choosing the telephone or face-to-face interviews, the size of the sample and any quotas for certain groups of respondents.

Timing and costs

By the time the research sponsor arrives at the section laying out the timetable and the costs, the project will most probably be won or lost. Of course the price tag is important but research is not a commodity product. There are significant differences between research suppliers and this is recognized by clients. It is not a business where the cheapest product always wins.

SUMMARY

The idea for carrying out market research may ferment for a number of weeks before a commitment is made to obtain proposals. In briefing an agency the client should try to give answers to a number of questions:

- What action will be taken when the research is completed?
- What has caused this problem or led to this opportunity?
- What is known about the area of research already?
- Target groups for the research?
- What specific information is needed from the research?
- What is the proposed budget?
- Are there any initial ideas for the research method?
- Are there any reporting requirements?
- When are the findings required?

The market research agency will prepare a proposal (the return of brief) after weighing up what information is required, the accuracy of information required, the budget, and the timing. With these four factors in mind, a written proposal is prepared that covers the following issues:

- an understanding of the problem;
- the objectives in overall terms and in detail;
- the method that will be employed to achieve the objectives;
- the timetable;
- the credentials of the researchers;
- the fee.

The quality of the market research proposal plays a large part in whether or not the agency wins the project.

3 Desk research

WHY REINVENT THE WHEEL?

There is no point reinventing the wheel, and there are many metaphorical wheels available to the market researcher. The expert desk researcher can quickly and inexpensively dig out data from a wide variety of sources to answer many research objectives. So why do we spend so much on primary research? The reason, very often, is because we do not know how to locate the information. Or it may be information that is not in quite the shape we require and it escapes our notice that with a little bit of reworking, it could be very useful. Sometimes, desk research seems too easy. A big decision surely needs a lot of money spending on it and merits an original piece of research. It is not necessarily so.

Desk research provides information that costs next to nothing. This information sits underneath our noses. The do-it-yourself researcher can easily obtain it. Moreover, for the 'do your own' researcher, desk research is a very practical tool – in most cases he or she is not at any disadvantage compared to a professional agency. A couple of days of desk research have a very big yield and the benefits of more time searching quickly diminish.

Desk research is a term that is used loosely, and it generally refers to secondary data or that which can be collected without fieldwork. To most people it suggests published reports and statistics and these are certainly important sources. In the context of this chapter the term is widened to include all sources of information that do not involve a field survey. This most certainly will include searching libraries and the

Internet but it could also include speaking to someone at a trade association or carrying out interviews with experts.

Before we talk about the public sources of desk research, it is worth emphasizing how much useful information often sits in the desks and on the shelves of the very companies that are seeking that data. This information could be in old reports that are forgotten or deemed useless because of their age. It could be in sales or market statistics and, with a bit of imagination, these could be re-worked to produce a valuable picture. Sometimes information is devalued simply because it seems to be too easily available. Our first plea is to make sure that there is no desk research lurking inside the company before moving the search to the wider outside world.

RESOURCES

Until the advent of the Internet and online databases, access to libraries was the only important resource needed to carry out desk research. Despite the marvels of the information highway, some data are easier to access from hard copy and off the library shelves. Indeed, the Internet for all its value is still not as comprehensive in its coverage of statistical data as it is in product and company information. Desk researchers should acquaint themselves with the nearest commercial library.

All major cities have at least one good municipal or university library and few researchers will be more than an hour's travel from such a resource. From time to time the reference books in the main body of the library will be useful but for the most part, it is the commercial section which is of greatest interest.

SOURCES OF SOURCES – THE HIGH LEVEL VIEW

Before exploring some of the popular sources of information to market researchers, it is worth pointing out that there are some useful 'sources of sources'. These range from inexpensive books such as *How to Find Information – Business: A guide to searching in published sources* (How to Find Series) by Nigel Spencer (available from amazon.com) through to the much more expensive *Croner's A – Z of Business Information Sources* (this lists some of the best Web sources and is available on CD-ROM).

There are also other general guides that can be used to track down sources of data including those covering published research, the press, directories and statistics. For international markets there are comparable 'sources of sources' including *European Directory of Marketing Information Sources* and *Directory of International Sources of Business Information*. Some or all of these 'sources of sources' will be found in a good library. The library's own cataloguing and indexing systems also provide a means of systematically searching out data. With experience, sources likely to be relevant to a particular field will become familiar and provide short cuts.

Encyclopaedias are useful storehouses of information for the market researcher, either to check out a technical issue or to obtain a closer definition of the subject and its associated terminology. Now that *Encyclopaedia Britannica* is on line (www.britannica.com) it has become universally accessible for browsing alphabetically, by subject, or for a quick word search.

The United States has led the world in the collection and dissemination of business information for many years. The Central Intelligence Agency uses its expertise on our behalf to bring together basic intelligence which began as the National Intelligence Survey and is now an online Factbook that can be very easily examined country by country (www.cia.gov/cia/publications/factbook/). The whole database can be downloaded though this requires either considerable patience or a broad bandwidth connection. Virtually every country in the world is covered. The Factfile gives geographical statistics on countries, the demographic breakdown of their population, economic overviews (in some detail), transportation, government, and maps galore. Another route to similar information is www.geographic.org.

INDUSTRY EXPERTS

Another means of locating data sources is through direct contact with organizations and individuals who have knowledge of a particular field. Trade associations and the publishers of information are examples. This sort of approach strays outside desk research in the strictest sense. However, a two-way traffic between sources (which identify potential contacts) and expert interviewing (to identify sources) is a means of getting the most value from desk research at little extra cost, (possibly at a saving if sources are identified more efficiently).

You could also try FIND/SVP (findsvp.com) which has a Quick Consulting and Research Service that aims to answer questions on markets through a fixed-fee retainer system and deliver the results by phone, fax and e-mail at a quite modest cost.

THE INTERNET

Accessing information via the Internet is the modern alternative to hours spent in libraries. For market researchers, the Internet has two important sources of information: the sites that companies, organizations and individuals have created to promote or communicate their products, services or views, and user groups that are made up of people who have an interest in a particular subject.

Web sites are recognized by the prefix www. Companies operating in the United States (and those elsewhere in the world, aiming at international audiences) are likely to be referenced as www. companyname.com. Other countries have citations which use a summary of their name such as www.companyname.co.uk (United Kingdom), www.companyname.de (Germany) and so on. A non-profit-making organization often has the suffix .org after its name, as in www.charity.org, and a university or academic institution is completed by the initials ac, as in www.university.ac.

The World Wide Web is estimated to contain over 2 billion pages of publicly accessible information. The problem is not the volume of information but finding that tiny bit that you need in this enormous ocean. Fortunately for researchers, search engine technology has increased by leaps and bounds, and an appropriate word string in a search engine such as Google, Alta Vista, or Yahoo will usually deliver thousands of hits. This too is a researcher's problem, for who ever looks beyond page three of these?

Search engines use programmes based on a spider or a crawler, which looks for key words or a word string in those billions of pages. The results are copied into a huge database (an index or list of information) and you are presented with the summary contents of the search at each site together with a hyperlink, from which a click will take you to the reference. Meta search engines such as Dogpile or Metacrawler use several search engines all at once, and then blend the results into a convenient form, such as listing the references in declining order of appropriateness to the search request.

In this massive sea of information it may be difficult to find what we require because:

- We are using the wrong search strategy – a different word or arrangement of words may yield more precise hits.
- We are using the wrong search engine – even the very best search engines do not cover all the pages on the Net so the vital piece we are looking for may never be uncovered. A different search engine could produce a different result.
- We are using the wrong word – the use of the American spelling of 'tires' would miss out on Web references to the British spelling of 'tyres'.
- The information we are looking for may not be available in the precise form we are hoping for. A search for the volumes of tires bought as original equipment by Ford may come to naught, but it would be easy to derive the figure by finding out the number of Ford cars produced per year and multiplying by five (one per wheel plus the spare).

A search strategy with a suitable arrangement of words may well hit the bull's eye and locate the information that is being sought. When typing in the search string, it may be helpful to use double quotations to enclose the phrase so that 'world health organization' will only deliver references to those three words in that combination. Without the quotation marks references, most search engines look for each of the three words separately and would deliver hundreds of thousands of irrelevant references to world, to health and to organizations. (Note that the Internet is indifferent to capital letters.)

Thinking laterally is certainly the first principle of desk research using the Internet. Avoid using very common terms (for example, Internet or people) as this will lead to thousands of hits but irrelevant results. Where possible, use a phrase (in quotation marks) or proper name to narrow the search and therefore retrieve a smaller number of more relevant results. If too many results are generated, it is easy to refine the word string in the search box and carry out an advanced search, or simply renew the search since the speed of delivery of new results will be on the screen in fractions of a second.

More often the search will start a trail that follows the links between related sites. The searcher must learn to surf from one site to another, book-marking those that are useful for downloading or copying into a work file. Here it is worth emphasizing that a crucial rule of desk research is always to note the reference of the data. Referenced data allows the credibility to be judged and it facilitates re-examination.

There are over 10,000 user groups (also called news groups or discussion groups) on the Internet covering almost every subject. They are roughly organized by topic, ranging from hobbies and recreation (prefixed by rec) through to computers (comp), science (sci), culture, religion, as well as 'alternative' subjects (alt). A question posted within an appropriate user group by a researcher may well find an answer from one of the millions of Internet users. An easy way to access user groups is through a search engine such as Google Groups.

At the time of writing, the best search engine for market researchers appears to be Google. It offers speed and consistent high quality hits through a programme built on algorithms.

ONLINE DATABASES AND MARKET DATA

Many databases of articles and reports can now be accessed via the Internet. Sometimes the information required by market researchers is available from commercial providers who charge significantly for access either as an up-front sum or on a pay-as-you-use basis – for example, Reuters, or Dialog DataStar. The user of such sources has to become a subscriber and must learn how to carry out searches efficiently (to minimize costs). Free or low-cost training is offered to new subscribers. In comparison with the Internet, searching online databases is more costly and typically could cost between US $5,000 and US $10,000 per year to a serious user. This is because the databases house collections of valuable reports, which, even though available on a page-by-page basis, still have a hefty price tag.

However, this begs the question of which database should be accessed in the first place – no one 'host' provides a direct gateway to all cyber-data. To fill the gap there are a number of database source books published, including *Directory of On Line Databases* (published twice a year by Cuadra/Elsevier, New York) or *Gale Guide to Internet Databases* that has 5,000 publicly accessible online databases. The major hosts (for instance, Reuters, DataStar) also publish their own guides.

The major benefit of any sort of online database is the speed of locating material using key word searching to match what is available to what is sought. This is particularly of benefit in searching press files (manually looking through the last few months' issues of even one paper is a daunting task).

There are an increasing number of Web sites that offer archive material to researchers without the need to sign up, although there is usually a fee for the report or part of it. The table of contents is available free and there are many synopses of reports, which may be sufficient for those requiring just an overview. The charges made for bought-in reports and similar sources range from the nominal to levels comparable to commissioning ad hoc research. Most fall within the US $500 to US $5,000 bracket. A good source of market research data, offering full or part reports is www.marketresearch.com which allows access to a collection of over 50,000 publications from over 350 research firms. One of the best general databases of commercial and financial news is ft.com – the Web site of the *Financial Times*.

Material such as abstracts, statistics and large directories are increasingly available on CD-ROM or by password from an Internet site (for example information on the chemical and rubber industry can be obtained from RAPRA – the Rubber and Plastics Research Association on a subscription basis.)

COMPANY DATA

Researchers need company data for competitor benchmarking, sourcing suppliers or building profiles of customers and potential customers. Only a few years ago company literature was a mainstay of product searches. Such literature is prepared for the public domain and will be sent readily on request. Today company Web sites are brimming with useful information. They contain pictures of products, maps of distributors, data sheets, company histories, press releases, and sometimes financial background. The information is nearly always more extensive and current than printed brochures and it is available in an instant. A request from the CEO for information about a competitor could be put together in couple of hours and contain an impressive amount of material.

The US Securities and Exchange Commission (SEC) requires all US public companies (except foreign companies and companies with less than US \$10 million in assets and 500 shareholders) to file registration statements, periodic reports, and other forms electronically, and anyone can access and download this information for free from its Edgar database on www.sec.gov. Searches can be made for individual companies or those within a standard industrial classification (SIC). The database allows access to all the reports that have been filed, including the most useful 10-K financial statements and directors' reports.

Financial data on companies is available in the United Kingdom from Companies House (www.companieshouse.gov.uk). The Web site of Companies House offers a searchable index which gives access to information on more than 1.5 million companies. Of these about 11,000 are public companies (PLCs) which issue shares and of the PLCs, about 7,000 are quoted on the Stock Exchange. Smaller companies file only limited information and this can reduce the value of company accounts in niche markets. Financial data on 30,000 companies worldwide can be obtained from Extel Financial Cards that can be accessed via one of the online databases such as Dialog.

GOVERNMENT STATISTICS

In most projects, the desk researcher will seek 'hard' statistical data and sooner or later this will point towards a government source. These cover most areas of business and social life.

A visit to US Department of Commerce site on www.commerce.gov offers a treasure trove of information from industry sector statistics to economic analysis to demographic data, and research publications. There is a good search engine to help navigate through this very large site.

There are also international bodies collecting and publishing statistics. For the European Union, the office responsible is *Eurostat* and this source will increasingly be important in projects covering the whole single market of the EU (www.europa.eu.int/comm/eurostat). Two other major publishers are the United Nations and the OECD.

In the United Kingdom, the National Statistics Web site (www. statistics.gov.uk) contains a vast range of official UK statistics which can be accessed and downloaded free. The site allows searching by themes such as agriculture/fishing/forestry, commerce, energy, industry, education, crime and justice, the labour market, the population and so on.

One of the cornerstones of any government's statistical service and a massive source of data for market researchers is the Census of Population. The US Census Bureau (www.census.gov) has a site covering every aspect of the population, including all key demographics such as age, education, labour, computer ownership and use, and income (to list but a few subjects). Marketeers use census output for segmentation by demographics and survey planning (for example, setting quota samples). The census is also the basis of geodemographic analysis systems.

TRADE AND INDUSTRY BODIES

Every trade, no matter how obscure, nearly always has some collective body to represent its interests (and also usually spawn several trade publications – see below). To meet members' needs, and for PR purposes, most of these bodies publish or can make available (sometimes to members only) considerable information about their industry. The organization and sophistication of these bodies and the volume of the information offered varies enormously. There are various organizations that can be used to access lists of associations. In the United States, the ASAE (American Society of Association Executives) is a gateway to 6,500 associations (www.asaenet.org). In Europe, the best source for associations is CBD who publish directories on various British and European organizations (www. cbdresearch.com).

MARKET RESEARCH REPORTS

A number of specialist market research companies speculatively carry out studies which are then sold as publications. Compared with privately commissioned studies these are incredibly good value. Often referred to as *multi-client reports*, these publications cover every subject imaginable from A to Z. There are over 30,000 multi-client reports available and they can be located through several sources. *Marketsearch* lists 20,000 published reports from 700 firms. The database can be searched in hard copy or from the company's Web site (www. marketsearch-dir.com). Another directory of published market research is *findex* (www.findexonline.com) which published over 10,000 off the shelf reports on world markets.

THE PRESS

The general, business and trade press are key sources for the desk researcher. As well as 'news', these sources include much background material, including special supplements on industries and markets. In the past, researchers relied on the clippings services of libraries and archive agencies but today's work is made easier by online search facilities on some newspaper sites. The best has to be the UK's *Financial Times* which has an archive facility available to everybody for simple searches and 'power' searches of a wider archive for a reasonable fee.

In industrial markets the trade press is a very important source of market research information. Every industry and trade has regular journals which can be identified in publications such as *Willings Press Guides* or *BRAD* (www.intellagencia.com). Many publications are not available online so there may be no alternative to reading through hard copy back issues.

DIRECTORIES

Directories are the staple diet of market researchers. They provide details of companies that either supply or consume goods and they are the usual source for preparing sample frames (list of companies or people to be interviewed). The directories may also provide a profile of a company, detailing its size by giving the number of employees, or whether it is an agent or producer.

One of the most comprehensive general directories is *Yellow Pages* (www.yellowpages.com in the United States and www.yell.com in the United Kingdom) since every company with a telephone number is given a free entry. These directories form the most comprehensive listing of small and medium enterprises (SMEs). For example, within the Yell Group, the Business Database supplies data on around 1.5 million

United Kingdom businesses sourced from the free-line entries in the *Yellow Pages* printed directories. From its Web site it is possible to run counts and download lists for sample frames.

Every country has its *Yellow Pages* on the Internet (www.gelbe-seiten.de, www.goudengids.nl, www.paginegialle.it, www.paginas-amarillas.es) from where it is possible to locate companies in the detailed product groupings used by the directory. For relatively small fees, researchers can order lists of companies' addresses and telephone numbers (in hard or soft copy) filtered by Standard Industrial Classification, company size (number of employees) and geographical region.

Other general directories, which comprise larger companies than those in *Yellow Pages*, include *Kompass* and *Dun & Bradstreet's*. These sources can be found in almost any library and they are now available for the whole of Europe and the United States on CD-ROM or on the Internet. The online facility allows entries to be abstracted using filters such as location, size of company and industry specialization. As well as these general sources, most industries have their own specialized directories, which may have a better listing of suppliers and buyers.

THE RANGE OF INFORMATION AVAILABLE FROM DESK RESEARCH

Sources such as those outlined above can be used to obtain data on the large majority of subjects likely to be covered in a market research project. These include those mentioned below.

The marketing environment

Markets do not exist in isolation and are shaped by environmental factors such as the state of the general economy, demographic trends, the legislative framework and various social factors. An understanding of these external factors is likely to be part of any full analysis of a market. The marketing environment is generally well documented, and desk research (rather than primary research) is the only practical source available. The economy, demographics and key social variables are all well covered by governments' statistical services and the many publications they produce. Other sources in this area include special reports (government and private), and press commentary.

Market structure and size

The structure of most business and industrial markets can be fully analyzed through desk research. Sources include the general and trade press, directories, company financial data, published reports, trade association output and government statistics. We have already pointed to the rich sources in the government statistical sites of the United States (Department of Commerce) and Europe (Eurostat, UK National Statistics and so on). The latter source includes *UK Markets* (formerly *Business Monitor*), which provides, for all industries, details of production, imports and exports with detailed product breakdowns on an annual basis. Government statistics such as *UK Markets* go back into long time series and provide a basis for historical and future trend analysis. This source or others may not provide market size estimates of the specific category of interest, but with ingenuity, reasonable approximations can usually be derived from top-down (making estimates from a wider classification which includes the one of interest) or bottom-up estimates (aggregating sub classifications). The skill in this sort of work includes bringing together disparate pieces of data from separate sources. For example, if a researcher has a reasonable idea of a market size in one country, it may be possible to make estimates for other countries by relating the known market size to readily available statistics on population or electricity production – which are available for nearly every nation state in the world.

Suppliers and brands

Data on suppliers and brands can be thought of as an extension of the sort of market structure analysis considered above, and may include profiles of major suppliers and their brands, marketing methods and advertising tactics, and factors making for success. Company Web sites are an obvious first source to be examined when researching suppliers and their brands. So too is the press (including trade journals), directories, company accounts and published reports. Advertising and trade literature (especially in technical markets) can usually be collected free and could add to the information obtained from Web sites. One important area of information, which is usually outside the scope of desk research, is consumers' attitudes to and satisfaction with suppliers. Generally this can only be obtained through primary research; although in some industries published reports may have relevant data.

DISTRIBUTION AND RETAILING

In most businesses, distributors are playing an increasing role as they provide a cost-effective means of supplying and servicing small (and sometimes not so small) accounts. Distribution structures can vary considerably, with many tiers ranging from importers, through to main distributors, local dealers and so on. Sources that provide an analysis of these structures are much the same as those just discussed for primary suppliers. Consumer markets are generally retail markets, and retailing generally is very well documented, including in the press and in published reports.

Products

Desk research can provide detailed product information. Web sites are a first port of call as they usually provide illustrations and specifications of products that can be captured and downloaded. Trade publications in some markets compare products from alternative suppliers. Mail order catalogues are another source of product details. Product literature is often particularly relevant in technical markets and is a valuable source for analyzing product features. Visits to exhibitions and trade fairs to collect this literature are an example of 'near' desk research, which can be used before moving into primary research. Pricing information may also be available from the sources just mentioned, although the difference between list prices and what is actually paid may reduce the value of such information.

Desk research is not usually thought to have a role in new product evaluation, and certainly consumer reaction to a new product has to be established through primary research. However, the fate of other new launches can provide very useful information and can be accessed from the trade press and other sources.

PLANNING, RECORDING AND EVALUATING DESK RESEARCH

A plan is needed if the search for published data is to be efficient. A written plan is a help to desk research, whether it is utilizing library or online sources. Before visiting a library or logging on, you should specify the information sought in some detail, although flexibility and some ingenuity are also needed (for instance, looking for relevant data under wider or narrower classifications and creatively making connections).

The desk research plan should also include a timetable. How long should be spent on the desk research part of a project? This will depend on the breadth of the information sought, the type of data and the resources to be used. It is difficult to generalize. However, what can be said is that diminishing returns apply and after quite a short time the extra information gained falls in proportion to the time spent searching.

Once found, data needs downloading into files. The source of any data should always be recorded, so that its accuracy can be both evaluated and, if necessary, retraced. In long projects and repeat work, this will provide useful short cuts to the most valuable sources and ensure that the same blind alleys are avoided.

Information needs not only collecting but also evaluating. In part this is a matter of making judgements about its validity. We are often fooled into trusting data that is published. Once in black and white, we assume that it must be correct. The experienced desk researcher learns that market size figures that are published need to be cross-checked by two or three sources, and frequently there are some serious anomalies.

Most secondary data accessed through desk research was originally generated through primary research. Thorough validation requires going back to the source and understanding the methodology used: was it based on some sort of census, on a sample survey, on some crude formula using a ratio or merely on anecdotal evidence? Where possible two or more sources for the same data can be compared (although make sure that they are different). However, some sense of proportion has to be kept. It is simply not possible to validate all the data thoroughly and nor is it necessary to do so – as previously mentioned, market researchers can work within quite wide bands of accuracy for practical purposes.

As well as validating the data, evaluation also includes its integration into a meaningful whole. Looking for linkages and patterns can and should be part of the desk research process with initial material often pointing to other sources and subjects. That is why we stated earlier that although planning is needed in desk research, flexibility should be retained. Subsequent analysis and integration of data will be facilitated by good note and record keeping when the material is collected and, if this is voluminous, by reasonably organized filing.

THE LIMITS OF DESK RESEARCH

Desk research can be very fruitful. However, it has its limits and it may only provide part of the information sought in a project. As previously suggested, where a mix of desk and primary research is likely to be required there is everything to be gained by carrying out desk research first and then filling the gaps through interviewing. In this way, the more expensive primary techniques are used only where essential.

One limit of desk research is its unpredictability. At least for the novice or where the subject area is unfamiliar, there can be no certainty of what the desk research will yield and what gaps will remain. This is partly the reason that desk research is not a major service supplied by market research agencies. It would be difficult for an agency to quote for carrying out desk research, carry out the project and deliver a scant report at the end saying that despite a thorough search, nothing has been found. For this reason, internal researchers carry out much desk research in-house. At least a short desk research exercise will cost very little and may save on much more expensive fieldwork. Unlike an agency, a 'do your own' researcher can live with little to show for the desk research stage.

Some information is also in principle not available from desk research and with a little experience this is obvious from the start. Generally this includes most attitude-type data, especially where the subject of consumer attitudes is particular rather than general opinions – of your own and competitor companies, of a novel product, of a specific advert and so on.

SUMMARY

There have always been volumes of data available to market researchers via secondary data (that which is already in the public domain). The Internet has considerably expanded the sources and the ease of accessing the data. There are many sites that are rich in data for market researchers and government statistical agencies or trade associations often own these. Also, a quick search on the Internet will show if there is a published report on a subject, usually supported by a synopsis which could give sufficient information for a quick assessment of a market. In addition to becoming familiar with favourite Web sites, the market researcher should learn how to develop search strategies that deliver useful information.

Desk research is an excellent tool for putting together pictures of a marketing environment – showing the market size, suppliers, the products that they make, and the trends in the market. It is also a rich source of data on company information and therefore useful for profiling both customers and competitors.

Often the market researcher must piece together disparate information from desk research to provide a picture of a market. This requires skill in searching as well as lateral thinking – to work out how one piece of information provides an answer to another.

The Internet has revolutionized desk research. However, the market researcher should also remember that valuable sources of secondary data could be found in conventional libraries, in trade associations and from industry experts.

4 Focus groups

THE FOCUS GROUP

The focus group is a research technique used to collect data through group interaction on a topic. Essentially, it is a group experience comprising a small number of carefully selected people who are recruited to discuss a subject based on the commonality of their experience.

Focus groups have four key characteristics:

- They actively involve people.
- The people attending the group have an experience or interest in common.
- They provide in-depth qualitative data.
- Discussion is focused to help us understand what is going on.

The people

Focus groups typically are made up of 5 to 10 people. The group needs to be small enough to allow everyone the opportunity to share insights, and yet large enough to provide group interaction and diversity of experience. Larger groups inhibit discussion, as some delegates shy from venturing opinions, while smaller groups may be limited in their pool of ideas.

Commonality of experience and interest

Focus group participants have a degree of homogeneity, and this is important to the researcher. This similarity is the basis for recruitment, and indeed, specific requirements are usually necessary for attendance at the group.

It is common for researchers and clients to jointly identify the key criteria that identify the individuals for focus group discussions. For example, a focus group examining people's attitudes to Web sites would almost certainly require them to have access to the Internet and to use it fairly regularly (this would need defining).

Depth of information

Focus groups deliver qualitative data that is rich in words and descriptions, rather than numbers. The group provides the forum for discussion, and the group moderator (the researcher guiding the group) uses his or her skills to get the discussion going in order to flush out ideas, attitudes and experiences. The focus group is more than a group interview. The key is the interaction between the group members.

The topic for discussion

The questions in a focus group are carefully designed to elicit the views of the respondents. A discussion guide is prepared prior to the group meeting and the group moderator uses this as his or her aide memoir of what must be covered. Careful design of the guide ensures a logical flow of conversation around the topic area and a clear focus for the discussion.

The topic guide is reflective of how groups operate. Groups always start with an introduction from the moderator explaining the purpose of the meeting and what can be expected to happen. Encouragement will be given to say what is being thought, and rules suggested on speaking in turn and not over each other so that the tape can pick up the words of wisdom. Then participants are asked to introduce themselves and perhaps say a few words about their experience with the subject in hand. This serves to get people talking and feeling comfortable enough to develop their opinions and experiences as the discussion progresses. Questions are tossed into the arena and the group members are encouraged to comment, debate and adjust their views so that the subject gets covered from all angles, and points of dispute become reconciled as far as is possible.

WHEN TO USE FOCUS GROUPS

Focus groups are used to identify and explore behaviour, attitudes and processes. They are best used to throw light on the 'why?' 'what?', and 'how?' questions. They can be used in three ways in the research design:

■ *Stand-alone method:* where the focus groups are the sole data collection method and they serve as the principal source of data.
■ *Supplementary to a survey:* where focus groups are used to enhance alternative means of data collection. Typically this would be as a precursor to a quantitative stage – determining the issues to be covered in the structured interviewing and giving insights into the problems or opportunities that are being researched.
■ *As part of a multi-method design:* where studies use several sources of data collection and no one method determines the use of the others.

When focus groups are used as the sole source of data, the objectives will be explorative and diagnostic (what is the problem, how can we solve it, how will the market react?). When it is important to also get a fix on the number of people that think or behave one way or the other, a multi-method design will be required with a quantitative stage to follow.

Group discussions are especially useful for researching new products, testing new concepts or determining 'What would happen if...?'. They work because delegates can digest the points raised by other members and, as they consider the implications of issues raised, further ideas may be sparked off which would remain untapped in a personal interview. This interaction creates a 'dynamic' in the group, as if the eight or nine separate brains have been wired together, ideas bouncing from one to the other in an easy fashion, and issues are challenged until a general consensus is achieved.

Typical applications for focus groups are:

■ to unravel complex processes from the basics, for example, a complicated buying process;
■ to identify customer needs, that is, where there is a complex interaction of factors influencing motives;
■ to identify how products are used;
■ to test new products, that is, where something needs showing to people;

■ to explore a concept, perhaps with stimulus aids so that people can visualize what it would look like;

■ to explore and identify issues of satisfaction (or dissatisfaction) for customers, staff or suppliers;

■ to explore perceptions of brand and service elements associated with the brand.

The decision to carry out focus groups or individual depth interviews is based on several factors. Focus groups are not always practical, and within the business community, it has to be accepted that geography often precludes the bringing together of participants. For this reason depth interviews are and will remain (until multiple verbal/visual link-ups become feasible) the most widely used qualitative research technique.

In general, focus groups are *not* the preferred option where:

■ measurement of size and distribution is required;

■ the sample base is widespread and small;

■ there is the need to protect respondents from possible bias introduced by others;

■ the topic area is sensitive, for example requiring disclosure of sensitive issues that could be an embarrassment in the company of others;

■ respondents require preparation to answer knowledgably;

■ respondents need to be able to show the researcher something in their home or business.

AREAS OF SPECIAL CONSIDERATION

The biggest potential problem of focus groups is the bias that can occur from the small number of respondents, the interaction with each other and the subject of discussion. These need not create problems if they are considered beforehand.

Culture

In many cultures, particularly in western countries, people have less difficulty sharing their views with others and engaging in debate even though their views may differ from others within the group. The West has a culture of free speech and therefore group discussion comes naturally. However, this cannot be assumed for all cultures. In many

Asian countries it is considered rude and inappropriate to openly crit-icize products, services and suppliers. The natural response is to be polite and present a view that is expected. It is also more difficult to get a group dynamic amongst Asian participants as the culture is to take everyone's views into consideration but to defer to the most senior per-son. We were reminded of these difficulties by an event in a focus group in Japan that was exploring attitudes to showers. Towards the end of the focus group the moderator (a Japanese lady) left the room to check with the client if any subjects needed further coverage. During her absence from the room, for what amounted to nearly five minutes, the members of the focus group did not speak a word to each other. This would be unthinkable in similar circumstances in a Western focus group.

Sensitivity of the focus topic

Focus groups are an excellent tool for getting people to open up and for flushing out ideas. However, there will be subjects where sensitivity of the topic is an issue.

It is not surprising that the toilet seat has not changed in design over the years; that condoms do not come in a variety of sizes and that per-sonal hygiene products tend to be developed through test marketing. To carry out research which requires disclosure of sensitive, personal information and experiences in a group setting is confounded with inherent problems. Such sensitive and potentially personally embar-rassing topics are best discussed in a private non-threatening setting. This is better achieved through a feeling of anonymity, with the researcher being distanced from the respondent, that is, collection by self-completion questionnaire or over-the-telephone interview.

The effect of the group hierarchy

Every researcher has to recognize the inherent imbalance of authority in the group situation. In general, if people feel equality between the group members and the group moderator, they are more likely to feel at ease and share their views in lively debate. For example, if you were tasked with researching the needs of people using hearing protection in the work place (ear plugs and ear defenders) and had chosen to use focus groups, you would have to think about the consequences of mixing plant workers, supervisors and purchasers in the same group. Plant workers may find it difficult to discuss their experiences in front of supervisors, particularly if some of their actions contravene company policy. Therefore, in planning focus groups, keeping respondent types as similar to each other as possible facilitates more open and candid discussion.

Difficulties with disclosure

Some people find self-disclosure more difficult than others. People can feel self-doubt and may lack confidence in expressing their views. Listening to others who are articulate and confident may make them still more fearful of showing themselves up. The group moderator needs to be sensitive to the differences among the group participants and help draw these out.

For example, focus groups with installers of central heating boilers may reveal practices which are considered substandard by other members of the group, and this may cause a group member to remain silent about his or her practices at work. Intimidation by more skilled, knowledgeable and confident plumbers may inhibit some group members and give a skewed view of plumbing practices.

Match of moderator

The role of the moderator is crucial to the success of the focus group. A skilled moderator uses considerable social skills to make people quickly settle down and open up. The body language of the moderator will help this process, including his or her attire. In most consumer groups the moderator dresses smart/casual to create a feeling of professional informality. However, if the focus group comprised accountants or members of the legal profession it might be more appropriate to wear a suit. The match between the moderator and the group participants has been the subject of much research on how the credibility of the moderator is viewed by the group participants and how much this affects the group dynamics.

The key point is that the moderator needs to be accepted by the respondents and has to have the ability to create a 'safe' environment where respondents feel comfortable and confident to freely express their own viewpoint.

The age, gender and experience of the moderator may be critical factors in some topic areas, but not in others. In general, the moderator's standpoint will be one of a researcher, not an industry expert, and usually his or her detachment from the topic area is an advantage. However, in some sensitive topics, it may be necessary to match the moderator to the group respondents – a female moderator for a female group discussing feminine issues, a male moderator for a male group of heavy beer drinkers.

PLANNING AND RECRUITING GROUPS

Between 5 and 10 members normally constitute a group, though there are no precise rules as to the ideal number. However, if there are more than 10 people, and everyone has their say, over the hour and a half of the group, each member is limited in making a significant contribution to the discussion and is inhibited from spontaneous chat.

As few as three to five group members can still be effective since even with this small number there is sufficient scope for the cross-fertilization of ideas. These small groups (mini groups) can be used where respondents are thin on the ground and the brainstorm effect of the focus group is still required.

NUMBER OF GROUPS

There are no hard and fast rules for deciding how many group discussions are needed to cover a subject. One focus group could give a rogue answer. Even two is on the light side as there could be differences between the two groups that would raise doubts as to which was correct. To obtain a better feel and counter the possibility of a biased response, it is advisable to conduct three or four groups. If the number of groups goes beyond six or eight (with people of the same characteristic) the output from the groups becomes difficult to draw together and analyze.

VENUES OF GROUPS

Focus group discussions can take place in a number of locations. It is common for viewing centres to be used for both consumer and business groups. It is not uncommon for business groups to take place in hotels, at conventions or at trade exhibitions. The venue needs to be chosen carefully to match the respondents, and should suit the expectations of the respondent group. Specialist centres have many advantages. They provide facilities for good quality audio and video recording of the proceedings. They are used to hosting groups and so they have a holding room where delegates can assemble before being seated. And not least, they have a viewing room from which observers can see and hear the group through a one-way mirror.

The venue must be easily accessible, preferably well known in the area and with good car parking facilities. The memory lingers of holding a group for independent pharmacists at a hotel in a city centre location where the directions to the hotel were poor, and the parking turned out to be an expensive public car park with no concession for hotel users. Focus group respondents arrived late and annoyed, presenting an additional challenge to the moderator.

The room in which the group is held should be small and intimate. A consumer focus group may have a layout similar to a lounge, with easy chairs in a semicircle and a coffee table in the centre. A group of business respondents is likely to be set up in boardroom style. The aim is to make the environment appropriate to the proceedings while at the same time being easy and relaxed.

The audio and video equipment for recording the groups should be checked beforehand. If the group is being conducted in a viewing centre, this will be taken care of by the viewing centre; otherwise, the moderator will take this responsibility.

GETTING RESPONDENTS TO ATTEND

Because focus groups rely on such a small number of respondents, it is essential that care be taken to recruit the correct profile. The qualifications for attendees must be decided at an early stage and turned into screener questions for a recruitment questionnaire.

The starting point for success in a group discussion is achieving an appropriate turnout from the targeted respondents. It always helps if the subject of the discussion sounds inviting. A good 'hook' helps. Of course, the recruiter needs to communicate enthusiasm for the event and to make the respondents feel that the success of the group is dependent on their attendance.

It is usual to give an incentive to respondents to encourage their attendance. The incentive is usually financial and will vary according to the expectations of the audience, usually amounting to around a half a day's pay (in cash).

THE GROUP MODERATOR

Groups are led by a researcher whose role differs considerably from that of an interviewer. The group moderator's role is:

- To steer the discussion through a range of topics which are relevant to the problem. There is usually an order to the 'unfolding' of these topics but there is sure to be some influence created by the spontaneity of the group itself.
- To act as a catalyst to provoke responses or introduce ideas. Sometimes the researcher should play devil's advocate or feign ignorance.
- To draw a response from those who are quiet and curb those who attempt to monopolize.

The way questions are asked in a focus group is quite different from a conventional interview. Empathy must be created with the members, relaxing them and generating a lively discussion. A brief introduction explains the proceedings including the tape recorder (there is little chance of the moderator taking notes as he or she will be busy keeping eye contact with the group). It is then necessary to break the ice by asking members to introduce themselves and their experience with the subject.

Working from the topic guide, developed prior to the group, the researcher moves the discussion from the broad to the particular. Members of the group are continuously encouraged to express their viewpoint and challenge the views of other group members. In this way all the issues unfold, supported by a discussion which gives a deeper understanding of the subject being researched.

Managing the group dynamics can be made difficult by a dominant personality who may attempt to run the group or whose views colour those of other members. Equally there may be slow thinkers, introverts, wits, compulsive talkers and the indifferent. Bringing out the best from each without insulting or embarrassing anyone requires both authority and tact. Groups generally take between 60 and 90 minutes to administer, depending on the complexity of the subject and interruptions from films or product presentations.

TOOLS OF THE GROUP MODERATOR

The group moderator will establish the stimulus materials prior to the group. The line of questioning will be defined through the topic guide, and any additional stimulus materials will be introduced at particular points in the discussion. This sounds as though it should be easy, but it requires particular skill to ensure that the questions asked deliver the necessary answers. For example, while we usually need the answer to 'Why?' questions, the way to discover this is often by asking 'How?' and 'When?', or 'What?' This is because the question 'why' may not have always been fully thought through and is turned into a justification or rational answer. Using *how, when, what* (as well as *why*) may get behind the question and help us arrive at our own interpretation. As with any depth interviewing approach, most questions are 'open' to keep the conversation going and to get the fullest answer.

We have already explained the importance of asking people to give personal introductions to ease themselves into a conversational mode. It is also important to ensure that early questions are non-threatening so that respondents feel comfortable. Good questions are conversational in nature; they use the vernacular of the respondent, and are easy to understand.

Group members are kept interested and stimulated by more than questions. Stimulus of one kind or another may be introduced, such as:

- visual stimulus materials (for example, video, story boards, photographs, advertisements, Web sites);
- auditory stimulus materials (for example, tapes, video);
- product trials and demonstrations.

In addition to stimulus materials, there are a number of specific techniques that can be used in focus groups. Many of these techniques are termed projective techniques and are borrowed from the field of psychology. They are used to seek information on a particular topic by asking about a different or easier topic. They work because they circumvent potential barriers to expression and tap into different ways of thinking.

Brainstorming is a common technique used in many business meetings in which a storm of ideas is encouraged – anything goes, and the more the merrier. In one of the ideas there may be something that can be developed and built upon. An important principle of brainstorming is

Figure 4.1 *Picture drawings showing attitudes to a university*

saying what comes to mind without too much forethought. It is also closely linked to word associations, where respondents are asked to think of words which are associated with a product or brand.

Sentence completion is a development of word association where the moderator presents the group with an incomplete sentence that they are asked to finish. This can be carried out individually and introduced into the group for discussion, or the group can engage in discussion to complete the sentence jointly.

Word sorting is a technique where the groups are presented with a number of words or sentences and asked to sort them into groups according to the attributes of a product, or brand, or need. This is commonly used in advertising research for identifying associations with brands.

Developing a campaign is a group activity in which everyone would work together to come up with a campaign around an issue, for example to get people like themselves to buy a product.

Some issues are difficult to express in words and *picture drawing* can be used to stimulate discussion. In a focus group with undergraduates, respondents were each asked to draw a heraldic shield and divide it into four quadrants, each with a simple drawing to describe their life before coming to university, something that characterizes their disposition, what it feels like at university and where they see themselves in the future. The foetus and the armchair in the drawings by two of the students (see Figure 4.1) were strong expressions of their feelings of safety and security at the university.

Other projective techniques that can be used in the focus group include:

- *Creating fantasy:* for example, if you had a magic wand and could change anything about the way you do your weekly shop, what would you change?
- *Creating analogies/questions:* for example, if this brand were a car, what would it be?
- *Personification:* for example, if this brand was a person, what would it be like, what gender, how would it behave? What would it look like?
- *Futuristic imagination:* for example, looking forward to the next five years, how do you think things will change in the way people book their holidays?
- *Role play:* for example, if you were the CEO of this company, how would you promote your products to people like yourself?

SUMMARY

Focus groups usually comprise 5 to 10 respondents who have been recruited to join in a discussion on a subject of common interest. Under the guidance of a skilled moderator, ideas are flushed out and developed in a way that is not possible in one to one interviews. It is the group interaction that makes focus groups special.

The findings from focus groups enable us to obtain a deep understanding of behaviour, motivations and attitudes. Although they are based on small samples, the insights that come from the group interaction almost always enable us to understand the real issues, though we may want to use quantitative research to measure their importance. The analysis of qualitative findings from focus groups is discussed in detail in Chapter 13 (Data analysis) and Chapter 14 (Reporting).

A small number of focus groups with a target audience, typically four, will ensure that all the issues have been aired and that the possibility of bias in a group is minimized.

The two most important ingredients for successful focus groups are the recruitment of the correct participants and a skilled moderator. Careful screening at the recruitment stage ensures that people with the right characteristics are recruited. The skills of the moderator will be used to open and direct the discussion so that everyone is included and all of the points of the debate are fully aired.

5 Depth interviewing

Interviewing implies a formality, structure and purpose. It suggests that there is a list of questions to be asked and answered. It is, of course, a dialogue between people, so to that extent it is a conversation. Ordinary discourse may take you nowhere whereas an interview needs to elicit information. The asking of questions through interviewing is central in our lives, and it is therefore no surprise that it is one of the most common methods of enquiry utilized in market research.

In this book, we divide research methods into the two traditional paradigms – qualitative and quantitative. Where the research sets out to measure and quantify, the interview will be structured with precise questions, a strict order of asking the questions and answers that have been anticipated and accounted for with pre-coded responses. This type of questioning is covered in Chapter 9.

The depth interview gives a different perspective to the highly structured interview used in quantitative designs where numbers and spread of response are crucial. In practice, many market research studies lend themselves to a multi-method design, incorporating aspects of both qualitative and quantitative methodologies. A customer satisfaction survey might require depth interviewing at the front end of the survey to establish issues that people should be questioned about. A survey on product development might begin with focus groups to explore unmet

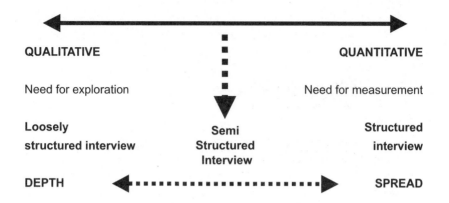

Figure 5.1 *Different types of interviews in market research*

needs, followed by structured interviewing to measure the size of these needs, and conclude with depth interviewing to test the concepts.

Where insights and exploration are required, the interview will be more loosely structured with flexibility in the construction of the questions themselves, the order they are asked and plenty of scope for respondents to answer in their own words without having responses boxed into pre-set classifications. This is the subject of this chapter.

The format of the depth interview is loosely structured, allowing freedom for both the interviewer and the interviewee to explore additional points and change direction if necessary. These interviews incorporate a good deal of the respondent's perspective into the findings and therefore increase the validity of the information collected. This is a very important feature where the research issues are not known, or where there is the feeling that decisions have been driven by assumptions which may, or may not be an accurate reflection of the views in the marketplace.

WHY USE DEPTH INTERVIEWS

Depth interviews are generally (but as we will see, not always) carried out face-to-face so that the interviewer can create a relationship with the respondent by taking the time to open up the subject, respond to body language and build trust that results in the truth coming out.

A small number of depth interviews increase our understanding of the issues faced by the respondent and can reveal practices that were previously assumed. By using depth interviews in a research design, the validity of the research is increased as the respondent's own perspective is incorporated into the research agenda.

Depth interviews can be carried out individually or in pairs. A husband and wife may be interviewed as a pair about banking choices. Two teenagers may be interviewed to find out what they think of parental controls.

Depth interviews compete with focus groups as a qualitative research method and are preferable in a number of circumstances:

WHEN TO USE DEPTH INTERVIEWS RATHER THAN A FOCUS GROUP

- Respondents are geographically scattered and it is not possible to convene a group.
- There can be no contamination of other people's responses in the discussion.
- Each respondent's story needs to be followed from beginning to end as in a case study of behaviour.
- Significant comment is required from each and every respondent (in a one and a half hour focus group each person only gets to talk for a maximum of around 10 minutes, whereas in a 45-minute depth interview respondents have the floor to themselves).
- Individuals' behaviours and responses need to be tracked over time, as with new product trials.
- The topic area is sensitive, such as personal wealth (or debt), personal hygiene topics, drug or alcohol use.

Depth interviews therefore are useful in market research designs where:

- research issues are not known;
- issues, attitudes and motivations need exploration;
- processes need describing in detail;
- contamination from other people's views is to be avoided;

- complex explanation and understanding is required;
- individuals need to test things and give their reactions to the products.

DEPTH INTERVIEWS IN MARKET RESEARCH DESIGN

As with focus groups, depth interviews can stand alone or be used as part of a multi-method design:

- *Customer satisfaction studies:* often in conjunction with a quantitative survey. Depth interviews can be used at the front end to identify satisfaction issues or at the back end to explore emergent issues from the main survey.
- *Market structure:* key respondents with a bird's-eye view of the market can be selected for their expert knowledge for depth interviews.
- *Product testing:* individual cases can be tracked through a trial of a new product through staged depth interviewing.
- *Needs assessment:* a small number of depth interviews can be used to identify current behaviours and identify unmet needs.
- *Advertising research:* testing of advertisements in many formats can be carried out using depth interviews. This allows the material to be shown and avoids the inevitable contamination from other respondents which occurs in focus groups.

HOW MANY DEPTH INTERVIEWS ARE NEEDED?

The number of interviews that are to be carried out is determined at the research design stage. In qualitative research we are more concerned with the quality and depth than the proportions of people that gave one response or another. As few as 10 depth interviews can be enough and 30 would almost certainly draw out all the issues pertaining to the research topic.

Carrying out and analyzing 30 depth interviews can be very costly. The depth interview, when carried out in a face-to-face situation costs around 10 times as much as a comparable interview conducted on the telephone. Much will depend on the circumstances such as the spread of the interviews, the ease of travel to the respondent, and the ability to combine other interviews in the same vicinity, when determining the number of interviews required.

QUESTIONS TO ASK ABOUT THE NUMBER OF INTERVIEWS TO BE USED:

- Are the interviews the sole data collection method?
- How specialized and unique are the practices or attitudes you are researching?
- What is the variability of the respondent types in the population – will 30 interviews cover all of them?
- How important is it that the range of responses sought is exhaustive?
- How important is it that the research diagnoses the problem rather than measures its size?
- How large is the population?

THE ROLE OF THE TELEPHONE IN DEPTH INTERVIEWING

There can be no doubt that face-to-face interviews offer advantages over the telephone in building rapport, watching and using body language as additional clues to the responses and allowing time to pace the discussion. The telephone is a restrictive tool demanding quick responses to questions and abhorring the vacuum of silence. In this respect it limits the time that someone can think about the answer to the question. It is also difficult to keep someone's concentration on the telephone for more than 30 to 40 minutes, although there are examples of discursive, unstructured conversational type interviews that have lasted 90 minutes.

However, face-to-face interviews are not without their disadvantages. They are expensive to set up. Normally they are preceded by a phone interview at which time the project is explained, some qualifying questions are asked and an appointment for the visit is made. So the cost of the initial telephone interview should be added to the cost of the face-to-face interview when comparing the total cost.

Just because a face-to-face interview has been set up it does not mean that the respondent will be there at the appointed hour. The logistical problems of sickness, absence and crises interrupting interviews should not be underestimated. 'No shows' form a significant minority of face-to-face interviews and they raise the cost of the project if a wasted journey is made.

Since the telephone is such an efficient medium for carrying out interviews, it is used widely for depth interviews and proves highly successful for a number of reasons. Nowadays, when time is at a premium, many respondents may prefer to carry out the interview using the phone. It can be argued that when visiting respondents on their territory, there are many potential distractions that could disturb the interview such as phones ringing, people interrupting, or distracting chitchat about the weather and the neighbourhood. Although these could be social niceties that lubricate the interview, they also burn up the interview time. In contrast, people with a telephone glued to their ear may be more likely to give their undivided attention.

There is, therefore, a trade off that researchers have to make when deciding their medium for the depth interviews.

WINNING COOPERATION FOR THE INTERVIEW

We live in a world of information seeking and information gathering, and this has undoubtedly affected compliance with market research studies, particularly where the respondent requires a significant investment of time. Compliance with depth interviewing can be a problem where there is no 'buy in' with the topic area and seemingly no advantage to the respondents to give up their valuable time. Where respondents already have a relationship with the research sponsor, that is, customer or consumer, the compliance will be higher, and a financial incentive either personally or to a selected charity can sometimes help. This is normal practice in the United States but not so in Europe.

THE PRINCIPLES OF INTERVIEWING

We have described interviewing as a conversation with form and purpose, where usually the interviewer and the interviewee are talking for the first time. This presents special problems beyond those that would be met in normal social interactions between friends. The interviewer has limited time to get the respondent to talk freely and openly about a subject. There are some guidelines that can help this process:

- *Listen rather than speak.* The role of the interviewer is to ensure that the questions facilitate rather than close down conversation. A transcript of the interview tape should demonstrate this, with a significantly smaller proportion of time given over to the interviewer's words.
- *Adopt a clear line of questioning.* The interview should have a flow that makes sense to the respondent. Questions should be non-threatening, but can still be challenging, straightforward and most of all should avoid confusing respondents or making them feel defensive.
- *Facilitate a permissive tone.* Any suggestion of 'correct' responses should be guarded against. It is easy for respondents to feel there is a 'right' answer and that the interviewer is seeking to elicit this from them. Questions which might be leading and body language encouraging certain responses must be avoided.
- *Demonstrate engagement with the respondent.* The interview will flow better if the respondent feels that the interviewer is part of the process. The interviewer's facial expressions, voice tone and intonation and body language can convey all kinds of messages to the respondent including interest and encouragement.

THE INTERVIEW ITSELF

Interviewing is a matter of style, and what works for one interviewer does not necessarily work for another. A businesslike approach with an aura of confidence and control will transmit positively to the respondent. Enthusiasm will help develop interest in the topic. There really is nothing worse than the disinterested interviewer.

At the beginning of the interview it is to be expected that respondents will feel a certain anxiety, not knowing what to expect, perhaps concerned

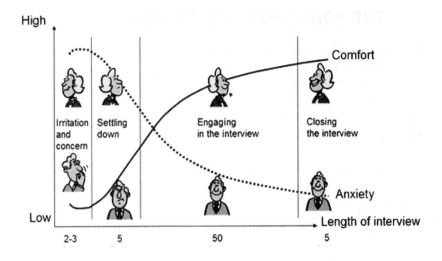

Figure 5.2 *The emotional state of respondents in different stages of the interview*

that they have let themselves in for something they would have preferred to avoid. Informing them that their words are being recorded could heighten this anxiety. They do not know what questions are in store or how long it will take, and they could fear the worst. They may even be unsure of their ability to answer the questions. Most of these feelings are rooted in ignorance – the anticipation being worse than the experience.

Skilled interviewers will create a rapport with respondents as quickly as possible and put them at ease. They will be assumptive about the tape recorder rather than making a big issue out of it. The sooner the interviewer gets the respondents talking, the sooner they will settle down and the greater will be the cooperation level. After the briefest of introductions, an easy question will start the ball rolling.

THE LINE OF QUESTIONING

There is no correct line of questioning in an interview, and much will depend on the topic matter. However, the stages in the interview need to be borne in mind at the planning stage. There is little point in launching into detailed questions in the first five minutes. The interview works because of the relationship between the interviewer and the respondent. The line of questioning must facilitate the development of the relationship and gradually build up to more searching questions.

As with focus groups, depth interviews are conducted around a topic guide. This is not set in stone, it is as its name suggests, a guide for the interviewer with sufficient freedom to allow the development of the interview at the respondent's pace and incorporate the needs of the research as well as the respondent.

The guide serves to ensure that all the research topics are covered in the discussion, but this does not mean that it is followed to the letter. The more skilled interviewer will hold the discussion guide in his/her head and make a mental note of coverage in the interview. This way, the interview flows in the form of a 'guided conversation' and appears 'natural'. As topics of discussion arise naturally, they can be followed and issues which have not occurred naturally can be raised by the interviewer. The discussion will be improved if subjects are raised by respondents in the natural course of the conversation. We cannot emphasize strongly enough the importance of listening to the responses, as many nuggets can be lost by the failure of the interviewer to pick up on issues either raised by the respondent or implicit throughout the interview.

DEVELOPING THE DISCUSSION GUIDE FOR THE INTERVIEW

The depth interview, being a qualitative data collection method, uses a loosely structured discussion guide similar to that used in the focus group discussion. This is opposed to the highly structured questionnaire that is used in a quantitative interview. It should follow a definite sequence. The conventional sequence is:

1. Introduction.
2. Warm up questions.
3. Main body of interview.
4. Thank and close.

The main body of the interview will be characterized by a number of specific sections relating the research objectives, and these are broken down into specific questions relating to that section, and the probes and prompts that can be used to develop the discussion and thus provide rich data.

As with the focus group discussion guide, open-ended questions are at the heart of the depth interview. They allow the flexibility to probe so that the interviewer may go into greater depth if required. They facilitate the development of a rapport between interviewer and respondent, encouraging cooperation and sharing of information. They also allow the interviewer to test the limits of the respondent's knowledge and experience, and as such can result in unexpected answers which may challenge the researcher's or the client's assumptions. A study commissioned to identify current practice in referral of business recovery work to accountancy firms revealed that a practice previously thought by the client to be the standard procedure was no longer operating and had not been for some time. These assumptions had been preventing the client seeking work from some of these lenders, as they falsely believed they were not in a position to refer work.

PROBES AND PROMPTS

A probe is a way of getting a respondent to expand further on his or her answer. The decision by the interviewer to probe further may be left to his or her discretion, or built into the discussion guide with reminders to prompt. Cues from the voice, body language and general tone of the interview can indicate that there is more that the respondent could and is willing to say. Silence itself can be a prompt as it encourages people to jump in and fill the space. An encouraging gesture and an enquiring look may be all that is needed. However, specific phrases and questions relating to the topic area can also be used:

> And what do *you* think about that?
> Can you talk me through that again?
> Anything more?

Whereas a probe is the enhancement of an answer, prompts introduce a subject that has not been raised. In most market studies, there are certain issues that need to be brought to the attention of the respondents to obtain their views. It may be necessary to remind a respondent about brands that have not yet been mentioned. It could be important to obtain his or her views on a process that has not been talked about.

The general rules for the development of the discussion guide are to follow a developmental sequence of discussion which will appear natural, building the conversation in depth, and to use questions that open rather than close down the discussion. The types of questions to avoid are:

- Long and complex questions causing respondents to become confused about what they are responding to, such as 'What do you think about the range of product available to you now, in the DIY stores and the supermarkets compared with a few years ago?' This also, in turn causes confusion at the analytical stage about which part of the question the respondent is referring to.
- Vague questions, such as 'What do you think will happen in the future?' The future in this question is open-ended and vague. Do we mean the next year, five years or ten years?
- Questions using technical jargon or company jargon that is not the language of the respondent, such as 'Have you got any use for SMS or GMS telemetry?' It is easy to forget that terminology used by the client is not always that used by the respondent.
- Leading questions, such as 'So you think Shell is a good supplier of LPG?' You will never know if the question led people to respond as suggested or if they rebelled at the suggestion, regardless of their viewpoint.
- Aggressive or threatening questions or comments, such as 'You seem to be avoiding answering me.' This may be the approach of the political interviewer, but in most marketing research, these questions serve to alienate the respondent and break down the rapport between interviewer and respondent

---

EXAMPLE OF AN INTERVIEW DISCUSSION GUIDE

Interviews with bankers and other lenders about using business recovery services and choosing suppliers of these services. Commissioned by Argent Fait accountancy company.

1. **Personal information.** Your job/responsibilities/position within the company.

---

2. **The market.**   Overall how has the economy changed in the last couple of years? PROMPT: chances of recession, and impact on businesses if there is a recession. How has the lending market changed in the last couple of years? Have you seen any changes resulting from the move towards a more rescue-oriented culture? What are these? PROMPT: fees, relationships, insolvencies.

3. **New legislation.**   What has been the impact of the New Insolvency Bill? What will be the future ramifications?

4. **Suppliers of business recovery services.**   What services are the most commonly used/most infrequently used? Who are the major players in business recovery service provision? What companies would you think of to use for these types of services? How do you get to hear about providers of such services?

5. **Choosing a business recovery service provider.**   How do you make the decision about which supplier of business recovery services you use? PROMPT: who is involved, how long does it take, company policy, relationships in the field, 'approved' suppliers. How many suppliers would you be able to choose from and how would you go about selecting one supplier over another? What factors might cause you to select?

6. **Dealing with suppliers.**   As a percentage of your total workload, how much time, on average, do you spend dealing with business recovery suppliers? Thinking of all the suppliers of business recovery services you have used, can you describe to me an excellent example of service? Use a case history. And similarly, can you describe to me the worst-case scenario you can recall?

7. **Magic wand.**   Let's now imagine you have a magic wand that you could wave to change the way business recovery services are commissioned. What would you do? How would that affect you? And also for the way business recovery services are organized, what would you use it for there?

8. **Argent Fait services.**   Thinking again now to the services of Argent Fait's business recovery team, how do you think they compare against other suppliers? What are their strengths/weaknesses? What do you think they could do better than they are currently doing to make usage easier and more efficient for yourself? PROMPT: contact, response times, availability, keeping to deadlines, clarity, knowledge, dependability, enthusiasm, efficiency. What do you value in their services over any of the other suppliers you use? PROMPT: fee levels, added

value, creativity of solutions. If you had the ability to change three things about the service Argent Fait provides, what would you change?

9. **Future trends.**   In the longer term, thinking about the next two years, can you see any changes that might influence the market for business recovery services? If you were the manager of the business recovery services department in a company, what would you expect to have to do over the next couple of years to keep your current level of business/increase the business you have?

10. Anything else you want to raise about business recovery services and providers?

THANK AND CLOSE

SUMMARY

Depth interviews are a qualitative data collection method which offer the opportunity to collect rich, descriptive data about people's behaviours, attitudes and perceptions, and unfolding complex processes. They can be used as a stand-alone research method or as part of a multi-method design, depending on the needs of the research.

Depth interviews are normally carried out face-to-face so that rapport can be created with respondents and body language can be used to add a high level of understanding to the answers. However, the telephone can be used to carry out depth interviews by a skilled researcher with little loss of data and at a tenth of the cost.

The style of the interview will depend on the interviewer. Successful depth interviewers listen rather than talk, have a clear line of questioning and use body language as a cue to building a rapport. The interview is more of a guided conversation than a staccato question and answer session.

The interview is conducted using a discussion guide (as in focus groups) that facilitates the flushing out of the respondent's views through open-ended questioning. As with focus groups, projective techniques can be incorporated into the interview.

6 Observation

OBSERVATION – A RESEARCH METHOD YOU CAN BELIEVE

It is worthwhile reflecting on the important role that observation has played in the formative years of the market research industry. In the 1930s companies such as AC Nielsen and Attwoods in the United States and Audits of Great Britain (AGB) began carrying out audits of product sales through retail outlets by counting stock levels in stores at periodic intervals and accounting for deliveries to the store during that same period. There were no questionnaires with questions to ask; the market researcher's role was simply to count stock and record purchases. As long as the recording was diligent and the sample of stores was representative, the result would be accurate.

Prior to the Second World War, the British government sponsored the Mass Observation Project to provide an anthropological study of the nation. During the Second World War this was extended to include a national panel of volunteers who kept diaries to track the mood of the war-beleaguered country using trained observers. They sat in pubs, watching and listening. They stood at bus stops and listened. They later captured their observations in diaries ready for analysis. A legacy of this approach is in the title of the market research agency, Mass Observation, which existed for about 30 years until being subsumed within a larger group. Its modern day equivalent is Video Research Ltd (located in Tokyo), one of the largest market research companies in Japan, whose title gives us a clue as to the tool kit the company used in its early years.

WHEN TO USE OBSERVATION

Since its origins in the 1930s the market research industry has moved on and the administered interview – either face-to-face or by telephone – has become the most common method of data collection. However there is still a role for observation, and indeed there has been something of a revival in its use, though usually as one of a mix of methods that form part of the whole research design. So, for example, the video camera has found a role for the market researcher. That camera positioned discreetly in the corner of the supermarket ceiling may not be there just to stop pilfering, it can also observe the shoppers and their behaviour. It can watch our procrastination as we buy our beans and collect behavioural patterns that may be automatic and which would not be recalled in a conventional interview. Do we deliberate over our purchase of a can of beans? Do we read the label? What influence and pressure comes from the accompanying kids? Do we pick up other brands and examine them or do we just fly down the aisles throwing cans in the trolley without even checking prices?

Observation is still used in a conventional sense, using the eyes and recording the data on pro formas. A telecom company wanted to consider the opportunity for offering information alerts to different industries, and chose commercial road transport as a potentially attractive sector. It was decided to commission a qualitative survey amongst transport managers to find out what type of information they needed in their daily round. Since it was believed that some of the information that was needed and used might be taken for granted, such sources and requirements may not be mentioned in conventional interviews. A sample of companies employing transport managers were persuaded to allow observers to spend two days in their offices finding out what was requested and how it was used. The observers watched drivers pop their heads around doors and share stories about traffic conditions, best routes and the weather. They heard phone calls being made to ferry companies to collect timetables. They observed juggling acts as the transport management team sought to optimize return loads and routes. In this way, the complex sources of information that are used as part of the natural cognitive process were noted and recorded, and they would not have been found by orthodox interviewing techniques.

Collecting information in this way need not be costly if the agent is the camera, but it is time-consuming and therefore expensive if an observer is required to hang around waiting, watching and recording. Observation can play an important supporting role in many different types of market research projects and it is these that we describe in the sections that follow.

THE AUDIT – A MAJOR APPLICATION FOR OBSERVATION

Traditionally researchers visiting stores on a particular date collected data for audits. At this time they would record the stock levels of all products of interest and check on delivery notes and purchase documents. They would return in one or two months' time and repeat the exercise. The data could then be used to calculate the sales of products by adjusting the retailer purchases by the difference between the two stock levels. Once the data had been collected from all the stores and pooled for analysis, it offered considerable insights into brand share movements over time, by retailer, by geography, and average prices.

Today the data are more likely to be collected by electronic means using bar codes (EPOS or electronic point of sale) and there is no requirement for a field worker to visit the store, though the principle remains the same. The key to audits is to set up systems for regular and continuous recording over years so that accurate trends are measured. This is a quantitative research tool and therefore the sample must be chosen with care to reflect the trade outlets that sell the products that are being tracked. Since just a few companies and outlets so heavily dominate the retail landscape, every effort must be made to be as inclusive as possible. If a leading outlet refuses to take part, it may scupper the whole scheme. As compensation for providing the data, the retailers either get paid or they get the data fed back to them against an aggregated figure for the rest of the contributors so that they can benchmark and track changes in their position.

OBSERVATION IN SHOPPING SURVEYS

Mystery shopping has become an important formalized part of shopping surveys. A fieldworker plays the role of a member of the public buying or enquiring about the product, and the fieldworker records the experience in as much detail as possible on a questionnaire (usually at a later time so as not to be obvious). This is common practice in hotels, restaurants and car dealers.

There are codes of conduct that researchers adhere to in mystery shopping. If the target of the mystery shop could lose out financially (as in the case of a car showroom where the fieldworker has no intention of buying a car) then the contacts are limited to members of the sponsor's outlets. In other words, only dealers within the research buyer's group are covered. Mystery shopping hotels involves paying the going rate for a room, and so allows the researchers to widen the net since a fair price has been paid and nobody's time has been wasted.

We have already referred to the use of observation in checking on the point of purchase – what do we actually do when we buy a product? The earlier example referred to the use of video cameras recording our shopping experience. There are many more complex buying situations where observation can be used.

Take for example the visit of a prospective customer to a car dealer's showroom. What do customers do when they enter the showroom? Are they purposeful and walk to look at one of the cars on display? Do they look around for help? Do the salespeople offer help and do they do so in an appropriate manner? How successful are the car salespeople in dealing with questions and helping move the sale forward? How do they deal with the tricky business of giving a price for the car? Do they follow up the enquiry?

The camera (or conventional observation) could be used to capture customers' reactions as they check into hotels, airports or restaurants. How friendly is the meet and greet? How efficiently does reception deal with the check-in process? Are customers offered all the information and help they require? And so on.

A key part of any shopping study is the measurement of footfall – that is the number of people passing an outlet or an advertising hoarding. Observation is an obvious means of recording shopping traffic, and it can be measured by fieldworkers counting heads. (Rather than keep a literal head count they are likely to use 'clickers' which are simple mechanical counters that are activated by squeezing/clicking the device.) Equally, it may be possible to measure the footfall electronically using optical scanners (more difficult than you might think in a busy thoroughfare with people pushing in crowds and not walking in an orderly manner).

Observation plays a very obvious role in shopping surveys, where a researcher can easily walk into a store to check if products are in stock and their ticketed price. This is not classed as mystery shopping as there is no communication with the retail staff (other than perhaps to ask if the product is sold at the store). The research task becomes more complicated if the researcher seeks to photograph the in-store display using a camera. For this, permission would be required from the manager and it cannot be assumed it will always be granted.

OBSERVATION IN PRODUCT RESEARCH

The traditional interview, especially one-to-one depth interviews in the home, in mall intercepts or in focus groups is an important contribution to product research.[1] These interviews provide occasions for respondents to evaluate products and talk about what they like and dislike. There is, however, always the danger that a 60-minute interview discussing a product will end up splitting the atom – in other words, yielding a great deal of information but not in the context of how real decisions are made. The decision to choose a particular brand of toothpaste may be complicated by a history of loyalty to that brand, but it is made in seconds in the superstore. It is not something that consumers agonize about a great deal and yet the interview asks them to do just this. There is always a danger that this extreme focus on a small decision achieves a result but that it is a little 'over cooked'.

A video camera in a store would capture any consideration of other brands at the toothpaste counter. However, if it were possible, observation in the bathroom would also establish if the tube is squeezed at the bottom, in the middle or at the top. We would see if the top of the toothpaste is replaced after use. We would see how much paste is squeezed onto the brush. A toothpaste manufacturer interested in packaging and product development might find value in all these findings.

Video cameras trained on the feet of runners in a marathon are played back at slow speed and accurate market share data can be determined for the different models and brands of shoes. In another piece of observational research Adidas noticed, almost by accident, that kids were leaving the laces of their trainers undone, and this prompted them to launch a highly successful shoe with a Velcro strap.

Grohe, a German manufacturer of mixer showers, ran workshops in which installers were observed fitting different makes of showers. The exercise prompted the development of an easy fixing kit to simplify and speed the work of the installer.

Marks & Spencer uses its Oxford Street store to watch how consumers react to new designs, and through observation of this type, quick decisions can be made to launch or kill a product.

OBSERVATION IN POSTER CHECKS

One of the problems of poster research is determining how many people see them. Posters form part of the backcloth of our streets. People seldom study them deliberately but take them in subliminally as they move around on foot, in the car or on public transport. Observation plays a role in providing answers to two important questions: first, what is the traffic count that passes the poster? And second, how visible is the poster (and what condition is it in)?

In order to obtain answers to these questions, visits must be made to the poster sites. From the traffic measures that are taken at the sites, researchers can develop predictive models to show the likelihood of viewing. These gross viewing opportunities are then adjusted by a visibility index assessed from cars, the sidewalk and taking account of any obstructions. This type of data is important to advertisers and their clients when setting charge rates for posters. A specific campaign would normally be tracked in the conventional way by interviewing a sample of people to determine their recall of the posters.

OBSERVATION IN CHECKING TELEVISION VIEWING

The television has become an integral part of the lives of people worldwide. In most Western societies, 98 per cent of households own a television, and many have two or more. Commercial television is financed by adverts costing thousands of dollars for a 30-second slot. Not surprisingly, the measurement of television audiences is taken very seriously.

In the early years of television, interviews with the viewing public were used to measure viewing, although before long a more sophisticated approach was required. Early electromechanical systems were devised that worked out from the heat of the television if it was on and recorded the event on long streams of paper tape. However, it measured television use and not television viewing, and more advanced methods have evolved.

Today the most common method of measuring television viewing is through 'peoplemeters' which are electronic devices that sit on a television and feed a data storage unit, also in the household, which in turn is linked to the telephone so it can transmit viewing data back to the market research company's central computer. In any one television region (or even a small country) a panel of around 400 households is signed up to have peoplemeters installed on their televisions. In the home equipped with the peoplemeter, the viewer uses a remote control unit which logs who is watching the television and what he or she think of the programmes. This is not observation in the classical sense as discussed earlier, but it is almost Big Brother watching you watching them.

SETTING UP OBSERVATION PROGRAMMES

Using observation requires imagination. Most of the occasions when we use observation it is in an artificial environment such as a focus group, a hall test or clinic.[2] These contrived occasions may be perfectly acceptable for simple checks. However, there is no substitute for watching consumers in the real world. The small instructions on a pack may be perfectly visible in a well-lit hall or focus group venue but impossible in a gloomy domestic environment. Installers of showers might be at pains to use screws for all parts of their installation when they know they are being watched in a clinic, whereas in the privacy of their own work environment the same installation might be put together with nails.

It is not easy to organize a fly on the wall camera to capture everything that goes on in domestic or business life. There are obvious issues of privacy to consider and in any case, fixed head cameras may not give the detailed picture that is required. However, video and cameras are superb ways of capturing a feel for the ways that products are used. A manufacturer of electrical cable reels (extension cable) believed that the display of his products in stores materially affected sales. He commissioned a store check which involved researchers visiting outlets and taking photos of the displays. Pictures came back of reels that were in jumbled heaps, and usually at floor level, because the flanges of the reels were not flat and would not stack. A small redesign resulted in a reel that worked just as well for the consumer and could be displayed to best advantage in the store.

Consumers can be asked to save their used discarded packs in a 'bin test'. The old wrappers, boxes or cans are thrown into bin-liners and saved for collection by the researchers. The trash is then examined to see how it was opened and used.

REPORTING OBSERVATIONAL DATA

In this discussion of the use of observation, it is clear that there is a high level of subjectivity (excepting audits and peoplemeters that record television viewing). There may only be a relatively small number of data sets to interpret. The observations may be capable of interpretation in different ways. The picture of what was observed may not be absolutely clear.

Despite the high cost of capturing and interpreting observational data, its impact can be considerable – it is said that a picture is worth a thousand words. A large ship repair company commissioned a survey to find out why it was losing share to Japanese yards. On conclusion of one of the depth interviews, a researcher asked permission to take a photograph of the respondent, a manager of a large shipping company. The photograph showed the respondent at his desk on which were two quotes: one was a few pages held together by a paper clip, the other was an impressive bound document. The impressive bound document was the bid that won, and it was from a Japanese competitor. The report on the findings contained 15,000 words of worthy analysis, but it was the one photo of the ship owner and his two bids that had most impact.

SUMMARY

Observation was the first method used by market researchers to collect data. It has been superseded in importance by interviews but there are nevertheless many opportunities where it could provide valuable insights.

Observation was originally used to carry out audits of products in supermarkets but today data is collected by swiping bar codes at the point of sale.

Mystery shopping is an important form of observation in market research, and is used to test customers' experience in buying situations such as at car dealers, hotels or restaurants.

The video camera has found a use for observing customers in supermarkets to find out how they choose products for their shopping basket. It is used in focus groups to watch the body language of the participants. In clinics it captures the reactions of respondents. It can be used to check on traffic flows or brands used.

The applications for observation in market research are increasing, helped by digital cameras and optical devices. It makes a very powerful supplement to other forms of more conventional research.

7 Sampling and statistics

THE PRINCIPLES OF SAMPLING

The theory of sampling frightens many would-be market researchers. There are all those formulae and so much science. Certainly the market researcher needs a good grasp of how to choose a robust sample but in truth, serious mathematics are seldom needed. Standard software and statistician colleagues do the heavy work.

Readers who want the mathematical side of the subject spelling out to them should read one of the many books that are devoted to this subject. In this chapter we will talk practically about how and why we choose samples in the way that we do.

The sampling that takes place in consumer markets is very different from that in business-to-business markets. We will take each separately.

RANDOM SAMPLING IN CONSUMER MARKETS

Consumer markets tend to be massive, with target audiences measured in hundreds of thousands or millions of people. Interviewing everyone, or indeed most people, in such large populations would be inordinately expensive and take a considerable amount of time. However, if we take a carefully chosen subset, then we do not need to interview many people at all to achieve a reliable picture of what the result is for the whole of the population. This subset is a sample; a group of people selected to represent the whole.

If the sample is chosen randomly, with everyone in the population having an equal and known chance of being selected, then we can apply measures of probability to show the accuracy of the result. If there is no random selection (we will come to this later), then there must, by implication, be an element of judgement or bias in determining who should be chosen, in which case it is not possible to measure the accuracy of the sample result. A random sample is often called a probability sample as we can determine the likelihood or chance of the result being within bounds of accuracy.

Random need not mean that the database has to be in one single pot. It is still random if the population is broken into smaller databases and a system is devised of selecting randomly from these. For example, surveys of a national population are more conveniently chosen by first breaking that population into districts such as states, or counties or boroughs, and carrying out a first cut to randomly choose a number of these districts. States, counties or boroughs that are chosen in this way are then used as the next level of a pool from which to carry out a random selection. This multi-stage or stratified random sample has all the principles of randomness and therefore qualifies as a probability sample from which the accuracy of the result can be determined.

If the selection of the sample were carried out manually it would demand some systematic approach such as choosing every nth number. In fact, we seldom need to worry about making the random selection in this way as the computer does it for us.

CHOOSING THE SIZE OF THE SAMPLE

We now have to decide on the size of the sample. This is where many people new to market research and statistics can become confused. They wrongly assume that the sample has to be some respectable proportion of the total population – say, 10 per cent. Think about it: if we carry out a 10 per cent sample of the United States we would need to interview nearly 3 million people. What matters is not the percentage of the sample of the whole population but its absolute size. In other words, as long as the sample is big enough, it will give us a picture that accurately reflects the total. But what is big enough?

Imagine that you had to test the quality of the water in Lake Michigan. How much water would you have to take out to do the test? There must be millions of gallons in that lake and you certainly would not want or need to take out 10 per cent. In fact, if you assumed that the water was well mixed, and you took a few bucketfuls from various points around the Lake and from its centre, you would get a very good picture of its water quality. It is the same with populations: only a few bucketfuls of people are required to give us a good picture.

Let us try to figure out how big a bucketful or sample size we need of a human population to give us an accurate picture. We will imagine that we want to find out what proportion of people in the United States eats breakfast. We randomly choose people from across the nation and plot the result. The first half-dozen interviews could give results that are all over the place and the picture is not clear. However, after a surprisingly small number of interviews, in fact around 30, a pattern will emerge. This is only a pattern and in no way does it allow us to predict the likelihood of the next respondent eating breakfast or not. However, by the time we get to 200 or so interviews, we will find that the result begins to settle at around 80 per cent eating breakfast, and even though we go on and interview hundreds more, the result will not change a great deal. The way in which the variability of a sample stabilizes as the sample size increases is illustrated schematically in Figure 7.1.

It will be noted from the figure that once our sample becomes larger than 30, the consistency of response (that is, it is less variable) markedly improves. Beyond the number of 30 we are moving from qualitative research into quantitative research and once the sample size reaches 200, we are very definitely getting into quantitative territory. The area between 30 and 200 is somewhat grey.

SAMPLING ERROR

It is worth repeating this very important principle of random sampling – the sample size required to give an accurate result to a survey bears no relation to the size of the whole population, it is the absolute size of the sample that counts. It does not matter if we are researching breakfast-eating habits in a small country like Ireland with a population of just

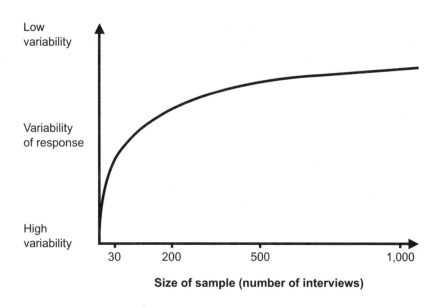

Figure 7.1 *Variability of response and sample size*

3.5 million or a large country like the United States with a population of nearly 300 million, a random sample of 1,000 people in each country will give us the same, very accurate result; in fact plus or minus 3.2 per cent.

What does very accurate mean? Because we have chosen the sample randomly, the accuracy of the result can be stated, at least within limits. These limits are expressed in terms of confidence or certainty. In most market research sampling, confidence limits are given at the 95 per cent level, meaning that we can be 95 per cent certain that if we carry out this sample again and again, choosing different people to interview each time, we will get a similar result. The result will only be similar – it will not be exactly the same. This is because there will be some degree of error from what would have been achieved had we carried out a complete census. However, with 1,000 interviews that error is only plus or minus 3.2 per cent of what the true figure would be from the census, which in the circumstances – not having to interview all those millions of people – is very good.

Hopefully, this is clear. A large, randomly selected sample size is all that is needed and it does not matter how many people there are in the total population. It now gets slightly more complicated because the error level is not always plus or minus 3.2 per cent for a sample size of 1,000:

it varies depending on the actual response that is achieved. The point is that when we set out to measure the proportion of people that eat breakfast, we do not know what the result will be. It could be everyone (or no one), in which case this would very soon become clear. For example, let us imagine that we interviewed 500 people and asked them the stupid question, 'Do you take a drink of one kind or another every day?' When all 500 tell us that they do, we can be fairly certain that the next person we speak to will also tell us he or she has a drink of one kind or another every day.

But imagine that we interview 500 people and ask them 'Do you drink tea every day?' and determine that half do and half do not. When we get to the 501st interview we cannot be certain whether this person will drink tea or not. This 50/50 split in an answer to a question is the worst case, whereas 100 per cent (or 0 per cent) is the best in terms of sampling error.

Before we carry out a survey we do not know what the result will be, and so we have to assume the worst case and quote the error assuming that 50 per cent will give a response to a question. And the plus or minus 3.2 per cent referred to for a sample of 1,000 is just that – it assumes that a response to a question from a survey will be 50 per cent.

So, we choose a sample size based on the worst case scenario (50/50) and quote sample errors at this level. Then once the survey is complete we have a result. In the case of the 'Do they eat breakfast?' question we find that 80 per cent of the people in the survey say that they do eat breakfast. We can then look up in tables or calculate using a formula what the error is around that specific figure. Figure 7.2 shows a 'ready reckoner' that can be used to check the sample error at the 95 per cent confidence limits. Look along the top row to the percentage that says 20 per cent or 80 per cent (the proportion that say they eat breakfast). Look down the left-hand column to where it says the sample size is 1,000. Where the row and columns intersect you will see the error is given as plus or minus 2.6 per cent. In other words, we can be 95 per cent certain that the true proportion of people that eat breakfast (if we were to interview absolutely everybody) is between 77.4 per cent and 82.6 per cent.

If we interviewed only 500 people the error on the 'Do you eat breakfast?' answer would be plus or minus 3.6 per cent, and it would be plus or minus 1.8 per cent if we interviewed 2,000 people. It is clear that the more people we interview, the better the quality of the result, but there are diminishing returns. Quadrupling the sample will usually double the accuracy for a given sample design.

% giving a response to a question

Sample size	1% or 99%	2% or 98%	3% or 97%	4% or 96%	5% or 95%	6% or 94%	8% or 92%	10% or 90%	12% or 88%	15% or 85%	20% or 80%	25% or 75%	30% or 70%	35% or 65%	40% or 60%	45% or 55%	50%
25	4.0	5.6	6.8	7.8	8.7	9.5	10.8	12.0	13.0	14.3	16.0	17.3	18.3	19.1	19.6	19.8	20.0
50	2.8	4.0	4.9	5.6	6.2	6.8	7.7	8.5	9.2	10.1	11.4	12.3	13.0	13.5	13.9	14.1	14.2
75	2.3	3.2	3.9	4.5	5.0	5.5	6.2	6.9	7.5	8.2	9.2	10.0	10.5	11.0	11.3	11.4	11.5
100	2.0	2.8	3.4	3.9	4.4	4.8	5.4	6.0	6.5	7.1	8.0	8.7	9.2	9.5	9.8	9.9	10.0
150	1.6	2.3	2.8	3.2	3.6	3.9	4.4	4.9	5.3	5.9	6.6	7.1	7.5	7.8	8.0	8.1	8.2
200	1.4	2.0	2.4	2.8	3.1	3.4	3.8	4.3	4.6	5.1	5.7	6.1	6.5	6.8	7.0	7.0	7.1
250	1.2	1.8	2.2	2.5	2.7	3.0	3.4	3.8	4.1	4.5	5.0	5.5	5.8	6.0	6.2	6.2	6.3
300	1.1	1.6	2.0	2.3	2.5	2.8	3.1	3.5	3.8	4.1	4.6	5.0	5.3	5.5	5.7	5.8	5.8
400	0.99	1.4	1.7	2.0	2.2	2.4	2.7	3.0	3.3	3.6	4.0	4.3	4.6	4.8	4.9	5.0	5.0
500	0.89	1.3	1.5	1.8	2.0	2.1	2.4	2.7	2.9	3.2	3.6	3.9	4.1	4.3	4.4	4.5	4.5
600	0.81	1.1	1.4	1.6	1.8	2.0	2.2	2.5	2.7	2.9	3.3	3.6	3.8	3.9	4.0	4.1	4.1
800	0.69	0.98	1.2	1.4	1.5	1.7	1.9	2.1	2.3	2.5	2.8	3.0	3.2	3.3	3.4	3.5	3.5
1,000	0.63	0.90	1.1	1.3	1.4	1.5	1.7	1.9	2.1	2.3	2.6	2.8	2.9	3.1	3.1	3.2	3.2
1,200	0.57	0.81	0.99	1.1	1.3	1.4	1.6	1.7	1.9	2.1	2.3	2.5	2.7	2.8	2.8	2.9	2.9
1,500	0.51	0.73	0.89	1.0	1.1	1.2	1.4	1.6	1.7	1.9	2.1	2.3	2.4	2.5	2.5	2.6	2.6
2,000	0.44	0.61	0.75	0.86	0.96	1.0	1.2	1.3	1.4	1.6	1.8	1.9	2.0	2.1	2.2	2.2	2.2
2,500	0.40	0.56	0.68	0.78	0.87	0.95	1.1	1.2	1.3	1.4	1.6	1.7	1.8	1.9	2.0	2.0	2.0
3,000	0.36	0.51	0.62	0.71	0.79	0.87	0.99	1.1	1.2	1.3	1.5	1.6	1.7	1.7	1.8	1.8	1.8

Figure 7.2 Sample size ready reckoner

The other important thing to remember about sample sizes is that they must always be judged in terms of their accuracy on the number in the group of people being examined – even if it is a subset of the whole. For example, the 1,000 people we interviewed to find out if they ate breakfast gave us a result which we are happy with plus or minus 2.6 per cent at the 95 per cent confidence level. However, if we get interested in the possible differences between children and adults or males and females, we have to take each subset separately. We may look at the female respondents in the sample and see that adolescent women appear less likely to eat breakfast than women over the age of 18. Let us say that the results show that only 70 per cent of adolescent girls eat breakfast compared with 80 per cent of those that are aged 18 or over. Can we be sure that the difference is significant? We need to know how many adolescent females were in the sample, and we find that it was only 75 out of 1,000 compared with the non-adolescent females where there were 400. Look on the error tables and see what the range of error is on these results.

We see that for the adolescent females the range of error for this result is plus or minus 10.5 per cent, or between 59.5 per cent and 80.5 per cent. The range of error for the non-adolescent female result is plus or minus 4.6 per cent, or between 75.4 per cent and 84.6 per cent. Because the ranges of error overlap between these two results, we cannot say that the difference is statistically significant – it lies within the bands of possible error and it could be due to sampling fluke.

A final word on error: it will be recalled that we said that very few samples are drawn from the total mass of population, rather the samples are selected in stages by randomly choosing a region (for example a state defined or political area) and then a random sample of sub-areas within that political region until finally, the households are drawn randomly from the electoral register. As a result of this procedure, the sample of households will be clustered into small areas which can be far more economically contacted and interviewed. Because of its economy over simple random sampling, multi-stage sampling is widely used in market research wherever random samples of the whole population are sought. The technique can be used with other sample frames as well as the electoral register. A problem with the technique, however, is that sampling error is always increased. Effectively, additional sampling error is introduced at each stage of the sampling process and needs to be allowed for when selecting an effective size of sample.

RANDOM SAMPLING AND NON-RESPONSE

From a sampling perspective, non-response is a major source of bias in the achieved sample. For one reason or another it is in practice impossible to collect data from every individual making up a sample. Some will not be contactable, some may have moved away or died and some will certainly refuse to participate. If respondents live in certain parts of an inner city it may be impractical to even approach them – interviewers increasingly will not go into some 'no go' areas. If for a random sample the response rate achieved is say 80 per cent (in practice now considered to be very high), the achieved sample from the 500 originally selected will be only 400, and possibly the accuracy levels with this smaller sample will be too low. Of course the problem can be apparently solved by sample replacement – take a supplementary sample and make contact until the desired 500 interviews are achieved. However, we are back to problems of bias. The non-respondents may in some way or another differ significantly (in relation to the aims of the study) from those who were interviewed and the results may not, therefore, be representative of the whole population. Certainly some non-respondents differ from respondents in that they refuse to participate in surveys, and this may well be very relevant in political polling or attitude research (that is, non-cooperators may be a certain personality type who hold more critical attitudes in general).

Non-response is a major problem for market researchers, particularly because average response rates to surveys are falling year by year. One advantage of random and pre-selected samples in relation to non-response is that at least the level of response achieved in a survey can be quantified – with a complete list of the sample the results of contact with each potential respondent can be logged. Also, because of contact records, rigorous callback procedures can be enforced to increase response: interviewers can be required to return up to three times at different times of the day to homes where there was no reply at the first call. Such procedures cannot be used in quota sampling (or at least their implementation cannot be assured), the subject to which we now turn.

QUOTA SAMPLES

In reality, very few samples in market research are truly random in the way that we have described them so far. This is because random samples are quite difficult and expensive to administer. In order that we have a random sample, we must have the whole population available to us from which we can make our selection. In Europe, the interviewing amongst households may be carried out face-to-face, calling at dwellings that have been identified in some systematic and random fashion. Typical of these is a random walk in which a street is randomly selected, a house is randomly selected on that street and then the interviewer has instructions to interview every nth house and to alternately choose an intersection to turn down. Special rules will cover blocks of flats and what to do when buildings are non-residential. Already you can see that it is getting complicated and there is scope for the instructions to go wrong.

Choosing the sample from an electoral register overcomes this nth number and left, right problem but there could still be quite some distances between the calls, making them very expensive.

And then who do you interview when the door is answered? The old fashioned notion of there being a 'head of household' is now blurred and the female may be earning far more than the male. Of course, we could have an alternate instruction here but there could prove to be many callbacks if the person we want to interview is not in. The random approach would not allow substitutes as this introduces bias.

In the United States there are very few door-to-door surveys. The size of the country and the possible dangers associated with knocking on strangers' doors in some inner city areas are two very good reasons this is so. Instead, the phone is more likely to be used for the interview. However, there is no perfect database of phone numbers. Significant numbers of people are ex-directory and they could represent a group of respondents with special characteristics – older and wealthier, more likely to be female. If the phone directories are insufficiently comprehensive then another means must be found of carrying out the random selection. All types of inventive methods are used here including random digit dialling (eventually a real number is found and starts ringing) or the selection of a number at random from the white pages and changing the final digit by increasing it by one number (say the randomly selected number from the directory was +1 972 735 0537 then it would be changed by adding one to the last digit to become +1 972 735 0538). Both random digit dialling and 'plus 1' dialling involves high costs of wasted calls – to non-residential subscribers, non-existent numbers and so on. Also, since among the reasons why people choose to be ex-directory undoubtedly is that they do not want to be bothered by people such as market research interviewers, response rates will be even lower than among listed households. (Response rates in consumer phone interviewing are low in any case.)

All this is avoided if we carry out 'quota samples'. The demographic structure of most populations is known. Previous surveys and census data tells us the splits by gender, age, income groups (or social grade), geography and many other key selection criteria.[1] Therefore, a simpler and cheaper means of obtaining a representative sample is to set a quota for the interviewers to achieve a picture that mirrors the population that is being researched. Filling the quota will provide a mix of respondents that is reflective of the population being targeted.

In effect, the choice of respondents in a quota sample is left to interviewers (unlike the case with pre-selected random samples) providing they fill the quotas to ensure the overall sample is representative, in key parameters, of the population being researched. In consumer research, demographics such as gender and income groups (or social grade) are common quota parameters, and they are often interlocked (for example, age group quotas for each income group). Table 7.1 illustrates this. In research using these quotas, respondents would be selected by the interviewing team to match the characteristics of each cell (for example, 12 respondents of the medium to high income group and aged 18 to 24), until all cells are filled. In Table 7.1, the quotas shown are for a total sample. Where a number of interviewers are involved, each is given his or her own individual sheet.

Table 7.1 *Example of interlocking quotas*

Age	Numbers of people in income group (which would be defined in dollars)				
	High income group	**Medium to high income group**	**Medium to low income group**	**Low income group**	**Total**
18/24	2	12	8	11	**33**
25/44	12	19	18	16	**65**
45+	17	24	25	36	**102**
Total	**31**	**55**	**51**	**63**	**200**

One practical problem with quota sampling is that the numbers required within a subgroup (for instance, higher income groups) may be sufficient to meet the needs of the total sample size but too small to provide reliable results about a subgroup which may be of particular interest. The common solution to this problem is to 'over-sample' the subgroup (for example, instead of 10 per cent of the sample being in the 'heavy consumers' group this is increased to 25 per cent) and the results adjusted back to the true profile of the population at the data analysis stage through the use of weighting techniques.

Quota samples are very commonly used in market research. Their chief practical merit is low cost: there are no clerical costs of pre-selecting the sample, the interviewers' productivity (interviews per day) is higher because they are not following up initial non-responses and the technique can be used with low-cost mall or street interviewing (where obviously pre-selection is a non-starter). The theoretical disadvantages are, however, considerable. There is the bias of respondents being selected by interviewers, who may consciously or otherwise reject potential respondents who appear 'difficult'. Also since initial non-responders are not followed up, there is a bias against those respondents who are less accessible – for example, people working long hours. In fact the response rates (or interviewer avoidance rates) are unknown with quota sampling.

Then there is the problem of non-computable sampling error. Quota samples, like random samples, are of course subject to sampling error but in this case there is no simple way of calculating what it is. Often the sampling error is calculated as if the sample was random but there is no theoretical basis for doing this. The likely sampling error of quota samples is subject to some dispute, but some consider that the rule should be to assume that it is twice that of the same-sized random samples.

As well as its application in quantitative research, quota sampling is widely used to recruit qualitative samples for focus group discussions and so on. In a fairly loose sense the intention is to cover a sample which is broadly representative of the target population in terms of demographics, product usage or even attitudes to critical issues. However, since there is no attempt to quantify from the research in any rigorous sense, questions and problems of sampling error do not apply. Problems of interviewer bias in selection, however, still need to be considered.

SAMPLING IN BUSINESS-TO-BUSINESS MARKETS

Business-to-business research is concerned with populations of not individuals but organizations (companies and so on, and often in defined sectors by industry). Surprisingly, there is no universal sample frame, or even comprehensive ones for most sectors, that is anywhere complete. Directories such as *Kompass* and *Dun and Bradstreet* (available in various forms including online, CD-ROM, and hard copy) for example, although widely used, miss out many smaller businesses and include names of businesses that are in unrelated fields. Also where research is of a sector, the definition of the sector relevant to the research objectives may not match the classifications used in sample frames.

These comments may suggest that reliable sampling is not possible in business-to-business research but this is to overstate the problem. In practice, samples taken from such directories, and often built from several sources, while not completely free from bias, are good enough for most purposes. There are also other issues important in business-to-business research apart from sample frame limitations, and particularly those relating to the fact that the companies in the population are not of equal size. Take for example the chemical industry. At one level there could be a small company employing one or two people and mixing chemicals with a bucket and a stick, through to the DuPonts, the BASFs and the Dows. In most business-to-business markets the distribution of companies fits the 80:20 or Pareto rule; that is 20 per cent of the units account for 80 per cent of the market being studied. The domination of most business markets by a small number of large companies means that it is crucial they are included in the sample. In fact, the researcher may seek (so far as cooperation levels allow) to carry out a census of the largest companies, and a sample of the rest (see Figure 7.3).

This singling out of specific companies to interview is judgemental, although there will be some guiding principles such as the number of employees, the output of chemicals, and turnover.

Not only does the business-to-business researcher have to contend with wide differences of size of company, there are also complications caused by the intricate nature of the decision making unit (DMU). Whereas decisions in most households are made by the partners and the children (or even by just one person), in businesses there are inputs from purchasing,

Large companies

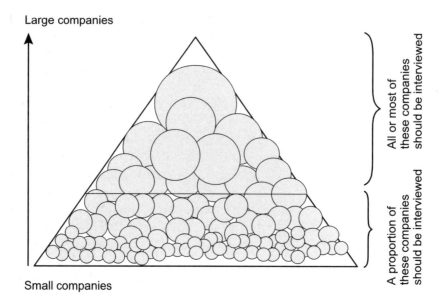

Small companies

Figure 7.3 *Domination of companies in business-to-business markets*

technical, production, and possibly finance and marketing. These inputs change over time. At the point where a product is being specified or evaluated for the first time, the technical team is likely to have a strong voice. Once the product is in the routine reordering stage, the purchasing and production people have more influence. So who do you select to interview? In theory you may set out to build up a picture across the board by selecting people from each group. However, since many business-to-business samples are small (200 interviews is quite a respectable size), the subcells of respondents in a particular job responsibility end up being too small to analyse separately. For these reasons the business-to-business researchers may compromise and decide to concentrate the interviews on just one group such as the key decision maker (thankfully there is usually one person who holds most sway in the decision).

USING STATISTICS TO DERIVE IMPORTANCE OF FACTORS

The discussion so far in this chapter has been on the subject of sampling. The availability of statistical processing software tools such as SPSS means that researchers are constantly looking for means of squeezing the data for more meaning. One common application that researchers should be aware of is the use of regression techniques to work out the importance of the various factors that are rated in customer satisfaction surveys.

Customer satisfaction surveys have two important components – the measurement of the importance of the many factors that are part of the offer from a company (for example, delivery on time, consistent quality, technical support) and satisfaction with these factors or attributes. However, researchers are constantly plagued by the measurement of importance because what people say are important may not be the issues that influence satisfaction. This we know because when we attempt to correlate all the attributes with the score given to overall satisfaction, we find different drivers of satisfaction from those which people stated were important. For example, we find strong correlations between the 'softer' service and people-related issues and overall satisfaction. These softer factors are shown to drive satisfaction and so they must be assumed to be important.

Some researchers believe measures of derived importance are more relevant than the answers to direct questions on what is important (stated importance) as the derived importance figures show where improvements will raise the overall satisfaction score. However, there are dangers in ignoring the stated importance. Although these may not be a complete guide to what drives satisfaction, they are basic requirements that are so important they have to be provided, at an acceptable level, by every supplier. In effect they are hygiene factors and typically include product quality, value for money and quick delivery. They may not drive satisfaction, but they do determine whether you 'play in the game'. If these slip, you are out of it!

USING STATISTICS TO ARRIVE AT NEEDS-BASED SEGMENTATIONS

Segmentation is concerned with ascertaining the size and nature of subgroups of a population, and it may be based on any number of characteristics. Consumer segments can be recognized according to demographics such as gender, age, income, geography or their different needs.

The classification data on questionnaires provide demographics

95

data, while questions in the body of the interview determine aspects of behaviour. Cross-tabulations of data on these criteria allow us to see the different responses among groups of respondents. This is segmentation at its simplest level, and every researcher uses the computer tabulations of findings to establish groups of respondents with marked differences.

However, we can use statistical techniques, in particular multivariate analysis, to allow more sophisticated segments to emerge. In a segmentation study (or even in a customer satisfaction study), respondents are asked to say to what extent they agree with a number of statements. These statements are designed to determine the needs and interests of the respondents. Typically there are a couple of dozen such statements, sometimes more. The possible combination of groupings from 1,000 interviews is literally millions of millions, and we need some means of creating combinations that have a natural fit.

Using a technique known as factor analysis, statisticians can work out which groups of attributes best fit together. After this grouping has taken place it is usually possible to see common themes such as people who want low prices with few extras, people who want lots of services or add-ons and are prepared to pay for them, people who are concerned about environmental issues and so on. Factor analysis reduces the large number of attributes to a smaller but representative subset. These subsets are then given labels such as 'price fighters', 'service seekers' and any other such terms that help the marketing team know exactly who they are addressing.

The groupings of needs that have been worked out by factor analysis are now run through further computations using a technique known as cluster analysis. These factors are inserted into the cluster analysis, whose algorithms rearrange the data into the partitions that have been specified and so determine how neatly the population fits into the different groupings.

The statistical approach to a needs-based segmentation has become extremely popular, and it is certainly an important objective means of finding more interesting and possibly more relevant ways of addressing the customer base. However, the tastes and needs of populations are constantly changing, and we should always be mindful of new segments that may not show up as more than a dot on the current radar screen. For example, if Guinness had carried out a needs-based segmentation amongst its customers in the 1960s, it might not have recognized the opportunity to reposition the drink as being young and trendy. This segment was developed by a series of astute marketing campaigns.

SUMMARY

Every market researcher needs to understand the basics of sampling. The only surveys that can be measured in terms of their accuracy are those based on a census or a random sample. Sampling enables us to take a small proportion of the total population and to establish a result that is representative of the whole.

The variability in the responses to a survey question begins to settle down once there are more than 30 completed interviews. The more accurate the required result, the larger the sample needed. It is the absolute size of the sample that matters. A random sample of 500 people will produce a survey result that we can be almost certain (95 per cent confident) will be plus or minus 4.5 per cent of what would be achieved had we interviewed everyone in the population. A sample that is four times larger will deliver a result that is twice as accurate because there are diminishing returns from increasing the sample size.

There are practical problems associated with random samples. Most market research surveys are based on quota samples, which ensure that the composition of the sample is the same as the overall breakdown of the population.

Industrial and many business-to-business markets require a different approach to sampling because the members of the population are (unlike in consumer markets) of widely differing size. Lists are built up of the companies that make up the market, and they are stratified on the basis of size. The small numbers of companies that dominate the industry are selected for interview as they account for 80 per cent of total consumption.

Statistical modelling is used widely in market research to derive the importance of factors that drive customer satisfaction. This type of analysis often shows that softer issues such as friendliness of staff and good communications affect customer satisfaction in a more positive manner than some of the hygiene factors such as price, product quality and delivery.

The analysis of findings almost always involves comparing the results of different segments (groups of respondents). More sophisticated statistical techniques are used to discover needs-based segments. Factor analysis is used to distil the many attitude ratings into groups of common themes. Cluster analysis is then used to find out the size of these segments within a population.

8 Questionnaire design

WHAT IS SO DIFFICULT ABOUT DESIGNING A QUESTIONNAIRE?

Asking questions and getting the right answers is not always as straight-forward as it may seem. Someone beginning their market research career may presume that questionnaire design is a clear-cut process – ask the question to the right respondent and you will get the answer. How hard can it really be? It is true that anyone can string some questions togeth-er, and normally you will get an answer in some shape or form, but the problem is, it may not be the answer you were looking for.

Questionnaire design is one of the hardest and most important parts of market research. Given the same objectives, two researchers would probably never design the same questionnaire, as questionnaire design is an art form that allows individual license to the creator. However, there are guidelines and these are outlined in this chapter.

THE ROLE OF THE QUESTIONNAIRE

The questionnaire plays a number of important roles. Its primary purpose is to facilitate the extraction of data from a respondent. It serves as an 'aide memoire' to the interviewer so that there is no necessity to learn the questions off by heart. It provides consistency in the way the interview is conducted, especially as frequently a number of interviewers are working on a project at the same time. Without a questionnaire, questions would be asked in a haphazard way at the discretion of the individual. Questionnaires are also an important part in the data collection methodology. They allow responses to be recorded in a consistent way to facilitate data analysis.

THE DIFFERENT TYPES OF QUESTIONNAIRE

A questionnaire can be administered in three different ways: by phone, face-to-face and self-completion (through mail/Internet). These three incongruent methods require different forms of questionnaire.

Table 8.1 *The three different types of questionnaire*

Questionnaire type	Area of use	Method of administration
Structured	Large, quantitative studies	Telephone/face-to-face/self-completion
Semi-structured	Qualitative consumer studies, business to business studies	Telephone/face-to-face
Unstructured	Qualitative studies	Depth telephone/face-to-face/group discussions

Structured questionnaires consist of closed or prompted questions (pre-defined answers – see next section) that require the designer to be aware of or to anticipate all possible answers. They are used in large interview programmes (anything over 30 interviews and more likely 200 plus in number) and may be carried out over the telephone, face-to-face or by self-completion depending on the respondent type, the content of questionnaire and the budget.

Semi-structured questionnaires comprise a mixture of closed and open questions. They are used in business-to-business market research where there is a need to accommodate a large range of different responses from companies. The use of semi-structured questionnaires enables a mix of qualitative and quantitative information to be gathered. They can be administered over the telephone or face-to-face.

Unstructured questionnaires are made up of free-ranging questions that allow respondents to express themselves in their own way. Unstructured questionnaires are made up of a list of questions with an apparent order, but they are not so rigid that the interviewer has to slavishly follow in every detail. The interviewer has the flexibility to go down separate lines of questioning and to probe or even construct new lines of unscripted enquiry. They are used in qualitative research for depth interviewing (face-to-face, depth telephone interviews) and they form the basis of many studies into technical or narrow markets.

THE DIFFERENT TYPES OF QUESTIONS

Questions can be classified in different ways. An important distinction is made between *open questions* and *closed questions*.

Open questions gather free responses that are usually collected as they are given. Since the respondents have the freedom to express an answer in any way they like, this type of questioning is highly appropriate for exploratory research as it offers useful insights into a subject area or product. Open questions are also used where the range of possible responses cannot be tightly classified.

Open questions are used where a researcher may be unsure about the responses at the time of designing the questionnaire. In fact to close down the question would restrict the answers. Open questions permit the respondents to say what they think in their own words.

Open questions present problems for researchers. First, they are difficult to evaluate as they must be grouped together before any statistical analysis can take place. Second, comments must be captured verbatim and this presents problems. Interviewers must take down every word in the interview and either write it onto the questionnaire or type it into the computer. They need speed or typewriting skills to do this and in any case may add their own interpretation to the precise words that are given.

The second style of question is the closed question. These take the form of single or multi-response questions. Single response questions can, as the term suggests, have only one possible answer. Perhaps the most typical of these is the *dichotomous* question that has just two possible options 'yes' or 'no'. (Of course there may be questions where the answer is 'don't know'.) Many attitudinal questions are single response in that respondents have to choose where they sit on a predetermined scale. They have to choose one response code that reflects their feelings and they cannot be both 'very satisfied' and 'very unsatisfied' at the same time.

Multiple response questions allow the respondent to offer more than one answer to a question, and are typically about awareness and use, asking which brands are known and which brands are used. A number of brands may well be mentioned.

Most closed questions are prompted in that respondents are told what response codes they can choose. However, this need not be the case. For example a questionnaire could contain a question that seeks to find out the awareness of brands, and this is achieved by a simple question such as 'Which brands do you know?' with no further prompts. Most likely the questionnaire would have all the brands listed to ease the task of the interviewer who needs only circle the code next to the brands that are mentioned. This is an open question with a closed response.

All closed question replies are anticipated. They are listed on the questionnaire and may or may not be read out or shown on a card so that respondents can choose their answer. The predefined answers are worked out by common sense, industry knowledge, or following qualitative research or a pilot study.

In general, closed questions offer efficiencies to researchers. They are certainly easier to analyze and are usually quicker to administer and ask. Thus, they are often used in large samples and in self-completion interviews. The consistency in the response categories allows trends to be tracked over time if the same questions are used.

Questionnaires can also be classified by their purpose. Questions are designed to collect three different types of information: information about behaviour, information about attitudes, and information that is used for *classification* purposes. Table 8.2 summarizes the three different types of information that can be gathered and the surveys in which they are used.

Table 8.2 *The three different types of questions*

Question type	Information sought	Types of surveys
Behavioural	Factual information on what the respondent is, does or owns. Also the frequency with which certain actions are carried out, where people live etc	Surveys to find out market size, market shares, awareness and usage
Attitudinal	What people think of something. Their image and ratings of things. Why they do things.	Image and attitude surveys. Brand mapping studies. Customer/employee satisfaction surveys
Classification	Information that can be used to group respondents to see how they differ one from the other, such as their age, gender, social class, location of household, type of house, family composition	All surveys

BEHAVIOURAL QUESTIONS

Behavioural questions are designed to find out what people (or companies) do. For example, do people go to the cinema? How often do they go? What type of films do they watch? Who do they go with? These questions determine people's actions in terms of what they have eaten (or drunk), bought, used, visited, seen, read or heard. Behavioural questions record facts and not matters of opinion.

Behavioural questions address the following:

- Have you ever...?
- Do you ever...?
- Who do you know...?
- When did you last...?
- Which do you do most often...?
- Who does it...?
- How many...?

- Do you have...?
- In what way do you do it...?
- In the future will you...?

ATTITUDINAL QUESTIONS

People hold opinions or beliefs on everything from politics, to social precepts, to the products they buy and the companies that make or supply them. These attitudes are not necessarily right, but this is hardly relevant since it is perceptions that count. People's attitudes guide the way they act.

Researchers explore attitudes using questions that begin with who? what? why? where? when? and how? as well as other exploratory phrases such as 'would you explain ...?' Attitudinal questions address the following:

- Why do you...?
- What do you think of...?
- Do you agree or disagree...?
- How do you rate...?
- Which is best (or worst) for...?

Scales are commonly used to measure attitudes. Scalar questions use a limited choice of response, chosen to measure an attitude, an intention, an opinion or belief of a respondent's behaviour. Scalar questions always involve numbers for measurement (even if this is tied to a verbal rating). The numbers help communicate to respondents their agreement or disagreement with a posed question, as well as facilitating statistical analysis of the final data.

There are five different types of rating scales that researchers commonly use.

Verbal rating scales

These are the simplest of all scales, in which respondents choose a word or phrase on a scale to indicate the level of their feeling. They are known as Likert scales after the person who popularized them and typically present five choices.

Q. Here is a pack design for a new type of Stilton cheese. Please look at it and, using a phrase from this card, tell me how appealing you think it is:

Very appealing
Quite appealing
Neither appealing nor unappealing
Quite unappealing
Very unappealing

A common verbal rating scale is one that asks about people's likelihood of doing something.

Q. And how likely would you be to try this product?

Very likely
Quite likely
Neither likely nor unlikely
Quite unlikely
Very unlikely

Numerical rating scales

This is a very similar approach to the verbal rating except the respondent is asked to give a numerical 'score' rather than a semantic response. The scores are often out of a number, with 5 and 10 being popular choices (where the large number is the best and 1 is the worst). It should be borne in mind that the bigger the scale, the more discrimination is required from the respondent. Thus narrow scales, such as those out of 5, work well on the telephone where the limited choice of numbers makes it easy for respondents to select an appropriate score. Also, 5-point ratings fit neatly with the Likert semantic scale.

Q. How would you rate the pack on the following?
Very convenient   5   4   3   2   1   Not at all convenient

Questions that use numbers for ratings do not have to lay out the complete string of possible responses. Respondents can be asked simply to write in the appropriate score (1 to 5 or 1 to 10) on a line or in a box.

There is much debate in the research community about which scales should be used, whether 5-point, 7-point or 10-point. The traditional choice of market researchers has been to use a 5-point scale, so allowing a neutral or no opinion mid-point response (the 7-point scale provides a greater degree of response sensitivity than a 5-point scale but still has a neutral point). Other schools of thought state that an even number of choices is best because it prevents middle-of-the-road answers and avoids a bored respondent to slip into the 'sitting on the fence' category. However, this may force inaccurate responses because some respondents may truly hold a middle-of-the-road opinion.

For questionnaires that test opinions on a very large number of issues, such as in customer satisfaction or segmentation studies, it is often wise to use a 10-point scale as this gives the greatest differentiation of response and therefore the greatest sensitivity, with no mid-point. This therefore allows a more in-depth statistical analysis using techniques such as factor and cluster analysis (see Chapter 13, Data analysis).

Researchers carrying out surveys in German-speaking Europe need to be careful of rating scales in which a high figure (such as 5) is considered very good and a low figure (such as 1) is very poor. The convention in German schools, when marking homework, is that 1 is the best score and 5 is the worst. Unless the respondents are warned that the 'poles' of the scale are reversed and that 5 scores good and 1 scores poor, the results could be confused.

The use of adjectives

A variation on the verbal/semantic scale is to ask respondents which words best describe a company, a product or, as in the next example, a person. The adjectives could be both positive and negative and they need not be opposites.

Q. I would like to read out some words that describe people. You have to choose one word from each pair to describe yourself. If you think neither fits, you must choose the one which is closest. Would you say that you are:

Introvert	1	or extrovert	2
Traditionalist	1	or an experimenter	2
Stylish	1	or fashionable	2
Ambitious	1	or content	2
Independent	1	or gregarious	2
Intellectual	1	or practical	2

The use of positioning statements

Here respondents are asked to agree or disagree with a number of statements. It is important that respondents are readily able to identify with one of the statements and are not left feeling that somehow they do not capture their mood.

> Q. I will read out some statements that people have said about the xxx car. Would you give me a score out of 5 to say whether you agree or disagree with the statement? A score of 5 means you agree strongly and a score of 1 means you disagree strongly. *Score 6 for don't know/cannot say.*

	Strongly disagree			Strongly agree		Don't know/ cannot say
A car that is a pleasure to look at	1	2 3	4	5		6
A car I hope says something to others about me	1	2 3	4	5		6
A car that is distinctive but not flashy	1	2 3	4	5		6
A rational choice of car	1	2 3	4	5		6
An emotional choice of car	1	2 3	4	5		6
The cheapest suitable car I could find	1	2 3	4	5		6
A car I enjoy driving fast	1	2 3	4	5		6
A car that doesn't attract too much attention	1	2 3	4	5		6
A car with a happy personality of its own	1	2 3	4	5		6
A car that tells people I am different	1	2 3	4	5		6

Ranking questions

Researchers often need to find out what is the order of importance of various factors from a list. Typically this is achieved by presenting the list and asking which is most important, which is second most important and so on. In ranking questions it is usually not valid to ask respondents to rank beyond the top three factors. This is because the less important the factors, the harder it is to assign a level of rank.

Q. I will now show you a card on which is listed a number of factors which could be important to you when choosing a combined weed killer and fertilizer. Would you look at the list and tell me which is the most important factor in influencing your choice? READ LIST. ROTATE START. TICK START. RANK JUST THREE FACTORS.

And what would be the second most important factor?

And what would be the third most important factor?

Factor	Rank
Available in the garden centre	_____
A competitive price	_____
Works at any time of year	_____
Kills weeds and moss	_____
Not poisonous to children or pets	_____
Made by a well known company	_____

Ranking questions that are read out must not be too long or otherwise the respondents will forget what has been said.

Ranking is a simple means of determining the importance attached to items and it works very well for the most and second most important factors. However, it can be misleading for the lower ranked issues because although they may appear as third or fourth on the ranked list, they could still be really important to the respondent.

CLASSIFICATION QUESTIONS

The third group of questions are those used to classify the information once it has been collected. Typical classification questions are used to build a profile of respondents by finding out their age, their sex, their social class, where they live, their marital status, the type of house they live in, the number of people in their family and so on, but they are also used to check that the correct quota of people or companies have been interviewed. Most classification questions are factual or behavioural.

A number of standard classification questions crop up constantly in market research surveys. These are:

Gender

There can be no other classifications other than male and female.

Marital status

This is usually asked by simply saying 'Are you ...'

- Single
- Married
- Widowed
- Divorced
- Separated

Socio-economic grade (SEG)

This is a classification peculiar to UK market researchers in which respondents are pigeonholed according to the occupation of the head of the household. Thus, it combines the attributes of income, education and work status. In addition to social grades, researchers sometimes classify respondents by income group or lifestyle.

In summary the socio-economic grades are:

- A: Higher managerial, administrative or professional
- B: Intermediate managerial, administrative or professional
- C1: Supervisory, clerical, junior administrative or professional
- C2: Skilled manual workers
- D: Semi-skilled and unskilled manual workers
- E: State pensioners, widows, casual and lowest grade workers

For most practical purposes these can be reduced to just four:

- AB
- C1
- C2
- DE

Alternatively, a question may be asked about the income of the respondent or the combined income of the household. The question can be desensitized by using income bands.

Industrial occupation

Countries have standard classifications for business types. In the United States the NAICS (North American Industry Classification System) was specifically introduced in 1997 (with revisions in 2002) for governmental regulations and census reports. In Europe companies are classified according to their Standard Industrial Classification (SIC). Often researchers condense the many divisions into more convenient and broader groupings such as:

- Accommodation and foodservices;
- Administrative and support and waste management and remediation services;
- Arts, entertainment and recreation;
- Auxiliaries;
- Construction;
- Educational services;
- Finance and insurance;
- Health care and social assistance;
- Information;
- Management of companies and enterprises;
- Manufacturing;
- Mining;
- Professional, scientific and technical services;
- Real estate, rental and leasing;
- Retail trade;
- Transportation & warehousing;
- Utilities;
- Wholesale trade;
- Other services (except public administration).

In surveys of the general public, it may be relevant to establish the level of employment of the respondent. For example:

- Working full-time (over 30 hours a week);
- Working part-time (8–30 hours a week);
- Housewife (full-time at home);
- Student (full-time);

- Retired;
- Temporarily unemployed (but seeking work);
- Permanently unemployed (for example, chronically sick, independent means and so on).

Number of employees

The size of the firm in which the respondent works can be classified according to the number of employees:

- 1–9
- 10–24
- 25–99
- 100–249
- 250+

Location

Depending on the scope of the survey, this can be a country code, or in any single country a code indicating the domicile of the respondent, such as state in which they live or a broader grouping such as East Coast, Central, West Coast.

We have described the different types of questionnaires and the different types of questions that are used to create a questionnaire. Figure 8.1 is an example of a questionnaire. The questionnaire was administered by telephone and the interview took less than five minutes to complete.

THREE STEPS IN QUESTIONNAIRE DESIGN

There are three steps to successful questionnaire design: formulate the questions; arrange the questionnaire layout; and test the draft.

Formulating the questions

The researcher should begin by making a rough listing of all the points to which answers are required. In building this list of questions it will be necessary to keep the objectives of the survey in mind. If one of the objectives is to assess the market size, a question must

Good Grub Restaurant – Customer Satisfaction Survey

Good Morning/afternoon. My name is................., I am phoning from B2B International, a research agency in Manchester. We are carrying out research for Good Grub restaurant and we are contacting all recent visitors to the restaurant. Do you have five minutes to help us with a few questions about your visit?

Q1   Have you visited the restaurant in the last month?

Yes..........☐
No ....☐   THANK AND CLOSE

Q2   When did you last visit the restaurant?

DAY	DATE	MONTH

Q3   How often on average, do you visit this restaurant?

At least once a week.............☐
At least monthly ....☐
Less often than this..............☐

Q4   How many people were in your party on the last occasion you visited the restaurant? ENTER NUMBER

Adults ....☐
Children (under 15yrs) ....☐

Q5   What did you, personally, order from the menu?

Pasta ....☐
Steak.....................................☐
Chicken.................................☐
Pizza ....☐
Salad ....☐
French Fries ....☐
Ice Cream ....☐
Coffee/tea ....☐
Soft drink ....☐
Other.....................................☐

Q6   In total, how much did your party spend on this visit?

ENTER TOTAL: [$]

Q7   Based on your last visit, how do you rate the following?

	Very Poor	Poor	OK	Good	Very Good
Speed of service	☐	☐	☐	☐	☐
Cleanliness	☐	☐	☐	☐	☐
Quality of the food	☐	☐	☐	☐	☐
Choice of the food	☐	☐	☐	☐	☐
Value for money	☐	☐	☐	☐	☐

Q8   How do you rate the overall performance of the restaurant, using a scale of 1 to 10, where 10 is excellent and 1 is very poor

[   ]

Q9   Are there any other comments that you would like to make about the restaurant?

[   ]

And finally, a few questions about yourself...

Q10 How old are you?

Under 18..............................☐
18–24 ....☐
25–44 ....☐
45–60 ....☐
Over 60................................☐

Q11   What is your zipcode?

[   ]

Q12 CODE gender

Male.................................... ☐
Female................................ ☐

THANK AND CLOSE

Figure 8.1   *Sample Customer Satisfaction Survey*

be posed which establishes the respondent's purchases of products over a given period. If another objective is to measure the market shares of suppliers, a question must be asked about the respondent's source of purchases.

In preparing the listing of questions, it is important to include classification questions that are used to group responses when analyzing the data.

Each of the questions in the rough listing should be scrutinized to establish whether they are vital to the survey, since long questionnaires threaten the consideration given to the later questions as interview fatigue sets in.

Once the questions have been roughly drafted, they can be refined taking into consideration the following points.

Ensure that questions are without bias

Questions or answers should not be worded in such a way as to lead the respondent into the answer. A bad question:

Q. How would you rate your recent experience from the service provided by company X?

> Excellent
> Very good
> Quite good
> Fair

(Respondents are not allowed the opportunity to say that they think the experience was poor or very poor.)

Make the questions as simple as possible

Questions should not only be short, they should also be simple. Questions that include multiple ideas or two questions in one will confuse and be misunderstood. A bad question:

Q. What do you know about company X and what do you feel they do well?

(The respondent may not answer both parts of the question and in any case, the responses will be difficult to analyse.)

Make the questions very specific

Words such as 'usually' or 'frequently' have no specific meaning and need qualifying. A common mistake is to be vague about time periods. A bad question:

Q. How often do you visit your local supermarket?

> Very often
> Quite often
> Every now and then
> Very rarely
> Never

(We will never know how often the respondent visits the supermarket, as 'very often' to one person could be every day, and to someone else it could be every week.)

Avoid jargon or shorthand

It cannot be assumed that respondents will understand words commonly used by researchers. Trade jargon, acronyms and initials should be avoided unless they are in everyday use. If the research is to taste test a new ice cream aimed at kids, then the language used by children should be that of the questionnaire.

Steer clear of sophisticated or uncommon words

A questionnaire is not a place to score literary points, so only use words in common parlance. Colloquialisms are acceptable if they are used widely (some are highly regional).

Avoid questions with a negative in them

Questions are more difficult to understand if they are asked in a negative sense. It is better to say 'Do you ever ...?' than 'Do you never ...?'

Do not use words that could be misheard

This is especially important when the interview is administered over the telephone. On the telephone, 'What is your opinion of religious sects?' could yield interesting but not necessarily relevant answers.

Do not ask questions that are outside the frame of reference of the respondent

One of the keys to good questionnaire design is to imagine the response at the same time as designing the question. Imagine that your aim is to work out consumers' annual milk consumption. If the question is framed as 'How much milk do you buy each year?' it is far more difficult to answer than 'How many litres/pints of milk do you buy in a typical week?'. The researcher can do the 52 times calculation much easier than the interviewer.

Use response bands

Most numeric data that is collected in market research surveys is analyzed in bands, and so it may be easier to ask the question in bands. For example, 'How many litres of milk do you buy each week?' could be made easier by putting in response bands such as:

- None
- Less than 1 litre
- Between 1 and 4 litres
- Over 4 litres.

The response bands should make sense within the context of the survey. For example, the simple split on milk consumption may need to be broken into more bands if such level of detail is required in the analysis.

Questions that are sensitive can be desensitized with response bands; for example questions about income or age, or in a business-to-business interview, company size. For example:

Q. Can you tell me what band your company's annual turnover falls into from the following choices?

< US $200,000
US $201,000–500,000
US $501,000–1,000,000
US $1,001,000–3,000,000
US $3,001,000–10,000,000
> US $10,000,000

Ensure that fixed responses do not overlap

The categories that are used in fixed response questions should be sequential and not overlap. This is a question with poor response bands:

Q. Can you tell me what age range you fall into?

> Below 21 years
> 21 to 30 years
> 30 to 40 years
> 40 to 50 years
> Over 50 years old

A person aged 30 or 40 would be caught on the cusp.

Allow for 'others' in fixed response questions

It is quite probable that the pre-coded answers do not allow for every conceivable response. It is good practice therefore to allow the option for other/additional responses. For example:

Q. Can you tell me which brand of dog food you normally buy?

> Barko
> Wuf
> Yummy
> Other (STATE)

Arranging the questionnaire layout

Every questionnaire needs 'boilerplate' or standard information such as the name and address of the respondent, the date of the interview and the name of the interviewer. Usually it is also necessary to capture the telephone number of the respondent and in the case of a business-to-business interview his or her job title and e-mail address. Some researchers prefer to place the boilerplate information at the beginning of the questionnaire, whereas others position it at the end.

The introduction and first question are key elements of any questionnaire, as they address the hurdle of achieving cooperation. Once an interview is started there is a very good chance that it will be completed. Therefore, the introduction should be designed to quickly and concisely communicate the legitimacy of the survey and win cooperation.

Classification questions may be asked at the beginning to screen respondents for interview, while many are left until the end. (Respondents may fail to understand why they are asked lots of personal questions about their income, composition of their household, age of leaving final education (and so on) at the beginning of an interview, whereas at the end, these classification questions are seen in the context of the complete subject.)

The flow of questions should be logical and make sense to the respondent. Where a mixture of open-ended and closed questions are used, the sequence is always open followed by closed. For example: Open question: 'What do you like about this brand of coffee?' Closed question: 'I will now read out some features of this brand of coffee that other people have said they like. After I have read them out I would like you to tell me which one of these features has influenced you most in your choice of the brand.' READ FEATURES. ROTATE START. TICK START. SINGLE CODE ONLY.

Open questions do sometimes follow closed questions, the most common one asking for more feedback on the respondent's answer – typically, 'Why did you say that?'

A mixture of question types and styles, such as open-ended questions, closed questions and scales, gives texture to an interview and helps maintain a respondent's interest.

Many telephone interviews are carried out using screen-based questionnaires (CATI or computer aided telephone interviewing) and the computer programme neatly arranges the formatting. Routing questions are taken care of and different responses automatically bring up different questions. However many paper questionnaires are still used, and the layout and format of the questions needs to be designed with the interviewer in mind. This means clear instructions as to what to do at and after every question. These instructions are normally written in capital letters to distinguish them from the questions themselves that are read out.

Response codes (normally numbers next to the answers for the interviewer to circle) should be clearly laid out close to the pre-coded answers. A dot leader from the end of the pre-coded answer to the number is helpful to ensure that the correct code is circled in the heat of the interview.

There should be adequate space (and lines) for writing in the answers to open-ended questions. The number of lines is an indication to the interviewer of approximately how much of the verbatim response he or she is expected to capture.

Piloting the questionnaire

At last the questionnaire is ready for piloting. In many surveys, half a dozen to a dozen interviews will be sufficient to establish if the questionnaire really does work. So far as is possible, the pilot should be carried out in the same conditions as the survey proper. A telephone interview should be tested over the phone, a street interview in the street.

During the pilot the researcher is looking for:

- comprehension (do the questions make sense as they were intended?);
- language and phraseology (are there any words that are creating difficulty?);
- ease of answering (are the answers within the capability of respondents?);
- cooperation (will all the questions be answered?);
- flow (does the interview flow easily from one topic to another?);
- instructions (does the interviewer know what to do next?);
- practicality (is the formatting easy for the interviewers?);
- the length of the interview in time (does it take too long and overtax the respondent?).

All too often there is not time to carry out a proper pilot, but at the very least, the questionnaire should be tried on someone in the office, preferably someone not involved in the survey. Someone who was not involved in the design of the questionnaire should play the role of interviewer while the questionnaire designer looks on.

The person that is in charge of analyzing the questionnaire should also be allowed the opportunity to sign it off before it goes into the field, as he or she may well spot coding or routing problems.

SPECIAL QUESTIONNAIRES – CONJOINT ANALYSIS

Conjoint analysis is concerned with understanding how people make choices between products or services, with the purpose of working out what combinations of features people like and are prepared to pay for. If you just ask people what they want in a conventional way, the response is likely to be the first thing that comes to mind and may not necessarily reflect what people actually do want. All choices involve compromises and trade-offs, as the ideal is rarely attainable, so we need an approach that allows us to simulate this decision making in the questions we ask.

Conjoint analysis provides the framework for asking these questions. In order that we can develop appropriate questions, we need to break the products and services down into their features and benefits, which we call attributes. These attributes can be offered at different levels – high quality/low quality; delivered in an hour/delivered in a week and so on. It is these attributes and the levels of the attributes that we show to respondents, and we ask them which they would choose.

	Envelope A	Envelope B
Colour	White	Brown
Sealing	Glue	Self-seal
Window	No window	Window
Price	50 cents	40 cents

Conjoint analysis takes these attributes and level descriptions of product/services and uses them in interviews by asking people to make a number of choices between different concepts. In the following example there are two concepts (envelope A and B) with three attributes and a price at two levels. Which would you choose?

We could easily add more concepts such as envelope C which is the same as concept A except it is brown. Concept D would be the same as A except it would be self-seal and so on. Each would have a different price. The design of the concepts is a crucial step in a conjoint project, and time is required to narrow these down to those that do really reflect buying decisions.

In order to arrive at reliable results it is necessary to carry out at least 100 interviews, and 200 plus would be more comfortable. These interviews are carried out face-to-face, at which time respondents view the different concepts as cards on the screen of a laptop computer. They make their choices, and specific software is able to calculate a utility value for each level of attribute by comparing the choices and therefore the trade-offs that respondents made in their answers.

A total utility figure can be calculated for envelope A and B, and thereby tell us which is preferred and by how much. (The utility values in the example are in brackets. Notice that a lower price has a higher utility as we typically prefer cheaper goods.)

	Envelope A	**Envelope B**
Colour	White (25)	Brown (15)
Sealing	Glue (5)	Self Seal (10)
Window	No window (10)	Window (15)
Price	50 cents (30)	40 cents (45)
Overall	(70)	(85)

The sawtooth Web site at www.sawtooth.com is useful for further information on conjoint analysis.

The problem for business researchers until now has been the cost of carrying out conjoint. Carrying out 200 face-to-face interviews scattered across Europe, North America or Asia is inordinately expensive. However, conjoint analysis can now be carried out online, and this is discussed further in Chapter 12.

TRADE-OFF GRIDS (SIMALTO – SIMULATED MULTI-ATTRIBUTE LEVEL TRADE-OFF)

Trade-off grids are an approach to collecting information from respondents that recognizes that an individual customer cannot have everything. A trade-off is inevitably made in order to get the best product someone can buy. The classic trade-off is between price and quality, but in practice when considering most purchases, we make trade-offs between different features and service levels, and even emotional factors such as brands. The trade-off grids are easier to administer than conjoint as they do not require a laptop. In a business environment respondents are phoned to check if they qualify for interview. A grid is faxed to them and in a follow-up phone call respondents and interviewers each have the grid in front of them as they run through the questions. A simplified example of a trade-off grid is shown in Table 8.3.

In a trade-off grid a product or service is described in terms of attributes and levels in much the same way as in conjoint. An attribute describes a generic feature such as time to answer the phone or delivery on promises. An attribute is then made up of levels: for instance, time to answer the phone has four levels in the above example. A typical product or service can be broadly defined in terms of as few as 10–15 attributes and can sometimes run to over 50.

The respondent then completes a number of tasks related to the grid. Typically the first task is to find out where he or she would want a 'first class supplier' to perform – this sets the ideal standard. Next we can ask where the current supplier is performing. We can then ask the respondent to do a number of different things – for instance to prioritize improvements in the current supplier's performance one square at a time, or to answer questions such as, 'If you had points to spend to make an improvement, where would you spend them and in what quantities?' Answers to these questions are marked on the grid by the interviewer.

Table 8.3   *SIMALTO trade-off grid*

Attribute	Levels			
Time to answer the phone	Phone can ring and ring	Always answered before 10 rings	Always answered before 6 rings	Phone always answered before 3 rings
Delivery on promises	Only meet 30% of promises	Meet 50% of promises	Meet 80% of promises	Always live up to promises
Knowledge of my business	Take no interest in knowing about my business	Know nothing, but seem keen to learn	Understand business in general	Very familiar with the detail of my business
Quality of advice	Advice is poor and can be incorrect	Advice is factually correct but limited in helpfulness	Advice is accurate and useful, but can miss bigger opportunities	Advice is accurate and identifies new possibilities for my business

One useful aspect of measuring performance by levels, is that you can clearly see where the next performance target is – it is not a question of guessing how to get from a score of 7.8 to 8.1 on a satisfaction score out of 10. The levels give specific objective information about the performance required.

The outcome is thus a detailed understanding of where the customer would like improvements and what those improvements should be.

SUMMARY

Questionnaires are at the soul of market research surveys. They drive interviews to find out behaviour and attitudes to products and services. Questions are always required to classify respondents for the purpose of analysis.

Questionnaires can vary from those that are highly structured and used in large surveys through to unstructured topic guides used in depth interviews and focus groups. There are a number of special types of questionnaires for testing the values people attach to different attributes and different levels of the attributes. Conjoint analysis uses sophisticated modelling to compute the utility or value that is attached to different product scenarios. Trade-off grids can be used in a simpler way to find out where improvements can be made to products and services and how much would be paid for those improvements.

Market researchers can ask open-ended questions or closed questions. Open questions allow respondents free expression in their answers but they are difficult to analyze in any large number. Closed questions are the mainstay of questionnaires.

In summary there are 10 things to think about when designing a questionnaire:

1 *Think about the objectives of the survey*: this will ensure that the survey covers all the necessary points.
2 *Think about how the interview will be carried out*: the way that the interview will be carried out will have a bearing on the framing of the questions (self-completion questionnaires need a different construction from an administered interview).
3 *Think about the introduction*: this is very important in capturing the respondent's interest and answering any queries over the legitimacy of the survey.

4 *Think about the formatting*:   the questionnaire should make effective use of white space so that it is clear and easy to read. Questions and response options should be laid out in a standard format and where appropriate, there should be ample space to write in open-ended comments.

5 *Think about the respondent*:   questions should be framed in a respondent friendly manner.

6 *Think about the order of the questions*:   the questions should flow easily from one to another and be grouped into topics in a logical sequence.

7 *Think about the types of questions*:   a mix of different styles of questions will create interest throughout the interview.

8 *Think about the possible answers at the same time as thinking about the questions*:   if you cannot fully anticipate what the respondents may say, the question needs redrafting.

9 *Think about how the data will be processed*:   how will the data be lifted from the questionnaires and analyzed? (This could vary from proprietary software used by market research agencies to an Excel spreadsheet.)

10 *Think about interviewer instructions*:   someone other than the designer usually administers questionnaires, so the interviewer (or the respondent in the case of self-completion questionnaires) needs clear guidance what to do at every stage.

Once the questionnaire is designed it should be piloted in circumstances that are as similar as possible as to those that will be encountered in the main survey.

9 Face-to-face interviewing

Interviewing the general public in person is the traditional and still very common method of collecting market research data. It competes with telephone and self-completion research as a mainstream quantitative data collection method although it has lost ground, especially to telephone interviewing, in the last few years. In the United States, the problem of interviewer safety has wiped out the traditional street and in-home interview which nowadays is largely confined to the security of special rooms in or close to shopping malls.

Whether face-to-face interviews are carried out in special venues, or in the home, they have a number of distinct advantages over the major alternative method of the telephone.

ADVANTAGES OF FACE-TO-FACE INTERVIEWS

Better explanations

In a personal interview, the interviewer can gain a deeper understanding of the validity of the response. In a face-to-face situation better explanations are possible as the respondents' body language offers additional clues to the answer. Longer explanations are possible. There are many occasions, particularly associated with advertising and product research, when the interviewer needs to show samples, or advertisements, and this demands face-to-face contact.

Depth

Following on from the above point, it is easier to maintain the interest of a respondent for longer if the interview is face to face. It is easier for the interviewer to use social niceties to maintain interest in the discussion if there is eye contact with the respondent. There is less chance of mishearing or misunderstanding. Deeper explanations can be offered to answers.

Legitimacy

In an over-researched world, respondents need to be able to justify giving up their time to help in the interview (this, in spite of the fact that many surveys also have financial inducements). Face to face with the respondent, it is possible to give a more comprehensive explanation about the purpose of the survey. Concerns about confidentiality can be more readily satisfied than with an 'anonymous' person at the end of a phone. An interviewer in the high street can show his or her identity card.

Greater accuracy

In a face-to-face interview the respondent has time to reflect on the questions and so give a more considered reply. If required, products can be shown, and in a business-to-business interview a colleague could be consulted to confirm a point. The interviewer is in a better position to judge the accuracy of the answer.

DISADVANTAGES OF FACE-TO-FACE INTERVIEWS

Although there are advantages to face-to-face interviewing, there are also a number of disadvantages.

Organization

Face-to-face interviews are more difficult to organize compared with those undertaken from a central location by phone. A consumer face-to-face survey of 1,000 interviews needs around 50 interviewers spread around the country. If the subject of the study is complex, a personal briefing is necessary and it is time-consuming and expensive to bring the interviewers together. On completion of the interviews the questionnaires must be safely despatched to head office on time. A batch that does not arrive on time will hold up the analysis. Computer aided personal interviewing (CAPI) overcome the problems of collecting paper, but the method has the added complication of dealing with laptop computers and downloading data.

It is more difficult to supervise face-to-face interviews than telephone interviews. Face-to-face interviews must have a supervisor in attendance for part of the time and check-backs have to be made to ensure quality. For the most part, face-to-face interviewers work on their own and the quality of their work depends largely on their conscientiousness. Telephone interviewing, carried out from a central location and with constant supervision, eliminates these problems.

Cost

Face-to-face interviews are nearly always more expensive than those carried out by phone. Household interviews that are based on pre-selected addresses are in turn more expensive than those related to a quota. In general, street interviews cost the same as telephone interviews. In some cases, street interviews offer advantages by allowing showcards and visuals, while at other times the telephone would be preferred as it facilitates sampling a wider audience.

A comparison between face-to-face and other methods of data collection must take into consideration all of the costs. Face-to-face interviewing may use interviewers employed at the same rates as (say) telephone interviewing, but work in the field incurs more expenses. Allowances also have to be made for bringing people together for briefings, additional supervision costs plus out-of-pocket expenses for lunches, travel, parking and post. These 'extras' will, in some cases, equal the cost of the labour.

In business-to-business surveys the difference between the cost of telephone and face-to-face interviews is even greater. A face-to-face interview with a respondent in business needs a telephone discussion in advance to set it up and this, in itself, is similar in cost to a telephone interview. In business-to-business research it is not unusual to have to travel (there and back) a few hours to obtain an important interview which itself may only last an hour. The cost of travel is enormous compared with the cost of a phone call. Normally a good average for business-to-business face-to-face interviews is one or two a day, though this figure could rise to four or five if they are concentrated in a conurbation. Allowing for the time taken to set up the interviews, carry them out, write up notes and make the necessary travel arrangements, visit interviews cost 10 times as much as those carried out by telephone – and this is assuming that the same consultant grade interviewer does both. In reality, telephone interviews are usually carried out by specially trained staff working at lower labour rates than business-to-business research consultants who travel to carry out the interviews face-to-face. Therefore, the savings resulting from using telephone interviews are actually much greater; sometimes less than 5 per cent of the cost of personal visits.

STREET INTERVIEWS

For many people, the image of an interviewer (usually female), clipboard in hand and standing in the street, epitomizes market research. Street interviews are still an important research method in Europe. They are used:

- *Where the people in the street are likely to be the target group*: if the subject of the survey is food or shopping, it makes sense that the interviews are carried out close to a busy shopping area. A shopping survey should cover each day of the week including any late nights that could attract different groups (for example, husbands and families). Because weekends are a busy time for shopping, these too need to be given an appropriate weighting. In addition, a good place to interview commuters is at airports, railway stations, bus stations and car parks. The commuter survey, as with the shopping survey, needs to be spread over different times and locations.
- *Where the questionnaire is short and simple*: using a short questionnaire (five minutes), and assuming that the questions are applicable for most of the passers-by, an interviewer can achieve 30 and sometimes more interviews in a day.
- *Where the questions appertain to a local issue*: a survey investigating a local issue could be suited to street interviewing. Interviewers positioned in a busy town centre would be able to collect the views of local people as they travel to work or go shopping.
- *Where cost and time are vital issues*: wherever there are serious time and budgetary constraints, street interviews have an advantage. They are quicker and easier to organize than house-to-house visits and can be cheaper than phone interviews.

There are some limitations to street interviews:

- *Where the interview is long or complicated*: the street is not a place to carry out interviews that take more than 5 to 10 minutes. Shoppers with their arms laden or dashing home may not be cooperative. The interviewer avoidance factor is impossible to measure, but at times it is obvious from the space surrounding the interviewer that many people are crossing to the other side of the street.
- *Where it is necessary to show many visuals*: it is difficult to show visuals or prompt cards in a street interview. Respondents could be caught without their glasses, the light may be poor, the rain or wind could cause problems, and if the shopper's hands are full, the showcards cannot conveniently be held.
- *Where the targets for interview are not likely to be around*: the street is not the best place to obtain interviews with working people who, by definition, are likely to be at their desks or in their factories when the shops are open. Old people who cannot easily get about, people who are ill and people who dislike shopping are not going to be in the street and eligible for interviewing.
- *Where it is necessary to calculate the accuracy of the results*: street interviews may not provide a representative cross-section of the population. As noted above, those in full-time employment could escape the net of street interviews. It is usual, therefore, for street interviews to be carried out against a quota to ensure that all groups are included in the correct proportions. Quota samples do not allow the calculation of sampling error.

HOUSEHOLD INTERVIEWS

The advantages and disadvantages of household interviews are, by and large, the corollaries of those for street interviews. They are nevertheless worth stating to highlight the strengths and weaknesses of the method. Home interviews (or those carried out in a interview/viewing centre) are suited to certain situations:

- *Where the interview is long and complicated*: an interview of more than 10 minutes needs to be carried out in a specialist interviewing centre or at the respondent's home.

■ *Where there are products or visuals to show*: visuals (showcards, advertisements, storyboards and products) need to be shown in a controlled environment. Similarly, demonstrations of products sometimes have to be made in the home.

■ *Where a probability sampling method is used*: random sampling demands the selection of households or people from the electoral register or by a random walk.

■ *Where special addresses form the sample*: a special list of people may be used as the sample. These could be customers who have returned a guarantee card, people who have enquired about a product, or people who read certain magazines. As the sample is made up of pre-selected addresses, the interviews must be carried out at the household (although telephone interviews would also be a possibility and in many cases the better option).

■ *Where the questions are of a sensitive nature*: if the questions are personal or sensitive in any way, they require an environment where people can settle down and feel safe and secure in their answers. There may not be enough time to build up a rapport and to settle people down in street interviews or over the phone.

■ *Where the interviewer needs to check out something in the house*: research into what has been purchased may require the interviewer to actually see the product. A serial number may have to be noted, a brand name checked, or a receipt examined. If, for example, the interviewer needed a sample of people with solid fuel appliances, then these people could be easily identified by walking round housing estates looking for houses with chimneys. Owners with double glazing, cars, certain types of garage doors and burglar alarms can all be spotted from the road.

Home interviews have limitations:

■ *Where time and cost are paramount*: household interviews are time-consuming and costly to carry out. Interviewers have to find the householder at home or otherwise they have to call back a number of times until successful. Expenses run high, and the number of interviews that can be carried out in a day is much less than is possible in the street. Seven home interviews per day would be a good achievement.

■ *Where the home environment could influence the response*: a survey carried out in the home, exploring teenagers' attitudes to drugs, could be swayed by fear of an eavesdropping parent. Some people may not wish to discuss personal matters such as sex, finances, politics or religion if they are within earshot of others – even their partners. The street is a public place but in certain circumstances it can offer more privacy than the home.

QUESTIONNAIRE DESIGN

The subject of questionnaire design was covered in detail in Chapter 8. Face-to-face interviews as discussed here are a quantitative research technique, and they need structured questionnaires with clear routing and interviewer instructions.

The formatting of the questionnaire is especially important for street interviews where laptops and CAPI (computer aided personal interviewing) is not possible. Questionnaires should be designed so they are easy to read and complete in the dark and dingy lighting that may exist in the street, on the doorstep or in people's homes.

The questionnaire must be piloted prior to use. Ideally this should be done in the field so that problems can be identified in the environment where the interviews will be carried out. Since field piloting is so expensive, a thorough office pilot usually suffices, although it helps if the interviewer is someone that has not been involved in the design of the questionnaire so that he or she can more readily pick up problems that could be missed by those too close to the subject.

RESPONSE RATES TO SURVEYS – AN INDUSTRY PROBLEM

One of the most serious problems faced by the market research industry is the falling level of cooperation to surveys. Each survey has a 'strike rate' that measures the successful interviews against the failures. The reason for non-achievement could be the person was not at home or there was a straight refusal to take part. Strike rates vary survey by survey, with some groups of the public being more heavily researched than others. However, in many surveys the strike rates are hovering dangerously close to the 50 per cent level. When strike rates fall below 50 per cent of the people who have been approached to take part in the survey, researchers become seriously concerned about the validity of the findings. Busy people who are never in when the interviewer calls, or those that refuse to take part in the survey, could have different behaviours and attitudes from those that are interviewed.

Interviewers make a concerted effort to make contact with potential interviewees by calling at different times of day on different days (up to three times). Once contact is established, the interview is won (or lost) depending on a number of factors:

- *Legitimacy*: respondents need to understand the reason why research is being carried out. The more they can justify it to themselves, the more likely they are to see the validity of the survey and their role in contributing to it. Surveys are more likely to be seen as legitimate if the sponsoring company or organization is made known. The interviewer also needs to be seen as legitimate and for this purpose, most carry identity cards issued by official market research trade organizations.
- *Financial incentives*: in the United States respondents are frequently offered a financial incentive (honorarium) to take part in a survey. This is also the norm in Europe in surveys of the medical profession and with attendees of focus groups. Europe is likely to follow the lead of the United States in the greater use of financial incentives.
- *Interviewer approach*: an interviewer who sounds confident, assumptive and businesslike is more likely to achieve cooperation than one that is diffident or apologetic.

Survey introductions are best if they are short so they quickly communicate why the research is being carried out. They need to involve respondents as quickly as possible for we know that once the first question has been answered, most people will finish the interview.

On completion, respondents deserve a thank you. Sometimes they are handed a card which explains who carried out the interview and why. In street interviews it is normal practice for the interviewer to ask respondents for their name and addresses. This is used to carry out a check-back on a percentage of the interviews (usually 5 to 10 per cent) to ensure the work has been carried out satisfactorily. Diplomacy and a special explanation may be needed as many people are reticent about giving their address to a stranger.

The interview may be complete but the interviewer has not finished. A final check is needed over the basic details. All questions should be legible and have been answered. The name of the interviewer, the date, and the respondent's name and address should be checked to ensure that they are filled in. Finally the completed questionnaires must be parcelled up for despatch. The postal instructions should be carefully followed. The field force administration at the office is unlikely to believe stories of recorded delivery or registered post slips which disappear along with a batch of questionnaires – they have heard the excuses too often.

HALL TESTS (MALL INTERCEPTS)

Mall intercepts (hall tests or central location tests) are used when it is necessary to test reactions of people to a product or concept that it is impractical to take to homes or into the street. For example, food and drink products need to be carefully prepared and presented at the right temperature and in the right conditions if a fair reaction is to be obtained.

Hall tests (as they are commonly known in Europe) are so named because they involve hiring a suitable hall or venue close to a busy shopping centre. In the United Kingdom many of these venues are church halls, hence the term. This contrasts with the United States where special facilities in shopping malls are owned by research companies and hired out to other research agencies, together with interviewers. Such special facilities are becoming increasingly available throughout Europe. 'Clinics' refer to a similar method in business-to-business markets where a hotel or a viewing centre is hired so that respondents can observe, try and comment on products.

At a typical mall test, half a dozen interviewers recruit people from the busy mall or streets and persuade them to come to the venue where they can taste or comment on the product. The number of interviews that can be completed in a day depends on the screening criteria for respondents and the length of the interview. If 50 people per day were interviewed, the test would probably run for three or four days in order to achieve a large enough sample to be statistically robust. The tests may be carried out in different cities to overcome regional bias.

Central to the purpose of holding a hall test is the need to show something to respondents. Usually this is a product, and hall tests and product testing are often regarded as synonymous. However, this is not necessarily the case. Hall tests are also used to test packs and advertising material. Mall intercepts are the normal venue for conventional face-to-face interviews in the United States.

When a product is the subject of a hall test, the objective is usually to establish consumers' acceptance, preference and attitudes. Often the product is new and the respondents have not seen it in the shops. The market research is carried out to measure overall liking plus some limited evaluation of the products. In many food tests, reactions are required to the product rather than to the brand, and so the test is often 'blind' with the respondents unaware of which brands are being tested. This type of taste testing is very different from the sensory evaluation carried out by panels of specially trained tasters who have learnt to feed views back in such a way that the formulation of the product can be changed.

In real life, products are bought in a context of choice. A person goes into a shop and chooses one chocolate bar rather than another. Product testing should, therefore, normally be comparative; the product being compared with other products that the new one will replace, perhaps against the leading competitive products. This is a dyadic test or a paired comparison. If a product is tested in isolation it is known as a 'monadic' test.

Products tested in a hall should be capable of being evaluated in this artificial environment, and most items of food and drink fall into this category. Eating a chocolate biscuit in a hall is no different from eating one at home. Similarly, products whose key characteristics can be seen or smelt, or that can be used in a simple way, can all be objects of a hall test. Products inappropriate for hall tests include personal hygiene products (for instance, deodorants), products that have to used over time (for example, a soap powder) or in a fairly complex way (for example, a window cleaner), or when using the product would be simply impractical in the hall (for instance, shampoo). Similarly, products where a conditioning process is necessary to gain acceptance may not be suitable to hall tests, and this presents problems for certain drinks and foodstuffs. For example, sweet and gassy drink formulations tend to score quite well in hall tests, but a beer that scored well in such a test would rapidly lose appeal if drunk in quantity, night after night. When a hall venue is not appropriate, it is necessary to consider testing the product in the place of normal consumption (the home, the pub and so on).

Hall tests are a quantitative technique, and use structured or semi-structured questionnaires with answers fed directly into computers at the time of the test so that the data is captured immediately. The aim is to make specific measurements on:

- *Acceptance*:   will the product be considered?
- *Preference*:   which product is preferred?
- *Attitudes to attributes*:   a product can be considered as a collection

of attributes, colour, texture, smell, taste and so on (and each of these can be further subdivided). What are the attitudes to these different attributes in terms of satisfaction or preferences?

As well as product testing, hall tests are often used for pack testing. For many consumer products the pack is a major element within the purchasing decision. Indeed, it may be the only way in which it differs from competitive brands. Getting the pack right is therefore critical.

Generally, pack tests are carried out for a new product or when an established product is being changed. The object is usually to compare a few possible pack designs either with each other or with competitors. This is done by showing mock-ups that are as near the finished packs as possible. As in product testing, packs are tested for specific attributes – colour, legibility, perceived appropriateness to the product and so on. The specific questions asked about the pack are structured and usually closed. If required, any qualitative probing of the pack concept will have been carried out in group discussions prior to the hall test.

Hall tests also have a role in advertising research. Again, the aim is to obtain quantitative responses to specific aspects of an advertisement such as the impact of its headlines and communication or memorability of the copy and visuals. If the advertising medium covered is the press, a hall test might be used for speed and convenience although alternative methods could be chosen (for example, home or even street interviewers).

SUMMARY

Face-to-face interviews with the general public have a number of advantages. They allow eye contact and body language which helps build rapport and gives a greater understanding of the answers. Products and adverts can be shown. If the interview is in a mall or in the home, the respondent is able to give more time to the consideration of the answers.

Many face-to-face interviews are carried out in the street or in the shopping mall, and it may not be possible to hold people for more than a few minutes as they are going about their daily business.

In certain product tests it is important to control the conditions of the test, in which case special venues in or near shopping malls are hired for a few days. People are screened as potential buyers and recruited to take part in the tests, where they give their preferences and attitudes.

10 Telephone interviewing

WHY INTERVIEW BY TELEPHONE?

The world in which we live today is a lot different from the world we knew just half a century ago. The majority of homes and businesses in the developed world are connected to a telephone network, and the density of mobile phone penetration is reaching saturation point. It is hardly surprising, therefore, that telephone interviewing has become commonplace and the preferred data collection method for market researchers.

Telephone interviews are, in the main, used for uncomplicated, structured interviews. It is common for most consumer interviews to last between 10 and 20 minutes, as any longer would result in interviewee fatigue and threaten the premature termination of the interview. In the case of business-to-business interviews, it is not unusual for interviews to last between 30 to 45 minutes providing the slot has been booked with the respondent and the subject matter is of interest and relevant.

Telephone interviewing is more common in the United States than in any other country, fostered by the easy availability of personal home telephone numbers and the ability to cover the large geographical area that would strain a national field force undertaking face-to-face interviewers. A concern about doorstep security also favours the telephone as an interviewing medium. Householders do not have to answer the door to a stranger while interviewers are spared the risk of entering dubious neighbourhoods.

The telephone allows us to gather information quickly over a wide geographical area at costs that are much lower than those for face-to-face interviews. Telephoning is carried out from central telephone units, and this facilitates easy monitoring, rapid feedback to interviewers, and the ability to capture information directly into computers at the time of the interview.

The greatest advantages of the telephone compared with personal interviewing are its speed and low cost. These are most evident in business-to-business market research. In favourable circumstances five to six 20-minute interviews with managers in industry can be completed in a day over the telephone. In the same time only one or two interviews can be achieved face to face.

In consumer research an accomplished interviewer may be able to achieve 10 to 15 10-minute consumer interviews in a day, but the time and cost advantages of telephone interviewing are not quite so clear-cut. If the comparison is between street/mall interviewing and telephone interviewing then there is probably little difference in either time or cost – in fact, mall interviewing might even be cheaper, but it still raises questions about non-representative samples (see Chapter 7, Sampling). However, when compared with in-home interviews, the telephone is both quicker and cheaper since there is no time wasted in travel between interview points.

CATI – COMPUTER ASSISTED TELEPHONE INTERVIEWING

Computers have replaced the clipboard and questionnaire in telephone interviews. Interviews carried out by telephone can be guided by a questionnaire displayed on the screen of a computer. The interviewer records answers via the keyboard, entering numbers that correspond with the pre-coded responses displayed on the screen. CATI is therefore the bringing together of computer technology and the telephone to improve performance and quality in market research data collection.

The considerable advantages that CATI interviewing offers are:

- The interviewer is left free to concentrate on the interview itself as the routing instructions are taken care of.
- Data is entered directly and the subsequent transactions of data processing are eliminated. Costs and punching errors are reduced.
- The whole process is speeded up because data is entered as it is obtained.

- The software programme easily manages the sample so that quotas are adhered to.
- At intervals during the survey, the researcher can interrogate the computer to examine the results.
- An analysis of results can be obtained immediately after the last interview has been completed.

There are some disadvantages to CATI interviewing. A conventional questionnaire can be drafted in no time and without the help of a technician who is required to make the conversion onto the computer screens. Getting a questionnaire up and running, fault free, on a CATI system takes time.

Capturing open-ended responses on a CATI system requires interviewers with good typing skills. Flexibility is lost as it is not as easy to refer back to an answer on the screen as it is by turning over the page of a paper questionnaire. In general, CATI is best suited to structured interviews carried out in large numbers, especially repeated surveys where all the possible answers have been worked out and can be listed as pre-coded responses.

THE ART OF TELEPHONE INTERVIEWING – CARRYING OUT A SUCCESSFUL INTERVIEW

Whether the interviewer uses a paper-based questionnaire or a CATI system, the principles of achieving a successful interview are the same.

The introduction – beating back the 'brush-off'

Obtaining a market research interview is not easy, especially given the large number of surveys that are taking place and the bombardment of our privacy through the 'cold call' selling of financial services or double glazing. The respondents believe (with some justification) that they are giving up their valuable time and may be getting little in return. The best way of approaching a respondent is to be confident, clear, pleasant and businesslike. As is the case with any interview, however it is administered, respondents will not participate if they fail to find the subject interesting or of relevance.

It is in the opening seconds of the introduction on the phone that the interview will be won or lost. The challenge is to introduce the survey, create a hook that interests the respondents, and to do so as quickly as possible so that the respondent can start talking. There may also be some other issues to communicate, such as how long the interview is expected to take, confidentiality aspects and an assurance that there will be no subsequent sales call directly as a consequence of the interview. The more the interviewer tries to pack in to the introduction and the longer it takes, the more time respondents have to think of reasons that they do not want to take part. A fast engagement is vital. The interviewer's approach really does make a difference:

- *Always be assumptive and confident*:   respondents like to feel that they are in the hands of a professional, someone that is businesslike without being pushy.
- *Create trust*:   respondents will talk to people they trust. Building trust in a few seconds is difficult when the interviewer has only a voice and words. However both can be powerful ordnance if they are used correctly. The right words and voice will create legitimacy for the interview. The wrong ones will result in a brush-off. It does help to have a script prepared before phoning to ensure that the introduction is, as near as possible, the best one to win trust and cooperation.
- *Respondents do not like to feel like they are being singled out unfairly*:   it feels good to know you are part of a nationwide survey.
- *Allegiances promote cooperation*:   if an earlier phone call resulted in contact with another member of the family (or a business colleague in the case of a B2B survey), it may help to name drop to create a sense of familiarity (assuming, of course, that permission has been obtained to name the contact).

Despite the most polished approach, difficulties will be encountered:

- *The person is always out or does not have the time*:   actually people are not always out, it just seems that way. There are certain times when a few minutes could be found for an interview. Family members or (in business-to-business interviews) a colleague could suggest the best time to catch the person.
- *The respondent is survey weary*:   some people (especially respondents in particular businesses) are constantly disturbed by market researchers. This leads to 'no survey' policies or a brusque 'Sorry, I've already been interviewed.' Market researchers have a special responsibility to these people to make interviews as interesting as possible – and that may

have to be the angle that is taken. It is a survey aimed at improving products (or services), and it has not been done before.

The best of planning cannot guarantee success every time. It requires people of considerable skill and tenacity to make the appropriate number of calls and win cooperation. It is not unusual in an interview programme to have to make over 100 dialled calls to achieve eight interviews. (Dialled calls do not always get answered. When they do get answered the person that is being pursued for interview may not be there, he or she may not have the time there and then, or he or she may refuse outright). Achieving telephone interviews is very much a numbers game.

The interview – keep the interest going

In most cases, once a respondent has started the interview, he or she will see it through to completion. We are not suggesting that compliance through the interview is a foregone conclusion; a different set of skills is needed for the execution of the interview itself.

The crucial requirement of any interview is to know the questionnaire thoroughly. This is especially the case with paper-based questionnaires, as complex routings could break the flow of the interview.

The interview is, of course, a script of a kind and the questions have to be read out exactly as stated. Good interviewers develop their own style, speaking at a moderate pace and with good clarity and diction. Although it may be the last interview in a busy and tiring day, the interviewer must sound interested. In fact, he or she will be interested because a good interviewer really does listen.

Although the questionnaire is a script, and it must be adhered to, there is scope to build in the social lubrication and verbal encouragements that indicate we are listening and are interested. The body language of the voice becomes even more important, given there is nothing else to create rapport.

The close

By the time the interview is finished a relationship will have been created with the respondent. Respondents deserve to be thanked for their time and effort, and it may be appropriate to ask permission to call again should it be necessary to clarify any of the answers. (This is more important in business-to-business interviews.)

SOME LIMITATIONS OF TELEPHONE INTERVIEWS

We have seen how the many positive attributes of telephone interviews have resulted in it becoming the main method used in quantitative research in the United States, and it is hot on the heels of personal interviewing in European surveys. However, there are sometimes occasions when it is not appropriate to use telephone interviews.

If something *has* to be shown, the telephone is not the right approach. Nor is the telephone suited when it is necessary to ask respondents to consider a number of pre-determined factors in order to test their views. More than five or six factors on a list are difficult to hold in the mind. In a face-to-face interview these would be shown on the laptop screen or a printed card so that they can be given fair consideration. That said, some of these limitations could be overcome by using a combination of phone, fax, post or e-mail. For example, the faxing or mailing (or e-mailing) of visuals or prompt materials would follow an initial interview by phone. The second phone interview is then carried out while the respondent is looking at the visual.

It is easier to say 'no' on the phone. It is easier for someone to say 'I have to go soon' and put pressure on the respondent to rush the final questions. Telephone interviews are always susceptible to distractions from television programmes, people knocking at the door, or in the case of business interviews, interruptions from colleagues or pre-arranged meetings. Telephone interviews are normally carried out in an impromptu fashion, while face-to-face interviews are often prearranged and so allow the respondent to set aside some time to participate.

In Asia, market research is not as established as it is in the United States and Europe. Asian respondents may not understand the direct questioning over the phone that is accepted by Anglo-Saxons. Indeed, telephone penetration throughout some Asian households and particularly in Indonesia is very low. It is more acceptable in Asian societies to use face-to-face interviewing.

In the United Kingdom, telephone ownership is approaching saturation but one in four hard-wired phone users is ex-directory. Younger people are increasingly relying on their mobile phones and may not have a hard-wired phone. Significant proportions of the population are inaccessible as a result of not being in telephone directories. As the number of people who are not listed in the telephone directory increases, there will be more difficulties for market researchers in finding representative samples.

Telephone interviewing is, on the whole, better suited to shorter interviews, and 10 minutes is probably the ideal length for a consumer interview, while 20 minutes to half an hour is the norm for business interviews. In telephone interviews the questions and answers are generally kept short, and so some researchers feel that this does not encourage discursive and insightful responses.

SUMMARY

Telephone interviews offer benefits of speed and cost, and their quality is easier to control than with face-to-face interviews. They have rapidly grown in importance over the last few years so that today they are equal to, if not more important than, face-to-face interviews.

The telephone interviewer requires special skills. Persuasion is required to win cooperation after which verbal and social skills will be needed to make the interview work. Above all, tenacity is essential as large numbers of calls have to be made to achieve a single interview.

Key requirements of a successful telephone interview are:

- Understand the subject and the questionnaire before picking up the phone.
- Check that the person on the other end of the phone is the right person to interview.
- Adopt a friendly, professional introduction that gives the survey legitimacy and a hook.
- Be clear and concise in the questioning.
- Listen, and make this evident with words of interest and encouragement.
- Ask questions to clarify responses and probe for a deeper understanding of the answers.
- Complete the questionnaire thoroughly, cross-checking responses where appropriate.
- Thank respondents for their time and valuable input and leave the door open if there is a possibility that they may need to be phoned back.

11 Self-completion questionnaires

THE UBIQUITOUS SELF-COMPLETION QUESTIONNAIRE

Self-completion questionnaires face us everywhere we go. They sit in our hotel rooms. They are thrust at us in airports. They drop through the mail box. We have all been subjected to self-completion questionnaires at one time or another, whether it is checking on satisfaction with a newly purchased car or the local utility company asking for views on its service. How many times have you actually filled one in? More importantly, how many have you ignored? We will discuss the pros and cons of self-completion questionnaires in this chapter, but we know that their major weakness is a very low (and often unpredictable) response rate. Our focus is very much on hard copy self-completion questionnaires which are mailed by post to respondents, or inserted in magazines, or left alongside the menu in a restaurant or hotel. There are many principles in the design and execution of these questionnaires that overlap with e-based surveys. However, because e-surveys have some special considerations they are considered in the next chapter (Chapter 12).

WHEN TO USE AND WHEN NOT TO USE SELF-COMPLETION QUESTIONNAIRES

Self-completion questionnaires are a perfect tool for the DIY researcher. A lone researcher sitting at a computer can mail out a questionnaire to hundreds of people for the cost of a stamp (or for nothing if it is sent by e-mail).

From the respondents' point of view, self-completion questionnaires may be a preferred method if they have difficulty finding the time to get to the phone or if they value privacy in their responses. A dentist or doctor can fill in the questionnaire in his or her own time. An employee of a company can fill the 'employee satisfaction' questionnaire in at home and be confident that the reply is confidential and anonymous.

Long, laborious rating questions, which are an important component of most satisfaction surveys, can be completed quickly whereas in an administered interview, each attribute and statement has to be read out. The administered interview takes much longer and feels more tedious. A self-completion questionnaire also presents a chance to use pictures as explanations, or it can be brightened up with pictorial scales of smiley and frowning faces.

Self-completion questionnaires are a useful means of collecting data from more than one respondent in a household or company. For example, a survey that seeks to find out weekly food consumption in households would enable two partners of the household to consult and ensures greater accuracy in the completion of the questionnaire. People can take their time. They can reflect on questions that need extra thought. There is a more considered response than one that is forced, 'off the cuff', in an administered interview.

For all their advantages, there are some major disadvantages with self-completion questionnaires. Probably the biggest shortcoming is that they generate low and uncertain response rates, which could be below 10 per cent of all the questionnaires sent out. It is an uncomfortable feeling if we know that 90 per cent of people have not replied. How certain are we that the respondents are representative? Are the replies we receive from people who want to complain? This we will never know unless we carry out control checks using conventional interviewing with a sample of non-respondents, and that is a luxury that is seldom afforded. If a very low response rate is anticipated, then nearly always this suggests the survey would be better carried out using an administered interview.

Self-completion questionnaires are not suitable for all respondents, such as the very young, people with learning difficulties, people with literacy problems, or the very old.

The questionnaires have to 'stand on their own' – there is no interviewer on hand to sort out a question if it is not fully understood. The questionnaires must be as near perfect as possible, with clear questions, clear instructions and adequate room to write in answers. 'Tick box' questions are easier to fill in and so are likely to dominate the questionnaire. Typically there are only one or two open-ended questions and these generally receive poor responses.

Clarity is also important in the formatting and layout of the questionnaire. A professionally typeset questionnaire manages to squeeze more questions on to the page and still maintain the white space that makes it look clean and neat.

We have suggested that self-completion questionnaires are a suitable instrument for the DIY researcher. However, there is a good deal of time required for the organization of the paperwork, printing, envelopes, the stuffing of the envelopes and the franking. Folding, stuffing and dispatching 1,000 postal questionnaires will require a day or more of someone's time.

IMPORTANT ASPECTS IN SELF-COMPLETION QUESTIONNAIRE DESIGN

The importance of the introductory letter

The introductory cover letter is as important as the questionnaire itself. This sets the scene for why the research is being carried out and plants the hook that encourages the response. The letter that accompanies the questionnaire is working like any good sales letter – it is seeking to persuade the respondent to take action. It must do so quickly so that, just as in the administered interview, the respondent is engaged in picking up a pen as quickly as possible. Once started, there is a good chance that the questionnaire will be completed.

A letter that is addressed to a person by name will have more impact than one that is simply addressed to 'The householder' or the 'Chief buyer'. Having said that, a misspelt name, the wrong name or the name of someone who has long since moved on will turn off response like an ice-cold tap.

The first paragraph should give the survey legitimacy. It needs a purpose that means something to the respondent. This could be the promise of improved products or service. It is worthwhile emphasizing that the respondent's reply is critical to the success of the survey, and this creates a burden of obligation. If the promise of product improvements is going to ring hollow, it may be necessary to offer a material incentive to reply. A small gesture such as enclosing a pen can help, but it is often necessary to proffer prize draws or monetary rewards.

The letter should give an assurance about confidentiality and conclude with clear instructions on what to do next. (Almost always a reply paid envelope is included with the cover letter and self-completion questionnaire, and reference should be made to this in the closing lines.)

Golden rules for writing good cover letters

- Write in an engaging style. Personalize the letter as much as possible. Be clear. Be brief.
- Explain the purpose of the survey and why the respondent has been selected – legitimize it and offer a hook (if necessary a material incentive).
- Give an assurance that completing the questionnaire is easy.
- If it is possible to do so, give an assurance that replies will be confidential.
- Give instructions as to what should be done – how to fill it in, and how to send it back.
- Thank the respondent.

An example of a cover letter for a postal survey is provided in Figure 11.1.

Question types, wording and sequencing

The golden rule of all questionnaire design is to think of all the possible answers at the time of designing the question. Most questionnaires fail because the researcher does not see them from the respondent's point of view.

Once respondents have the first question there is a good chance that they will finish the whole questionnaire. Simple routine questions help lead respondents into the main body of the questionnaire.

University of
HUDDERSFIELD

December 2002

Dear Student,

It has become increasingly important that Universities understand their student population in order to help them tailor the services and courses they offer to their students. The University of Huddersfield would like to find out why students choose Huddersfield University as their place of study, and what they think of the University when they get there.

To do this, they have commissioned us, B2B International Ltd, a specialist research agency, to carry out an independent study for them. The first stage of the research involved listening to the views of students through focus groups to find out the main issues that are important to students. Some of you may have been involved in these. We would now like to measure these issues across the whole University population and to do this we are seeking your co-operation.

I am enclosing the student survey questionnaire that we have developed from our discussions with students for your completion. We hope that you will use this opportunity to tell us why you chose Huddersfield and to have your say about what is important at the University, how it affects you and whether particular things should change. By spending ten minutes completing this questionnaire you can influence how the University develops.

The data from the survey will be used to build up a picture of the University and identify how the University can improve to meet the needs of the students who attend Huddersfield to study. Completed questionnaires should be returned **directly to B2B International by Monday 13th January 2003** using the reply-paid envelope enclosed.

To thank you for taking the time to complete the questionnaire, there will be a prize draw with seven prizes of £100 (one for EACH School). To enter the draw, please complete the slip below and enclose this with your completed questionnaire. The prize draw will take place in January 2003 and winners will be notified personally and results posted on the University website.

Thank you for taking part.

Carol-Ann Morgan
B2B International Limited
Telephone 0161 440 6000

✂ -

GRAND PRIZE DRAW Detach and enclose with your completed questionnaire.

NAME ....

CONTACT ADDRESS ....

....

CONTACT TELEPHONE NUMBER ....

SCHOOL ....

Figure 11.1 *Sample cover letter for a postal survey*

Open-ended questions are badly answered in self-completion surveys. Questions that ask for free-ranging explanations get inadequate (and often illegible) answers. Typical replies are 'Because it is good', 'We have always bought it', 'It does its job' and so on, and there is no opportunity to find out why it is good, why people always buy it or in what way it does its job.

Nor is it possible to ask complicated questions. It is no good asking householders how much they spent on leisure activities over the last year. The subject is too vague and householders do not keep annual expenditure figures of this type in their head. The researcher stands some chance if a question asks about the frequency with which people indulge in specific leisure activities (and then the researcher can do the maths to arrive at an estimated expenditure).

We have already emphasized that successful self-completion questionnaires should be easy to complete. Thus, wherever possible, questions should have pre-coded answers simply requiring a box to be ticked or a number circled. Pre-coded questions are suited to self-completion questionnaires as they save the respondent time writing in the answers. Scalar questions are highly applicable because they can be completed quickly by ticking boxes.

Although pre-coded answers do help the respondent, complicated routing can still be off-putting and must be avoided; especially because skipping questions creates confusion and can often lead to errors in completion.

Finally, with self-completion questionnaires it is not possible to disclose information in a controlled fashion as in a telephone or visit interview because respondents probably will read ahead and become aware of forthcoming questions.

Golden rules for writing good self-completion questionnaires

- Use short and simple questions (couched in the respondent's language and using measures of quantity or time that are respondent friendly).
- Have an easy question to get people started.
- Design questions that are absolutely clear and have no ambiguity.
- Questions should have pre-coded (appropriate) response codes.
- Response codes should be easy to complete, such as boxes to tick or numbers to circle.
- Make sure that the response boxes are in line with and close to the answers (or clearly linked to the answer with a dot leader).

- Leave sufficient space to be able to tick the correct box or write in the answer.
- Have a logical sequence to the questions.
- Use clear instructions for the routing (where to go next, what to do next).
- Make sure that the name and address of the researcher is clearly marked somewhere on the questionnaire (in case someone loses the reply paid envelope and wants to send it back in a different envelope).

Enhancing the appearance of the questionnaire

Most recipients view market research questionnaires as 'just another form to fill in', and since there is no compulsion to respond there is a danger that the form will end up in the waste paper basket unless it catches the respondent's interest. A clear and attractive layout is more important in a self-completion questionnaire than one used by an interviewer.

The more professional the production, the greater will be the response, so typesetting the questionnaire is worth considering. An attractive layout and the interesting use of space will also encourage replies. Colour can help a questionnaire to stand out in the sea of paper on most respondents' desks. There should be consistency of styles throughout a questionnaire for both spatial arrangement of information and the use of colours and logos. There are always exceptions to prove a rule and sometimes a simply formatted questionnaire, as if typed on an old-fashioned typewriter, will engage sympathy and interest, and win a response.

Figure 11.2 shows part of a sample self-completion questionnaire for a postal survey.

RECOMMENDATIONS FOR PRACTICE

Pre-testing and piloting postal surveys

It is especially important to pilot self-completion questionnaires because once they are printed and dispatched, there is nothing that can be done to rectify a mistake or omission. Organizing a pilot that is a real mini-survey is unlikely to be an option as it would require almost as much time and administration as the real thing. The best that the researcher

SECTION 2 -YOUR EXPERIENCE AT HUDDERSFIELD UNIVERSITY
This section is about what you think of Huddersfield University.

I.   YOUR PROGRAMME OF STUDY

Year of your course: 1☐₁   2☐₂   3☐₃   4☐₄   5☐₅   6 or more☐₆   (46)

Type of course: Full time ☐₇   Part time ☐₈

Level of course: Undergraduate ☐₉   Postgraduate ☐₀

Does your course involve a work placement?   Yes ☐₁   No ☐₂   (47)

Which type of award are you studying for?   (48)

Foundation Year	☐₁	Postgraduate award, eg. MA, MSc	☐₄
Pre-Degree, eg.HND, HNC, WITS course	☐₂	Other programmes, eg. ACCA, Cert Ed	☐₅
Undergraduate degree, eg. BA (Hons) BSc	☐₃	Postgraduate award eg. MA, MSc	☐₆

On average, how many days per week do you come into the University? (please circle)

0   1   2   3   4   5   6   7   (49)

Please rate the extent to which you are satisfied with the following issues in relation to your PROGRAMME OF STUDY (COURSE) and then rate how important it is to you.

(6) COURSE ORGANISATION	SATISFACTION			IMPORTANCE		
Not applicable	Totally Dissatisfied	Neither Nor	Totally Satisfied	Not at all Important	Neither Nor	Very Important
a) ☐₁ course induction	1 2 3 4 5 6 7 (7)			1 2 3 4 5 6 7 (11)		
b) ☐₂ information about your course (eg. course handbook) 1	2 3 4 5 6 7 (8)			1 2 3 4 5 6 7 (12)		
c) ☐₃ notification of alterations to the timetable	1 2 3 4 5 6 7 (9)			1 2 3 4 5 6 7 (13)		
d) ☐₄ how you are kept in touch with what is happening on your course	1 2 3 4 5 6 7 (10)			1 2 3 4 5 6 7 (14)		
(15) COURSE CONTENT						
a) ☐₁ content of your course	1 2 3 4 5 6 7 (16)			1 2 3 4 5 6 7 (23)		
b) ☐₂ opportunity for work related placements	1 2 3 4 5 6 7 (17)			1 2 3 4 5 6 7 (24)		
c) ☐₃ availability of placements	1 2 3 4 5 6 7 (18)			1 2 3 4 5 6 7 (25)		
d) ☐₄ extent to which your course motivates you to study	1 2 3 4 5 6 7 (19)			1 2 3 4 5 6 7 (26)		
e) ☐₅ extent to which your course meets your needs	1 2 3 4 5 6 7 (20)			1 2 3 4 5 6 7 (27)		
f) ☐₆ extent to which your course prepares you for work	1 2 3 4 5 6 7 (21)			1 2 3 4 5 6 7 (28)		
g) ☐₇ recognition of your course in the job market	1 2 3 4 5 6 7 (22)			1 2 3 4 5 6 7 (29)		
(30) THE TEACHING STAFF						
a) ☐₁ reliability of the academic staff (ie. don't cancel classes, punctuality)	1 2 3 4 5 6 7 (31)			1 2 3 4 5 6 7 (38)		
b) ☐₂ teaching ability of the academic staff	1 2 3 4 5 6 7 (32)			1 2 3 4 5 6 7 (39)		
c) ☐₃ knowledge and skills base of the academic staff	1 2 3 4 5 6 7 (33)			1 2 3 4 5 6 7 (40)		
d) ☐₄ the use of a range of teaching methods	1 2 3 4 5 6 7 (34)			1 2 3 4 5 6 7 (41)		
e) ☐₅ helpfulness of the academic staff	1 2 3 4 5 6 7 (35)			1 2 3 4 5 6 7 (42)		
f) ☐₆ the use of 'Blackboard' by lecturers	1 2 3 4 5 6 7 (36)			1 2 3 4 5 6 7 (43)		
g) ☐₇ supervision of your dissertation	1 2 3 4 5 6 7 (37)			1 2 3 4 5 6 7 (44)		
(45) ASSESSMENT						
a) ☐₁ flexibility of dates for handing in assignments	1 2 3 4 5 6 7 (46)			1 2 3 4 5 6 7 (53)		
b) ☐₂ information about assessment criteria	1 2 3 4 5 6 7 (47)			1 2 3 4 5 6 7 (54)		
c) ☐₃ consistency of marking standards	1 2 3 4 5 6 7 (48)			1 2 3 4 5 6 7 (55)		
d) ☐₄ methods of assessment used (eg. essay, exam, practical, etc,)	1 2 3 4 5 6 7 (49)			1 2 3 4 5 6 7 (56)		
e) ☐₅ speed of return of course/assessment results	1 2 3 4 5 6 7 (50)			1 2 3 4 5 6 7 (57)		
f) ☐₆ usefulness of academic staff feedback about assessments	1 2 3 4 5 6 7 (51)			1 2 3 4 5 6 7 (58)		
g) ☐₇ information about dissertation submission	1 2 3 4 5 6 7 (52)			1 2 3 4 5 6 7 (59)		

148

If you feel there are any questions which are not relevant to you, please tick the 'not applicable' box

(60) THE TEACHING RESOURCES		SATISFACTION							IMPORTANCE							
Not applicable		Totally Dissatisfied		Neither Nor			Totally Satisfied		Not at all Important			Neither Nor			Very Important	
a) ☐₁ provision of course material																
(ie. handouts, technology based material) 1	2	3	4	5	6	7	(61)........	1	2	3	4	5	6	7	(65)
b) ☐₂ equipment available for learning and teaching purposes..1	2	3	4	5	6	7	(62)........	1	2	3	4	5	6	7	(66)
c) ☐₃ the teaching facilities available, ie. rooms, labs, etc 1	2	3	4	5	6	7	(63)........	1	2	3	4	5	6	7	(67)
d) ☐₄ 'Blackboard' learning support 1	2	3	4	5	6	7	(64)........	1	2	3	4	5	6	7	(68)

(6) ACADEMIC AND PASTORAL SUPPORT																
a) ☐₁ your access to academic staff outside lecture time 1	2	3	4	5	6	7	(7)........	1	2	3	4	5	6	7	(13)
b) ☐₂ guidance and support from academic staff 1	2	3	4	5	6	7	(8)........	1	2	3	4	5	6	7	(14)
c) ☐₃ support whilst out on placements.....................................1	2	3	4	5	6	7	(9)........	1	2	3	4	5	6	7	(15)
d) ☐₄ support for learning disabilities (eg. dyslexia)..................1	2	3	4	5	6	7	(10)........	1	2	3	4	5	6	7	(16)
e) ☐₅ support for disabled students (eg. physical disabilities) ..1	2	3	4	5	6	7	(11)........	1	2	3	4	5	6	7	(17)
f) ☐₆ support for part time students...1	2	3	4	5	6	7	(12)........	1	2	3	4	5	6	7	(18)

2. STUDENT ADMINISTRATION

Please rate the extent to which you are satisfied with the following issues in relation to student administration both before and since you arrived at the University, and then rate how important it is to you.

(19) BEFORE YOU ARRIVED AT THE UNIVERSITY		SATISFACTION							IMPORTANCE							
Not applicable		Totally Dissatisfied		Neither Nor			Totally Satisfied		Not at all Important			Neither Nor			Very Important	
a) ☐₁ the open day 1	2	3	4	5	6	7	(20)........	1	2	3	4	5	6	7	(26)
b) ☐₂ information contained in the prospectus 1	2	3	4	5	6	7	(21)........	1	2	3	4	5	6	7	(27)
c) ☐₃ admissions process...1	2	3	4	5	6	7	(22)........	1	2	3	4	5	6	7	(28)
d) ☐₄ information through clearing 1	2	3	4	5	6	7	(23)........	1	2	3	4	5	6	7	(29)
e) ☐₅ availability of part-time courses at Huddersfield 1	2	3	4	5	6	7	(24)........	1	2	3	4	5	6	7	(30)
f) ☐₆ university website...1	2	3	4	5	6	7	(25)........	1	2	3	4	5	6	7	(31)

(32) STUDENT ADMINISTRATION SINCE YOU ARRIVED AT THE UNIVERSITY																
a) ☐₁ student handbook 1	2	3	4	5	6	7	(33)........	1	2	3	4	5	6	7	(40)
b) ☐₂ efficiency of the enrolment process 1	2	3	4	5	6	7	(34)........	1	2	3	4	5	6	7	(41)
c) ☐₃ timeliness and accuracy of invoicing for your course fee 1	2	3	4	5	6	7	(35)........	1	2	3	4	5	6	7	(42)
d) ☐₄ method of payment of the course fees (ie. installments)..1	2	3	4	5	6	7	(36)........	1	2	3	4	5	6	7	(43)
e) ☐₅ administration of student loans 1	2	3	4	5	6	7	(37)........	1	2	3	4	5	6	7	(44)
f) ☐₆ handling of general enquiries within your																
school/department..1	2	3	4	5	6	7	(38)........	1	2	3	4	5	6	7	(45)
g) ☐₇ procedure for handing in assignments/assessments..........1	2	3	4	5	6	7	(39)........	1	2	3	4	5	6	7	(46)

3. COMPUTING FACILITIES

Which University computing facilities do you MOST frequently use?

(Please tick only ONE box. If you use more than one facility, please tick the area you want to rate in the following questions.)

Central Learning Centre ☐₁   School facilities ☐₂   (47)

Do you have access to a computer at home?   Yes ☐₁   No ☐₂   (48)

If yes, is it connected to the Internet?   Yes ☐₁   No ☐₂   (49)

Figure 11.2 *Part of a sample self-completion questionnaire for a postal survey*

can hope for is to test for comprehension and clarity by having a friend, colleague or typical target fill it in. It is helpful for the designer of the questionnaire to sit next to the tester and hear a 'stream of consciousness' (verbal thoughts) as he or she is working out what the questions mean and completing the answers.

Project management and administration – planning, costing, timetabling

The starting point of any survey is to work out a timeline of what should be done by when and by whom. Postal surveys depend on suitable databases containing the correct names and addresses of respondents. If lists are out of date, contain inaccuracies in spelling of the names and addresses, or are made up of unsuitable respondents, the questionnaires will fall on stony ground and the response rates will be low. Work on the database to clean it up and de-duplicate will not be wasted. All databases are out of date as soon as they are created. Part of the study findings will be an analysis of the quality of the database measured by 'return to sender' envelopes.

If many thousands of questionnaires are to be sent out, it may be worth using a mailing house to fill and send out all envelopes.

Most people who fill in self-completion questionnaires do so within a day or two of receiving them, so the bulk of the returns will come back within a few days of mailing. A reminder will boost the response but this can only be sent out after a respectable period (after a week to two weeks). This will add a couple more weeks to the survey timetable. It is preferable that the reminder mailings miss out those who have already returned a questionnaire. This may not be possible if replies are anonymous.

Most self-completion surveys could be cut off after three weeks and, although stragglers will come in over the next weeks and even months, 95 per cent of the replies that are likely to come back will have been captured (see Figure 11.3).

Christmas, Easter and the month of August in Europe are difficult times to mail self-completion questionnaires. It is also worth thinking about when the mailing will land on respondents' mats. Friday could be a bad day to land a business-to-business mailer but a good one for a householder.

A summary of the project planning tasks in a mailing programme is shown in Table 11.1.

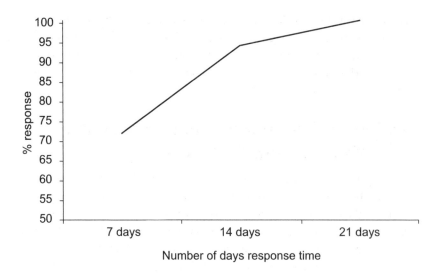

Figure 11.3 *Response rates over time from self-completion questionnaires*

Boosting response rates

Everything should be made as easy as possible for the respondent to reply and, as a result, raise response rates. The relevance, importance and interest of a survey to the respondent are important influences on response rates. However, other basics such as referring to the inclusion of a reply-paid envelope with the questionnaire will also help. There are a number of cross-checks to follow that will boost the numbers in any postal survey.

Interest

The one factor that influences the response rate of a postal survey more than anything else is the interest that respondents have in the subject. A postal survey of customers is likely to achieve a higher response than one of non-customers because there is an interest in and a relationship between customers and the sponsor of the study.

Response rates of 30 per cent and higher from a single mailing are quite common when the subject is about a new car or on behalf of a company with some apparent authority such as a utility company. In staff satisfaction self-completion surveys, response rates can be as high

Table 11.1 *Summary of key tasks in planning a self-completion postal survey*

Key tasks	Things to check
Buy or build the list of respondents	Can it be obtained on disk?
Obtain quotes from printers for questionnaire, cover letter and reply paid envelopes	Check quality of paper. Check on turn-around time.
Design questionnaire and cover letter	Obtain approval of client
Test questionnaire by watching half a dozen colleagues complete it. Amend the questionnaire.	Do they understand the questions? Do they follow the instructions? Did they find it easy?
Order stationery and printed material: outward envelopes, letter head, reply paid envelopes, questionnaire	Check licence number for reply paid envelope is up-to-date. Check that envelopes are of the right size for holding the return questionnaire and assembly of outbound pieces.
Book a mailing house for folding, inserting and franking mail OR ...	Check cost of outsourcing. Check on turn-around time.
If carrying out in-house, arrange for the franking machine to be filled and brief staff who will be helping with typing, and stuffing envelopes	Note that the Post Office offers a franking service for large quantities of mail. Arrange for checking a sample of each person's work to see it is being done correctly.
Advise Post Office if there are quantities of over 1,000	You may need to open an account with the Post Office or have a cheque for mailing cost
Mail the questionnaires	If the questionnaires land on any day of the week, will this adversely affect the response?
Brief staff who deal with incoming mail on requirements for opening (or not opening) the returned questionnaires	Is there a necessity to check the franked return questionnaire to determine the domicile of the respondent?
Track numbers of responses each day to determine when to close the survey	Consider data processing after two weeks or re-mailing with a reminder

as 70 per cent. In contrast, respondents receiving a questionnaire through the post enquiring about the type of washing liquid they use would most probably yield a low response (less than 5 per cent is likely).

Keeping it brief

The shorter the questionnaire, the more likely it will be completed and returned. Carefully laying out 40 questions on two sides of A3 (folded to make four pages of A4) can result in what looks like a shorter questionnaire than one with 20 questions spread over six single pages. However, the number of questions does not influence responses as much as the interest factor, and there are many examples of long, 12-page questionnaires obtaining high response rates.

Anonymity

Self-completion surveys that offer anonymity usually have a higher response than those where respondents must identify themselves, although much depends on the circumstances. In many business-to-business surveys, respondents may be happy to be identified as long as they are confident that the research is bona fide and not a surreptitious attempt at selling.

Householders like to be assured that their names will not be sold on to a mailing house, and that there will be no sales pressure to follow as happens with all e-enabled respondents with their e-mails. The ever-increasing problem of 'spamming' has resulted in people becoming very suspicious about disclosing their e-mail addresses (see Chapter 12: e-surveys).

Advance publicity

An advance letter alerting people that the survey is soon to be carried out will boost the response, and any other publicity will also help. For example, in staff satisfaction surveys replies are boosted by posters around the company asking people to respond. A company newsletter could be an excellent vehicle for pre-publicity about the survey.

Second mailings

A second mailing can boost response rates. If the first mailing yields a 25 per cent response, a second one could draw a further 10 to 15 per cent. The researcher needs, therefore, to consider whether it is better to send a second mailing to the non-respondents and live with a fall-off in response rate or mail to a fresh sample from which a further 25 per cent response should be obtained.

Incentives

The use of incentives has been shown to influence response rates. The incentive can take the form of a promise of better products, improved service or a prize draw for a gift such as a sum of money, a holiday or car. In business-to-business interviews, charity donations are more appropriate because of the fact that some respondents are not allowed to accept personal reward while others may see it as bribery.

SUMMARY

The initial reaction of most people is to discount postal surveys because they suffer from low and uncertain response rates. Where there is a strong relationship with a target audience, the response rates will be high, and in employee satisfaction surveys they often exceed 70 per cent.

Self-completion surveys have their advantages. They are an ideal tool for the solo researcher as there is no requirement for a field force of interviewers. They are best suited to surveys with lots of rating scales that would be tedious in an administered interview.

The key to designing good self-completion questionnaires is to imagine the difficulties the respondent will face during completion and take these into account in the formulation of the questions. Clear and simple questions with closed responses and tick boxes are ideally suited to self-completion questionnaires. An engaging cover letter that creates interest and offers an incentive for replying is as important as the questionnaire in generating a high response.

The organization of a postal survey requires strong project management skills to ensure that the administration and mailing goes to plan.

12 E-surveys

A NEW RESEARCH TOOL IN THE KIT BAG

The Internet has given researchers an additional route by which to collect data. It is used in desk research as a library in the sky (see Chapter 3), and it also provides considerable opportunities for new approaches to interviewing.

The Internet is establishing itself as an efficient mechanism for managing self-completion surveys. In other areas it is more developmental, such as hosting focus groups for respondents who are widely scattered or who wish to remain anonymous.

COLLECTING INFORMATION FROM A WEB SITE

A huge amount of data can be obtained about Web site traffic without any survey work. It is standard procedure to examine the number of visitors to the site, the number that have looked at each page, what search strategies visitors used to navigate their way to the site, how long they stayed on the site and so on. When these data are plotted on a daily, weekly or monthly basis, there is much to be learnt about how many hits the site is getting and what is found to be interesting (or easy to find) on the site.

These numbers tell a story but they do not enable us to profile the visitors or obtain feedback on what people like and do not like about the site. For this we need a more conventional questionnaire.

This is no problem for a Web site. A questionnaire can be designed to pop up and grab the attention of visitors, or they can be directed to a file on the site by signposts on the site map. Because it costs nothing to have a questionnaire on a site, and it frankly looks good to be seeking visitor feedback, these questionnaires are anything but novel. In fact, since they exist everywhere, they are shunned by most and obtain very low response rates – 2 per cent is typical and 5 per cent is very good.

The Web site questionnaires pass some messages back to us, but we are left wondering how typical they are given that they represent such a small proportion of traffic. They could be the views of people with time on their hands, complainers or nerds. It raises the constant problem with self-completion questionnaires that generate a low response: are we better with no information than information from a small and possibly biased group that could mislead us? There is no answer to this. Despite the bias, it could be worthwhile running a questionnaire on the Web site to see if there are any trends in the answers that are coming back and to at least get a feel for what irritates or pleases people.

SENDING OUT E-BASED SURVEYS

The Internet offers market researchers – especially do-it-yourselfers with few resources – the ability to collect information quickly and cheaply using an e-based questionnaire. This is even easier than in a postal survey as there is no print, post or typesetting to organize. Quite obviously the Internet provides the mail delivery network and a mail out presupposes that we have e-mail addresses for our target group. This in itself is one of the biggest problems in e-surveys for a number of reasons.

First, not everyone is on the Internet and so for some audiences it would exclude significant numbers and present a biased sample. Second, and possibly of greater importance, lists of e-mail addresses are notoriously inadequate. They are seldom comprehensive, and whatever addresses are listed could be wrong or neglected by their owners. Purchased lists are dubious in accuracy and coverage.

If there is no e-mail address list, it is surprisingly difficult to collect addresses through a quick phone survey. Addresses are given incorrectly, they are taken down incorrectly, and there is often a considerable reluctance to give the address for fear of it finding its way onto a spamming list. If you do not have a good e-mail address list, you should think of using a more traditional means of collecting the information such as 'snail mail' or telephone interviews.

However, there are some good e-mail lists. Companies collect e-mail addresses for their customers. Because there is a relationship between supplier and buyer, the e-delivered self-completion questionnaire has a good chance of being filled in. Respondents find it easier to check a box on an e-based questionnaire than deal with the paperwork and post in a traditional self-completion survey.

Also, e-surveys are an ideal method of carrying out staff surveys within companies. Most people in companies have an internal e-mail address, and the quick delivery of an e-questionnaire and the easy means by which it can be completed and returned, makes much more sense than using paper questionnaires.

In theory, it is possible to send a questionnaire, written in Word, as an attachment. In practice, this is failing to use the massive advantages offered by one of the many specialist e-survey software packages that exist. Most of the proprietary software packages used by market research agencies for computer aided interviewing facilitate the conversion of the questionnaire to a Web format. Equally, there are a number of excellent (and not expensive) software packages designed specially for e-surveys (for example Perseus or Sphinx).[1] These packages allow virtually anyone, with no training, to design attractive questionnaires for e-surveys. The respondent scrolls through the questionnaire, answering questions by marking the closed questions with 'radio' buttons and typing in numbers or text answers where appropriate (see Figure 12.1 for a sample page). There are options to remain anonymous (important in employee surveys) and a 'submit' button at the end of the process which delivers the completed questionnaire back to the researcher and into a 'pot' for analysis. From here the pooled data can either be analysed using the software resident within the package (most allow quite comprehensive analysis facilities) or exported into Excel or SPSS for statistical analysis.

A lone researcher, working from a PC equipped with the e-survey software, can have a questionnaire designed, sent out, returned and analysed in a couple of weeks at no cost other than that of his or her time.

Customer Satisfaction Survey

Please answer ALL questions in each section

Section 1 - Product

How important to you are the following issues relating to product and how satisfied are you currently?

Rate the issues on the IMPORTANCE scale where 7 is very important and 1 is not at all important.
Rate the issues on the SATISFACTION scale where 7 is very satisfied and 1 is very unsatisfactory.

	n/a		IMPORTANCE							SATISFACTION				
		1	2	3	4	5	6	7	1	2	3	4	5	6	7
a) The level of value CAP data provides to your business	☐	○	○	○	○	○	○	○	○	○	○	○	○	○	○
b) The benefit CAP data provides to your business	☐	○	○	○	○	○	○	○	○	○	○	○	○	○	○
c) The solution provided compared to competitor offerings	☐	○	○	○	○	○	○	○	○	○	○	○	○	○	○
d) The value for money provided	☐	○	○	○	○	○	○	○	○	○	○	○	○	○	○
e) Ease of use of the data	☐	○	○	○	○	○	○	○	○	○	○	○	○	○	○
f) Fit for purposes/appropriateness in meeting business objectives	☐	○	○	○	○	○	○	○	○	○	○	○	○	○	○
g) Quality of CAP data	☐	○	○	○	○	○	○	○	○	○	○	○	○	○	○
h) Accuracy/reliability of CAP data	☐	○	○	○	○	○	○	○	○	○	○	○	○	○	○
i) The CAP product range	☐	○	○	○	○	○	○	○	○	○	○	○	○	○	○
j) CAP's capability in providing innovative solutions tailored for your industry	☐	○	○	○	○	○	○	○	○	○	○	○	○	○	○

Figure 12.1 *Example of a Web-based questionnaire*

CONJOINT ONLINE

Trade-off interviewing such as conjoint, is expensive. It requires face-to-face interviews with at least 100 people and preferably 200 or more. Interviewers need to be equipped with laptop computers to present the randomized concepts that respondents are asked to sort by selecting, rejecting and ranking. In business-to-business market research the high cost of face-to-face interviewing has limited conjoint analysis to groups of respondents that are in dense geographical clusters – such as truck operators – or where there is a very high cost of failure to a pricing problem.

The Internet now offers a solution to the problem. It is not difficult to present randomized concepts, online, that people can look through and indicate their preference. Respondents can self-complete these interviews in exactly the same way as they would any other e-based survey (see Figure 12.2 for an example of a page taken from a conjoint survey on cars – see a demo on www.surveysite.com). The widespread penetration of the Internet in businesses and the use of broadband width are rapidly making conjoint online a feasible option to B2B researchers.

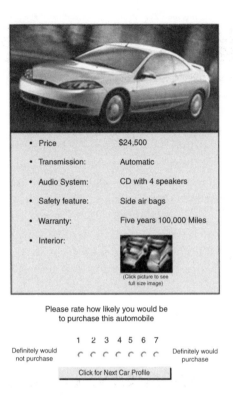

Figure 12.2 *Example of a conjoint online survey (courtesy of www.surveysite.com)*

E-FOCUS GROUPS

Carrying out conventional focus groups is difficult with scattered and niche audiences. Sometimes these hard to get at populations come together for conventions or they attend exhibitions, and this can provide the right circumstances to convene a group. However, the timing of the exhibitions and the conventions is seldom synchronous with the research timetable, and so for the most part we are precluded from using focus groups. Now imagine a chat room on a Web site where a moderator brings together this scattered audience. The net meeting technology allows discussions to be held by telephone, on the Internet, so the cost of the calls is minimal. There are blackboard facilities for those who want to jot down their comments, either because their language is not up to the spoken word or because the moderator wants to put the issues on to a sort of 'flipchart' for discussion.

Respondents need incentives to attend the e-focus group, and there are fees required by the moderator. However there are no viewing centre costs and no travel costs. The costs of this type of research are substantially less than if the focus group was at a venue.

At the present time this technology is more suited to participants who are in business and have the tools and support to plug into such a meeting, but it will not be long before it is being used in consumer markets. Focus group moderators will have to work on new skills.

They will need to be able to manage the technology and set rules and conventions for controlling the discussion from their remote position. They will also have to learn how to draw out the insights without being able to see body language. E-focus groups will not take over from conventional focus groups but they will find their place.

USING THE NET TO POSE QUESTIONS

In a recent survey we carried out into the future for biomass energy (think wood-burning power stations) a trawl was carried out of the subject on the Internet. This is a well-documented story with many interested parties who want to push biomass energy because it is a sustainable energy source. Contacts were identified from the Internet in organizations around the world and 'conversations' were carried out by e-mail. People proved eager and willing to join in the e-conversation, and many went to a great deal of time and trouble to provide supportive information. This is not interviewing in the conventional sense, but it is a useful new tool to researchers providing quick and low-cost access to experts worldwide.

In a similar vein, there are Web sites that host bulletin boards where a question can be posed and someone will pick it up and provide an answer or a lead. Take a look at www.freepint.com which is a kind of market researcher's bar on the Internet. You can drop by and talk to people in the bar or leave a message to see if anyone can help. A surprisingly large variety of technical subjects are answered, and some of the past questions and answers make interesting reading. User groups specific to an industry or a subject can be employed in a similar way to pose questions and seek leads.

SUMMARY

The Internet has opened up a new range of research tools to market researchers. As a library of easily accessible information it has changed the life of desk researchers. It has also provided links through e-mail addresses that can be used for e-based questionnaires. These remove many of the organizational problems of paper-based questionnaires, and there are opportunities to use specialist techniques such as trade-off interviewing.

The Internet is also allowing researchers in business to host focus groups in which respondents can either talk to each other through a net-phone arrangement or write their answers on a blackboard.

Finally, the Internet can be used to locate experts and in the right circumstances, e-mail conversations can provide a powerful qualitative research tool.

13 Data analysis

Towards the end of a market research project, the fieldwork is completed and the data must be analysed. Faced with a pile of data, it is not unusual for a market researcher to be subject to 'paralysis through analysis'.

Most market research surveys of 200 or more interviews are entered into computers and analysed on proprietary software that simplifies cross-analysis. This produces tables showing the numbers and percentages of people who answered each question for the whole sample, as well as the results for groups of special interest, for example male respondents versus female, different age groups, different income groups and so on. This cross-analysis of questions cannot easily be carried out in Excel spreadsheets. A typical page from a set of cross-analysis tables is shown in Figure 13.1. The table presents results from one question out of many that were asked in a readership survey of a company magazine mailed to customers. The total column shows that of the 176 respondents, most people flick through the magazine and do not read any of the articles. Looking across the 'cross breaks' that analyse the results for certain groups of respondents, there are no obvious differences amongst the industry groups but it seems that small companies and younger respondents are more likely to read the magazine (or ignore it). After a couple of minutes examining the data, it does not look so daunting, as patterns of response show through which enable us to make observations and arrive at findings.

We will return to cross-tabulations later after we have looked at the principles of analysis of closed questions.

Table 13 (continuation)
Q14 Which of the following statements best describes the degree to which you might have looked at it?
Base: All who have received the July edition of The Magazine

		Q56 What is the principal nature of your business								No of employees						Age			
	Total	Manu-factur-ing	Distri-bution	Retail-ing	Serv-ices	Govt	Leisure Industry	Agri-culture	Other	Less than 25	25–50	51–150	151–250	251–750	750+	Less than 35	35–44	45–54	55+
Base	176	76	8	3	27	32	8	2	14	30	23	43	14	25	40	28	49	58	40
I have read over half	9 / 5%	3 / 4%	1 / 13%	0 / 0%	1 / 4%	2 / 6%	0 / 0%	0 / 0%	2 / 14%	3 / 10%	1 / 4%	2 / 5%	0 / 0%	2 / 8%	1 / 3%	3 / 11%	2 / 4%	2 / 3%	2 / 5%
I have read a couple of articles	38 / 22%	17 / 22%	2 / 25%	1 / 33%	5 / 19%	8 / 25%	0 / 0%	0 / 0%	2 / 14%	8 / 27%	5 / 22%	6 / 14%	1 / 7%	5 / 20%	13 / 33%	9 / 32%	12 / 24%	13 / 22%	4 / 10%
I have read one article	15 / 9%	7 / 9%	0 / 0%	0 / 0%	2 / 7%	3 / 9%	1 / 13%	0 / 0%	2 / 14%	3 / 10%	1 / 4%	5 / 12%	0 / 0%	2 / 8%	4 / 10%	2 / 7%	4 / 8%	7 / 12%	2 / 5%
I have flicked through it but not read anything in any detail	62 / 35%	28 / 37%	3 / 38%	1 / 33%	9 / 33%	13 / 41%	2 / 25%	0 / 0%	4 / 29%	8 / 27%	10 / 43%	21 / 49%	7 / 50%	7 / 28%	8 / 20%	8 / 29%	17 / 35%	20 / 34%	16 / 40%
I haven't read it yet but I may get around to reading it	35 / 20%	14 / 18%	1 / 13%	0 / 0%	6 / 22%	3 / 9%	4 / 50%	2 / 100%	4 / 29%	2 / 7%	5 / 22%	5 / 12%	5 / 36%	7 / 28%	11 / 28%	2 / 7%	10 / 20%	12 / 21%	11 / 28%
I have not read it and don't intend to do so	15 / 9%	6 / 8%	1 / 13%	1 / 33%	3 / 11%	3 / 9%	1 / 13%	0 / 0%	0 / 0%	6 / 20%	1 / 4%	4 / 9%	0 / 0%	1 / 4%	3 / 8%	3 / 11%	4 / 8%	3 / 5%	5 / 13%
No response	2 / 1%	1 / 1%	0 / 0%	0 / 0%	1 / 4%	0 / 0%	0 / 0%	0 / 0%	0 / 0%	0 / 0%	0 / 0%	0 / 0%	1 / 7%	1 / 4%	0 / 0%	1 / 4%	0 / 0%	1 / 2%	0 / 0%

Figure 13.1 Cross-tab from house magazine readership study

THE ANALYSIS OF CLOSED QUESTIONS

A closed question is one that requires respondents to choose an answer that is presented to them in the interview. We will begin with a closed question that requires a single choice – only one response can be chosen out of the five options that are in the question.

Q5   How likely are you to buy a new car in the next two years?
  Would you say you are: READ SCALE. ONE RESPONSE ONLY.

  Very likely
  Quite likely
  Neither likely nor unlikely
  Fairly unlikely
  Very unlikely

The number of people interviewed in this survey was 200, and the responses can be presented simply as the number giving each response: very likely = 50, fairly likely = 80 and so on. However, it is better to set out the results in a more formal manner such as in Table 13.1. This gives the responses as percentages rather than numbers but the total number of responses on which the percentages are based – the base or sample size – is also shown. The inclusion of the base in a table is essential in presenting survey data as this indicates the accuracy or robustness of the result. Another point to note about Table 13.1 is that it has a clear title and says which respondents are included; in this case the whole sample – all respondents.

Table 13.1 *Likelihood of buying a new car in the next two years (all respondents)*

Likelihood of buying	%
Very likely	25
Fairly likely	40
Neither likely/unlikely	14
Fairly unlikely	18
Very unlikely	3
Total	**100**
Base	200

Table 13.2 *Likelihood of buying a new car in the next two years (owners of company cars)*

Likelihood of buying	%
Very likely	40
Fairly likely	0
Neither likely/unlikely	25
Fairly unlikely	30
Very unlikely	5
Total	**100**
Base	100

Possibly, however, it may be useful to present data for just part of the sample, for example for those respondents who own their own car as opposed to those who drive a company car. In order to obtain this sub-group we filter out those who drive a company car by using the answers to one of the other questions in the survey (see Table 13.2).

In nearly all quantitative market research, we need to compare the results of different groups of people. Table 13.3 shows a simple cross-analysis that compares the likelihood of purchase between private and company car owners together with the breakdown for the whole sample; the data for all respondents (total), private car owners and company car owners are shown as separate columns. Two points to note are that the figures in the column for company car owners are the same as in

Table 13.3 *Likelihood of buying a new car in the next two years (by company and private car owners)*

Likelihood of buying	Total %	Company Car owners %	Private car owners %
Very likely	25	40	10
Fairly likely	40	0	80
Neither likely/unlikely	15	25	5
Fairly unlikely	18	30	5
Very unlikely	3	5	0
Total	**100**	**100**	**100**
Base	200	100	100

Table 13.2 and that a base – the number of relevant respondents – is shown for each column. The inclusion of a base for each column is very important in order to judge the reliability of making comparisons between subgroups of the sample – in this case the two subgroups of company car owners and private car owners each have bases of 100 and at this sample size the range of sampling error is high (see Chapter 7).

In Table 13.3 the cross-analysis was very simple. It can be far more complex – for example, the likelihood of buying could be cross-analysed by any number of demographic groupings such as age, sex and income group. This sort of analysis is almost standard in most consumer market research. Other interesting cross-analyses could be achieved using any other question included in the questionnaire (for example in the survey we looked at the number of miles driven, and this could have an influence on the likelihood of buying a new car).

The question we have used is a *scalar* question, and a common way of presenting the responses from this type of question is by *mean scores* (average scores) as shown in Table 13.4. Each score (shown for each column) is a weighted average of the numerical values assigned to the pre-coded responses (+2 for 'very likely', +1 for 'fairly likely' and so on) and the numbers of respondents giving each response.[1] The resulting mean score in the example indicates the average likelihood of purchase for the whole sample and for the subsamples of both company car

Table 13.4 *Likelihood of buying a new car in the next two years by private and company car owners*

Likelihood of buying	Total %	Company car owners %	Private car owners %
Very likely (+2)	25	40	10
Fairly likely (+1)	40	0	80
Neither likely/unlikely (0)	14	25	5
Fairly unlikely (−1)	18	30	5
Very unlikely (−2)	3	5	0
Total	**100**	**100**	**100**
Mean score	*+0.66*	*+0.40*	*+0.95*
Standard deviation	1.14	1.39	0.59
Standard error	0.08	0.14	0.06
Base	200	100	100

owners and private car owners; comparisons are easier to make with only one figure per column to look at rather than the whole distribution of responses to the scale. In the table, private owners appear more likely to buy than company car owners – a mean score of +0.95 compared to +0.40.

Mean scores are just a form of averages – a way of describing a distribution with a single measure of *location*. However, in interpreting data it also important to consider its *dispersion* around the average. The standard deviation is the most commonly used such measure, and is an intermediate step to calculating dispersion in the population from which the sample was drawn – that is, standard error which can in turn be used to estimate sampling error or compare two measures (for instance, from different subsamples) for statistical significance. The specialized data analysis computer software calculates the mean scores and other statistics such as the standard deviation and the standard error automatically. Table 13.4 includes both standard deviation and standard error.

Interpreting scalar data just from mean scores does, though, have some dangers and the (contrived) example in Table 13.4 illustrates this. Comparison of the mean scores of company car owners and private car owners suggests that it is private car owners who are most likely to buy a new car. However, if we look at the distribution of responses we see that among company car owners, 40 per cent are very likely to buy compared with only 10 per cent of private car owners, and the higher mean score amongst private car owners is because, compared with company car owners, far fewer gave a fairly/very unlikely response. Which of these two ways of interpreting the data will give a better indication of future purchase intentions? Whatever the answer, it is clear that interpretation based on mean scores alone has limitations, and at the most should be regarded as no more than a useful way of summarizing data.

Drawing inferences from a sample to a population requires that the sample is representative – in other words it mirrors the population in its characteristics. However, often the sample of interviews we achieve is not representative, and it may over or under-represent population groups. Sometimes this may be by design so that adequate numbers of respondents of each important group are included (to allow for statistically meaningful comparisons). Table 13.5 shows the responses from another survey, this time asking if people own a particular type of domestic appliance – to which they answered either 'yes' or 'no'. These results were then cross-analysed by household tenure (owner-occupiers and tenants).

It will be seen that in the sample, owner-occupiers and tenants each

Table 13.5 *Ownership of an appliance by home tenure: weighted totals (all respondents)*

Own appliance	Total Unweighted	Weighted	Owner occupiers %	Tenants %
Yes	43	51	60	25
No	57	49	40	75
Total	**100**	**100**	**100**	**100**
Base	200	200	100	100
Sample (% across)		100	50	50
Population (% across)		100	75	25
Weighting factor			1.50	0.50

accounted for 50 per cent of the sample. However, among the population sampled it is known (from other sources) that in fact only 25 per cent are tenants and this group is, therefore, over-represented in the sample (and owner-occupiers under-represented). This was by design to provide an adequate number of both – 100 in each group – because a representative sample of 200 would have yielded only 50 tenants and this is too small a number for analysis. Because of the make-up of the sample, the total ('unweighted') column will not, therefore, be a reliable indication of appliance ownership among the whole population. A solution is to calculate a weighted total column. This is the result of multiplying the responses among owner-occupiers by a weighting factor, adding this to the responses from tenants multiplied by another weighting factor , then re-percentaging the combined values to give the weighted column.[2]

In the example, weighting was a simple calculation based on only one variable – household tenure. However, in practice, the sample may differ from the population in a number of important aspects (for instance, age and gender as well as tenure) and several variables may need to be used in weighting to replicate a representative sample. This is a simple task for the market analysis software to perform.

DATA ANALYSIS OF OPEN-ENDED QUESTIONS

Up to this point we have considered the analysis of closed questions. However, questionnaires often include open-ended questions of the type shown below. In principle, each response to such a question is unique. The responses given by just nine respondents are shown below the question.

Q. Why would you not consider buying a new car in the next two years?
DO NOT PROMPT. RECORD VERBATIM.

Respondent number	Response
1	My existing car is very reliable
2	I cannot to afford to buy one.
3	They depreciate too quickly and my own car is running well
4	My life seems uncertain at the moment
5	We own dogs and they wreck a new car
6	With only two of us at home we have no need of one.
7	I think that discounts will increase in the future
8	I may get a car with my job
9	I don't know really.

With only nine responses it is easy to read through them all and make some generalizations (or not). However, with say 100 respondents, each giving their own reasons for not intending to buy, it is much harder or impossible to see any common pattern. What we need to do is to arrange the individual responses into similar groups. This is illustrated below.

Each response group is designated a code which is entered into the computer for purposes of analysis. The process of categorizing individual responses to open-ended questions is called *coding,* and the list of codes is a *code frame.*

As can be seen in the example, an individual respondent (3) may give a response which falls in two groups. Grouping individual responses in this way involves a certain judgement – in the example, three responses

Code	Response group	Respondents included
1	Satisfaction with current car	1, 5, 6, 3
2	Monetary reasons	2, 3, 7
3	Job uncertainty	4
4	Could get company car	8
5	Don't know	9

have been grouped as 'monetary reasons'. However, one mentioned the inability to afford a new car, one mentioned depreciation, one mentioned the prospect of better discounts in the future. It may be more useful to group these in different ways (for example, high price issues, depreciation). There is no absolutely right or wrong approach; it all depends on what the information is to be used for.

It should be clear from this short discussion that producing the most appropriate coding frame requires skill and a holistic understanding of the project. It is a job for the researcher in charge of the project and should not be left to the data preparation team as they may not be aware of all the objectives of the study.

The result of this type of coding can be presented as a table such as Table 13.6. In this case the table shows the responses from 70 respondents (that is, those not intending to buy). Note that the column does not total 100 per cent; this is because of multi-response – some respondents have given reasons for not intending to buy that fall in two or more code categories. Tables showing this type of coded responses to open-ended questions can of course also include cross-analyses.

The coding of open-ended questions in market research is quite a problematical activity. The coding frame itself may be inappropriate and produce a data analysis output which leads to misinterpretation and possibly wrong conclusions. Also, even if the code frame has been well designed, the actual coding process may be poorly done – every response must be related to the frame, the 'correct' grouping selected and the corresponding code assigned. This work is usually carried out by clerical staff (the data preparation team) with little or no understanding of the overall objectives of the research, and even with the right aptitude and effective training, mistakes can be made.

Open-ended questions require coding which, as we have seen, is very labour-intensive (therefore costly) and highly judgemental. This type of problem does not exist with closed questions. The researcher should think very carefully at the questionnaire design stage if open-ended

Table 13.6 *Reasons for not considering buying a new car (those not considering)*

Reason	%
High prices/can't afford	55
Satisfaction with current car	35
High depreciation/high insurance	21
Job uncertainty	15
Don't know	10
Total	*
Base	70

*Multi response and therefore the column does not total 100

questions are really needed and be certain that it is not just negligence in thinking through and testing possible responses to arrive at a good pre-coded question. In most quantitative surveys, it is generally best to keep open-ended questions to an absolute minimum.

ANALYSIS OF NUMERICAL RESPONSES

A final type of simple analysis is of questions which produce responses in the form of numerical values, for example:

Q. How much did you pay for this appliance?
DO NOT PROMPT. RECORD ACTUAL VALUE
US$...

The individual responses can be listed, sorted into order (for instance, by descending values) and then classified into intervals as illustrated in Table 13.7 – analysis software can take the hard work out of this. It will be seen that the intervals are not of equal range, and this is deliberate since most responses fall into the narrow range of US$340 – 345.[3] The question responses could have been recorded by the interviewers under pre-coded intervals but without knowing the likely responses, it is possible that the wrong intervals could have been used – for instance, US$340 – 350 would have accounted for two-thirds of all responses and there would have been no indication of whether most would tend to the top or bottom end of this range.

As well as showing the distribution of numerical values by intervals (as in Table 13.7), various statistics could also be used to describe the responses, including measures of location (descriptive measures such as the mean, median and modal values) or measures of dispersion (showing variability in the range results using measures such as standard deviation). Such measures are often useful when grossing up from the sample to the total population (for example, having calculated the average consumption of a product among the sample, that of the whole population might be estimated by multiplying this average by the known total population).

MULTIVARIATE ANALYSIS

Cross-analysis enables the relationship between two variables or 'dimensions' to be examined – for example, the likelihood of purchasing a new car as in Table 13.3. The relationship between three dimensions can (if with more difficulty) be also examined in a table; we could for example take miles driven each year as the third dimension in Table 13.3 and have for both company car owners and private car owners, sub-columns of three categories of miles driven (say under less than 7,000 miles per annum, 7,000 to 15,000 miles per annum and over 15,000 miles per annum).

However, why stop at only three variables? The investigation of relationships between any numbers of variables may be worthwhile, and

Table 13.7 *Amount paid for appliance (those who have bought an appliance in the last two years)*

Amount paid $	%
Under 300	3
Over 301–340	19
Over 340–345	54
Over 345–350	13
Over 350	7
Don't know/can't remember	4
Total	**100**
Base	58

produce a model (a representation of the reality restricted to selected but critical variables) which offers useful insights into how a market works, and therefore provides guidance to effective marketing. The relationship between more than two or three variables is the outcome of *multivariate analysis*. In part the uptake of these techniques is because the mechanics of carrying out complex statistical operations has been made so much easier through widely available and user-friendlier software such as SPSS.

The statistical concepts and techniques underlying multivariate analysis are beyond the scope of a general introduction such as this book, and we limit ourselves to merely pointing to a couple of important applications, segmentation and preference analysis.

Marketing planning is now very much based on segmentation; the age of mass markets is waning and increasingly strategies are aimed at influencing specific market segments or niches. Segments can be defined as target groups with common characteristics. Traditionally, demographics have been the standard groupings used for segmentation. However, segments can be found by grouping people according to more subjective factors and especially their needs – these being determined by ratings of attitudinal questions in the interview. Using appropriate scalar questions any number of such attitude variables can be obtained, but the question then arises as to how these can be used to group consumers into homogeneous segments, based on common needs, which can be addressed through different marketing tactics. Two multivariate techniques used for such segmentation are *factor analysis* and *cluster analysis*.

Factor analysis focuses on the attitude attributes themselves and reduces them to a smaller number of *component factors;* groupings of attitudes which on the basis of responses appear to be empirically linked.

The focus of cluster analysis, on the other hand, is respondents themselves. As the term suggests, they are clustered into relatively homogeneous groups on the basis of their attitudes to the product. In the drinks market for example, one cluster may prefer drinks which are characterized by attributes that can be described as 'sophisticated' whereas another cluster may share attitudes more related to the intoxication effects of the products. Clusters are usually given contrived names to help the non-specialist (for example, 'vintagers' and 'guzzlers'). (See also Chapter 7).

One of the most testing challenges faced by market researchers is finding out what is really important to people in driving their purchasing decisions. In interviews we ask people what is important to them, but often the quick response we receive is related to one of the obvious and measurable issues such as price, product performance or delivery. Of course these things are important, but we know that people who claim that they are driven by price in choosing a supplier or brand often stay loyal to that brand for years, despite the fact there are many cheaper products around. Something else must be influencing them that they are not articulating. An alternative to simply asking for 'stated' importance is to link preferences for whole products (which can be purely artificial constructs of attribute bundles) or brands, to how these are described by respondents (in terms of attributes). The importance of the attributes is then derived from the two sets of data at the analysis stage.[4] A widely used multivariate technique to achieve this is conjoint analysis, which calculates 'utility values' for attributes. Trade-off analysis is a variant of this, based on respondents giving preferences for pairs of attributes. A major benefit of conjoint analysis is that it allows the researcher to carry out simulations and forecast the likely effect of changing attributes and, therefore, components of a product mix. This can include the effect of pricing changes; conjoint analysis is often used in pricing studies (see also Chapter 8).

Multivariate analysis is also used in statistical forecasting, with the relationship between a dependent variable (what is to be forecast; for example, market size, brand shares) linked to a number of other variables and possibly with time-lags considered (the effect of changes taking some time to work through to the dependent variable). Often such forecasting is carried out with data other than produced in primary research (for instance, using published macroeconomic variables), although it can be a useful technique in the analysis of continuous research programmes.

All multivariate analysis and for that matter all market research analysis seeks to represent key characteristics of markets and how they relate to each other. In other words data analysis is a form of statistical model building that helps us to understand how markets work, and can often be used to make predictions of the effects of taking certain marketing actions by asking 'what if' questions. But the output needs interpreting, particularly for the benefit of decision makers for whom the techniques may be a mystery. In turn this requires a real understanding of what is being done to the data and what the output actually means. Multivariate analysis, therefore, requires more than just acquaintance with the terminology. Statistical experts cannot always be relied on to interpret the output of the analysis in a useful and practical way. Finally, it should be borne in mind that the most sophisticated analysis is not necessarily the best. Often simple cross-analysis produces adequate results and ones that decision makers can feel confident to use.

QUALITATIVE DATA ANALYSIS

In qualitative research the samples are smaller than in quantitative surveys and the data is more subtle and complex. It is likely for example that the questions will be mainly open-ended and the interviewer will have prompted for full responses. Also the interview or discussion may be unstructured, with the sequence and even the range of topics varying between different respondents.

Some of the types of data analysis already discussed for quantitative research may also have a place in qualitative research. However, coding open-ended responses is seldom appropriate since too much detail is lost in this way, and it is more usual to list and compare full responses. If the number of responses are few enough it may be sufficient just to read through the relevant parts of the questionnaires or other records. It is also often useful to enter the verbatim responses into an Excel spreadsheet, together with a code or identifier that enables them to be sorted by different types of respondent. Often in the report produced of the research it will be appropriate to illustrate with verbatim quotations from individual respondents, and sorting in this way will make this easier. There are a few software packages around that aim to help in the process of sorting and analysing qualitative data by means of counting the frequency of mention of different words or word strings. However, the infinitely wide range of words and combinations of words that can be used to answer a question limits these.

Where interviews or group discussions have been tape-recorded – and this is common practice in qualitative research – it is generally considered good practice to transcribe them into typed-up text and carry out analysis with this material. It will be obvious that while tape recording interviews is a highly efficient means of capturing what is said at the interview, it imposes much additional work afterwards, and this is one reason why qualitative research is expensive.

175

Qualitative researchers still have to rely on immersing themselves in the scripts by thoroughly reading the transcripts and making notes on the salient points. This indicates the difficulty of carrying out qualitative research with more than (say) 30 interviews. At or beyond this number, the surfeit of interviews begins to blur in the researcher's mind and there is a tendency to selectively recall the latest or most impressive interviews that were carried out.

The analysis of qualitative research depends on the flair and particularly the interpretation placed on the data by the practitioners involved. No two qualitative researchers are likely to produce identical outputs from their focus groups or depth interviews. Nor will they analyse and interpret the data in the same way. This is one area of research where the researcher who has carried out the fieldwork should be deeply involved in the analysis, interpretation and presentation, for otherwise much will be lost.

SUMMARY

The final output of fieldwork is data. In quantitative studies, the data preparation team code and enter the data into computers, and proprietary software enables one question to be analysed by another. This cross-analysis is central to the researcher's task of determining different patterns of response among different groups of people.

The analysis of open-ended questions requires skill, and is costly as all the responses must be slotted into a specially designed coding frame.

Increasing use is being made of statistical and modelling techniques that provide greater insights into the data. Multivariate analysis is used to demonstrate relationships between data, and is used to identify segments and to show how people determine the importance of different issues when they are choosing products or services.

The analysis of qualitative data is in the main handled by the researcher who carried out the focus groups or depth interviews. Using the tapes from the interviews and the transcripts from the groups, the qualitative researcher draws out the findings and develops conclusions with few, if any, analysis tools.

14 Reporting

Market research reporting has changed over the years. The traditional 10,000 to 15,000 words written report is fast disappearing as many clients opt for content-heavy PowerPoint presentations. Market researchers therefore write fewer and fewer reports and prepare more and more presentations.

Writing reports is no longer the arduous task it used to be; word processing has changed the face of document preparation. Amendments, changes in structure, editing and grammar checking are all now ongoing tasks for the report writer. Similarly with presentations, PowerPoint has given the presenter the flexibility to prepare slides and subsequently hide some of the more detailed data-laden slides which are not required for the actual presentation. This feature gives clients the flexibility to use the prepared slides at a later date for any presentations they may be required to make within their own workplace.

Not only do the findings (in whatever form they are presented) leave documentary evidence of the study, they also leave a lasting impression of the project and the company responsible for conducting the study. Few clients will delve further into the data, therefore the direction and actions taken by the client will usually arise out of the evidence presented.

COMMON RULES FOR BOTH WRITTEN REPORTS AND PRESENTATIONS

- Know your audience.
- Get the structure right.

- Pay attention to detail with painstaking checking and editing.
- Make it look good.

Know your audience

Reports are written for people to read, digest, and develop action plans for the future. Targeting the audience for the research has its difficulties. Audiences are often varied and their needs can differ greatly. Typical audiences for research reports consist of the market research managers and other managers from areas such as business development, marketing and sales. Almost certainly there will be interested parties at director level. A researcher needs to balance the needs of these groups within the report.

Market research managers want the report to answer the research brief and give recommendations for action, but they also want considerable detail on the research findings (that is, the presentation of the data, sample breakdown, clearly labelled charts and so on). Other managers are more concerned with clarity and structure. They want reports that they can quickly and easily assimilate, and they place more emphasis on the outcomes of the findings – what action will be taken. These diverse interests make it especially important that there is close communication with the client to find out at what level to pitch the findings. It is usually at the most senior level!

Most failings in reporting are caused by the absence of structure, fuzzy findings and a lack of attention to detail. Audiences are distracted from paying attention to the valuable content by inadequate signposting, bad grammar, a poor writing style and mistakes in punctuation and spelling.

Get the structure right

The key to good market research reporting is structure. Structure is apparent throughout the research process: structure in the formation of the research aims and objectives, structure in the research design and structure in the data collection process. It is this structure that makes the market research study a systematic enquiry and not simply anecdotal feedback. Without structure, the mass of data can be overwhelming and serve to confuse rather than assist business decision making.

The report cannot be prepared without working out the structure first. Sometimes the structure of the report or presentation is clear from the outset, although in most cases the structure is worked out as the data is analysed and the storyline unfolds. This can be an intimidating time for the researcher, but once the structure has been established, either in the form of chapters in a written report or in the sections of a presentation, the task is much easier.

There are two starting points for getting a structure in a report. The first is the proposal that lays out which subjects should be covered and the second is the questionnaire. The data analysis arising from the desk research, the qualitative research, and the quantitative research is an obvious place to start. Tables and charts are assembled for each part of the study, and if they are in PowerPoint they can easily be regrouped to form partitions that fit with the outcomes. In this way, we start with a procedural approach and move on to a more analytical approach.

The main headings and the subheadings will come out of the knowledge that has been built up on the subject. The researcher will then be in a position to start writing text for either the slides or the narrative report. However, the structure should not be considered as set in stone, and it is important that the researcher keeps an open mind. 'Cut and paste' makes changing the structure very easy. The very act of writing or running through a presentation serves to focus the mind, and better structures may become apparent.

A report structure must have a beginning, middle and an end. The beginning consists of the introduction to the market and background to

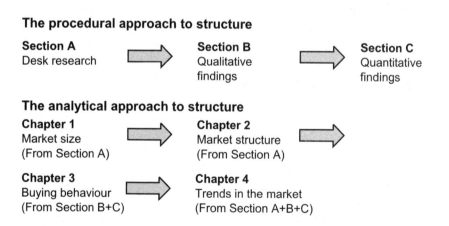

The procedural approach to structure

Section A
Desk research

Section B
Qualitative findings

Section C
Quantitative findings

The analytical approach to structure

Chapter 1
Market size
(From Section A)

Chapter 2
Market structure
(From Section A)

Chapter 3
Buying behaviour
(From Section B+C)

Chapter 4
Trends in the market
(From Section A+B+C)

Figure 14.1 *Arriving at a report structure by procedure and analysis*

the study, the middle is usually the bulk of the report – the detail of the findings – and the end brings the data together to form conclusions and recommendations. The typical 'procedural' structure of a report or a presentation for a customer satisfaction study follows roughly the line of questioning in the questionnaire: that is, an introduction, how suppliers are chosen, which suppliers are used, how the supplier is rated for satisfaction and importance on various issues such as product, price, availability and delivery, customer service and support, followed by the conclusion and recommendations. There is nothing inherently wrong with this structure, but it may be better to regroup the data into a story about loyalty and how it can be improved. For example:

Chapter 1. Introduction
Chapter 2. Executive summary
Chapter 3. The problem of customer churn

- The effects of high customer turnover for our company
- Levels of customer churn in our industry
- Trends in customer churn

Chapter 4. Factors building loyalty amongst customers

- The 'must haves': hygiene factors driving loyalty in the industry
- Differentiating factors driving loyalty in the industry
- Summary of factors driving loyalty in the industry

Chapter 5. Our performance in driving loyalty

- Levels of satisfaction amongst our customers
- Ratings of loyalty drivers amongst other key competitors

Chapter 6. Conclusions

- Factors driving loyalty in our business
- Differences between key suppliers
- Strengths and weaknesses of our company

Chapter 7. Recommendations

- Opportunities and threats for current and new business
- Areas where satisfaction can be improved to lead to greater loyalty

This is a structure built around the problem and the actions required. It focuses on the interpretation of the data and the translation to loyalty.

The changed structure of the report addresses the rationale for commissioning the research in the first place. It hits at the heart of what it means for the business and therefore will have more impact in driving actions, rather than gathering dust on the marketing manager's shelf.

Writing, checking and editing

A writing style for narrative reports and presentations needs to be developed which communicates the data quickly and clearly. The report must have impact so that a busy reader can quickly 'gut it' for content.

A few rules can be observed in relation to style and layout of a report:

- Make frequent use of headings to partition the subjects of the report.
- Use bullets and short paragraphs to quickly communicate ideas.
- Avoid the heavy use of text and use graphics and diagrams wherever possible.
- Clearly label all diagrams with headings (as well as sources of data).
- Avoid complicated words, jargon and slang.
- Avoid long ambiguous sentences making too many points.

After the report has been completed, the author checks the report for structure, readability and content. It may be that an alternative structure works better for the report, and this can be played around with to enhance the flow.

Second, the detail of the data has to be checked carefully for accuracy. Is the data correct? Does the data make sense? Does it need to be included? This stage requires a ruthless hand, and any superfluous data that does not support the conclusions and recommendations can be edited out. Remember the requirements of a report; clearly stated and easy to read.

The third check is for spelling, grammar, labelling of charts, indexing and readability. This is best carried out initially by the writer and then again by someone other than the writer. Corrections are made and the report is ready for printing and binding.

The same rules apply for presentations, although there will be less text. The structure, data consistency, spelling and grammar require the same checks as the written report. Where the client has opted for a presentation rather than a written report, the presentation will tend to be very content-heavy. In these cases, the researcher needs to check that the presentation, when used as a stand-alone document, tells the complete story even though there is no long narrative. It has to be prepared as if for someone who will pick it up in a year's time, knowing little about the subject will be able quickly to absorb the findings from the slide deck.

Make it look good

The report or presentation document is what the researcher leaves behind. This will be a lasting impression by which the research will be judged. In addition to the editing that we have discussed in the previous section, the report must be 'window dressed' to look good. In the main this means finding a house style and being consistent in applying it.

Some hints when window dressing the report

- Keep it simple (fussy borders and colourful templates detract).
- Do not use colourful backgrounds (they will not print clearly on black and white lasers and copiers).
- Have a title page that shows what the report is about, when it was presented, who wrote it, and contact details.
- Use page numbers.
- Label all slides and charts.
- Be consistent in all aspects of the layout – margins, fonts, heading styles, table labelling.
- Do not try to cram too much on to one page.
- If in doubt, leave it out.
- Learn from the designers – make effective use of white space.
- Use a report cover and binding that will stand the test of time.

REPORTING QUALITATIVE DATA

Qualitative reports need to tell a story, identify a process and make sense of perceptions and experiences. To achieve this, the researcher has to reconstruct the data through the analysis to locate the findings in a clear framework.

Most qualitative studies start with a very loose framework which has been developed at the proposal stage. At the time of reporting, this framework will have to be tightened. Qualitative data can be presented through analytical and flow diagrams which communicate complex issues (such as how buying decisions are made or how a process works), or they can be located in the well-known established marketing frameworks such as the four Ps, Ansoff's matrix and so on. Verbatim comments can add emphasis to a point as they are the words of the market place, not the researcher.

Quotes that are used should be carefully selected to typify the viewpoint under discussion, though this does not necessarily mean they are representative of the general view. The report may need to highlight the unique and peculiar as well as the general perspective. However, quotes should not directly identify any individual respondent and should respect the rights of individuals to anonymity.

Summary points when presenting qualitative data

- Data should be located in a clear framework.
- Frameworks can be presented diagrammatically as well as in text.
- Direct quotes, when used, should be indicative of a research finding and located close to that discussion in a presentation or report.
- Quotes should be grammatically 'doctored' to make sense.
- They should respect the confidentiality of the respondent.

Figure 14.2 *Using verbatim comments to communicate a point*

REPORTING QUANTITATIVE DATA

Quantitative data, on the other hand, is numerical in nature. For most types of data, there are several options available:

- charts;
- graphs;
- tables;
- diagrams;
- frameworks;
- text.

Using charts

The pie chart

These are used where the component parts of the whole need to be shown, that is, the data must add up to 100 per cent (see Figure 14.3). They are most frequently used to present:

- *Classification data:* where the detail of a sample is presented.
- *Market size data:* the share of the market, sales within a sector of the market.
- *Brand shares.*

Pie charts will convert actual values to percentages, therefore where there are a number of unknowns or 'not stated' responses causing the data not to total 100 per cent, they should be used with caution.

The spider chart

The spider chart is used to present numerical data. In the example shown in Figure 14.4 we see satisfaction levels with a supplier on six attributes across three different countries. It allows the presentation of complex, comparative data so that differences quickly become apparent.

The bar chart

Bar charts are a commonly used method of displaying data in quantitative studies. There are several different types of bar charts to choose from, depending on the type of data to be presented. They can be horizontal, vertical or divided. Horizontal charts are most commonly used with rated data. They have a huge visual impact and therefore

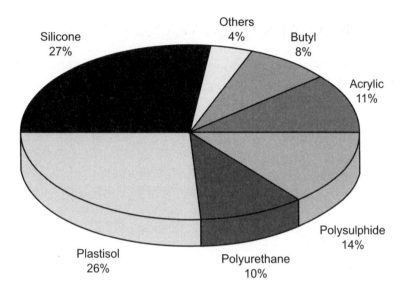

Figure 14.3 *Pie chart showing the European flexible sealant market*

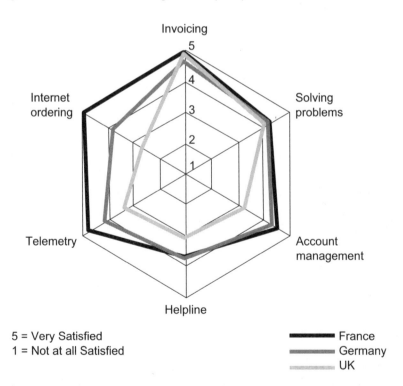

Figure 14.4 *Spider chart showing satisfaction with a supplier*

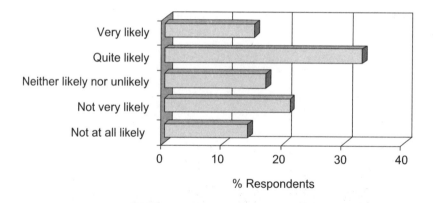

Figure 14.5 *Horizontal bar chart showing likelihood of purchase*

the order of the chart is important. The data is organized to display the charts in ascending or descending order. The only exception to this is the chart where it is the scale that is the important variable (as in the example of likelihood to buy, see Figure 14.5).

The horizontal bar chart is commonly used to present customer satisfaction and quantitative concept testing data. The key requirement is to display clearly the rated scale, either by mean scores or the percentage rating at a particular level.

It is also possible to compare the ratings of several groups of respondents on the one chart: for example, when looking at the attractiveness of a new concept, the reactions of men and women can be plotted against each other for comparison. A cautionary note, though: charts tend to look messy and cluttered if too many bars are plotted side by side, and this loses the power of the chart and makes it difficult to see what is going on.

The vertical chart is most commonly used where a measure of size or volume is needed for example in market sizing. Charts can be split to display the component parts or divisions and trends within a group, for example, sales trends over time (see Figure 14.6).

Using graphs

Graphs are used to present trends in figures over a given period. They perform the same function as bar charts, though they are often used where the prediction of a trend is required, for example, sales trends, population trends, economic trends. From line graphs, predictions can be made based on the trend.

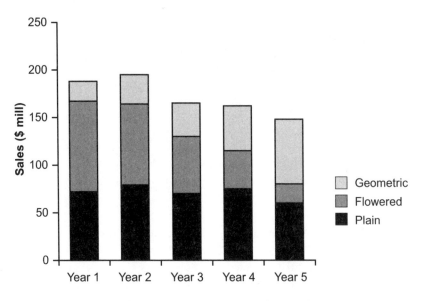

Figure 14.6 *Vertical bar chart showing sales of carpet designs*

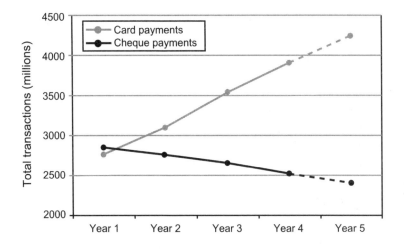

Figure 14.7 *Line graph showing trends in card and cheque payments*

Using tables

Tables are usually used in quantitative studies where there is a large amount of statistical data to be presented. This can be descriptive or inferential data. Tables quickly communicate large amounts of data, displaying any patterns within the data. However, there are some rules about how tables should be constructed to maximize their effectiveness:

- ▪ *Simplicity:* tables should be kept simple. This may mean using several tables rather than one complex table. All too frequently, even in the media, tables are overly complex leaving the responsibility of interpretation to the reader. The meaning of the table should, by and large, be immediately obvious.
- ▪ *Labelling:* tables should have clear headings identifying what the table is about. Columns should state their content along with the unit of measurement, that is, numbers, percentages, weight units, monetary value and so on. If appropriate, the question itself should be displayed and the sample sizes that the results are derived from. Short titles are better than long ones.
- ▪ *Displaying the totals:* tables should add up (or at least explain why they do not). The summary columns and rows are the ones to which we look for reference and which give meaning to the data.
- ▪ *Rounding the figures:* tables look better where the numbers are rounded. They make it easier for the reader to relate one figure to another. Of course, there are instances where numbers should not be rounded and decimal places are important (for example, a table of currency conversion rates).
- ▪ *Ordering rows and columns:* randomly distributed rows require the reader to work harder to interpret the table. Tables where the rows are organized in increasing or decreasing size should therefore always be used. For example, the most important attribute or the attribute with the highest satisfaction score should be at the top of the table. This serves to draw the reader's eye to the order as well as the data. Where several columns of data are used, the order should be made by the first data column. As with charts, the only digression from this rule comes with ordinal scales such as 'very likely', 'quite likely', 'not very likely', and 'not at all likely'. The sequence of these scales always remains the same whatever the result.
- ▪ *Format of the table:* several techniques can be used to present tables in a manner that easily separates the rows and/or columns, and cur-

rent word processing and report writing packaging have made this much simpler for the writer. The main method of making the data easily readable in tables involves the use of lines, text and colour. Most software packages have a range of automatically formatted tables available which incorporate the use of all these elements.

Using flow diagrams

Flow diagrams are a simple and effective means of presenting organizational data. This data can relate to anything from how the market is structured to how an organization operates, to how an individual makes decisions. The key issue for the development of a flow chart is the structure of a process. These charts need to have an input and a follow through. They are most commonly used to present supply chain data.

Diagrams should be labelled clearly and the stages and relationships should be easy to follow, however complex the structure of the data that is presented. Rather like a maze, the reader should be able to start at one point and follow it through to the end, no matter how many diversions and alternative routes there may be. Figure 14.9 (see next page) displays the complex route to market from shower manufacturers to end-user. This single chart has a far greater impact in describing this market than any number of words and paragraphs.

DRAWING CONCLUSIONS

The conclusions and recommendations section of a report is, arguably, the most important. Market research is commissioned to make changes, to re-evaluate the way things are done and make informed decisions about the future, and the report has to leave the client feeling they have data which gives a clear way forward.

It is helpful to use frameworks in the conclusions. These locate the problem in a context and bring the detail back into a bigger picture. There are a number of business and marketing frameworks which can be used to do this in market research. These frameworks offer a theory for showing how things work and are well documented in the literature. There are three broad classifications into which these frameworks fall, regardless of the methodologies adopted in the research design. Table 14.1 displays the classifications for drawing conclusions and making recommendations and the frameworks that fall into them.

	Impact on satisfaction	Average satisfaction with supplier*
Delivery of product	36%	4.1
Price	28%	4.2
Product	15%	4.6
Customer support	14%	3.8
Technical service and maintenance	7%	4.2
TOTAL	**100%**	**4.3**

* 1 is not at all satisfied and 5 is extremely satisfied

Figure 14.8 *Table to show satisfaction with a supplier*

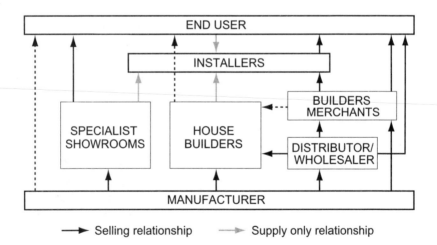

Figure 14.9 *Flow diagram showing route to market for shower manufacturers*

MAKING A PRESENTATION

Presentation of a market research study will normally last up to two hours. A presentation is almost always delivered using PowerPoint slides, which may be supported by other materials such as video and audio clips. Audiences of up to 10 are the norm, with those who have a key interest in the study in attendance, while others may be sitting on the sidelines. As with reports, knowledge of the roles and responsibilities of those attending the presentation beforehand can help the researcher tailor the presentation to the different needs of the audience.

What makes a good presentation is a good presenter. However, in market research, the slides play a more important role than in other presentations as they are the source of the data.

The presentation itself creates the opportunity to make a good impression, and the polishing of the researcher's skills in this area is essential. Skills of presenters are individual and dependent, to a large extent, on the personality of the presenter. However, there are some rules which can be observed to smooth the process.

Before a presentation, preparation is the key. The last thing people want to see at a presentation is a presenter reading aloud from the

Table 14.1 *Three classifications of frameworks for drawing conclusions and making recommendations*

Section of conclusions	Purpose of the section	Examples of frameworks
Situation analysis	To summarize the key issues and bring them together	Life cycle, Ansoff grid, SWOT, decision making models
Marketing and business goals	To show what can be achieved	Porter's generic strategies, adoption models for new products, hierarchical communication models (eg AIDA)
Recommendations	To show what action is required	Four Ps, XY grids, flow models process

slides – they can do that themselves. They want to hear what is behind the slides. They want to hear the presenter talk around the slides, expand on the bullet points, pull out the important data, draw their attention to the important words in a verbatim quote and to make links with previous slides (or even future slides, if appropriate). This makes a lively presentation and leaves the audience with a feeling of added value.

The presenter can take steps to ensure they will be able to do this. First, it is important to be immersed in the data; to know it inside out. Second, the researcher should know every chart and what is going to be said when that chart comes up. Finally the presentation must be rehearsed, even if this is to oneself in front of the computer. For the novice presenter, it is even better if this rehearsal is done out loud and, if possible, in front of a tame audience.

Preparation pointers for a good performance

1. Know the data inside out.
2. Know the presentation structure inside out.
3. Memorize the slides and the background to the points being made on the slides.
4. Practise the presentation and what you will say on the day.

On the day, different skills kick in. These are about the performance. It is perfectly normal to feel a bit anxious before a presentation. The presenter rarely knows everyone in the audience and it is usual to commence with a round of introductions. In the first five minutes presenters will need to control their nerves as well as memorizing the names and responsibilities of all attendees – a tricky task for the novice.

Controlling the nerves is one of the most important tasks. The nervous presenter does not inspire confidence, and the audience needs to be put at ease about what to expect. Your heart might be beating faster than it normally does, your breathing may be fast and shallow and your hands sweaty. The voice moves into tremolo. You fidget and adopt mannerisms that everyone else can notice except you. You repeat words and phrases again and again. Your focus is on yourself and you lose concentration on the presentation. There are some techniques that can be used to control this, and it is worth looking into them if you suffer from nerves. Confidence can also be built by taking a course on presentation skills. However, more than anything, practice at presentations makes perfect. The more you do, the better you become.

The pace of the presentation in relation to the timing must be borne in mind throughout. It is very easy to become submerged in questions pertaining to the minute details of the data slides and then skip over the all-important conclusions and recommendations. It is the responsibility of the presenter, not that of the audience, to keep an eye on the timing.

Performance on the day

1. Dress for the occasion.
2. Control your nerves in a way that works for you. Settle yourself and the audience. Write down their names.
3. Prepare your introduction and set the scene on timing and content.
4. Control any unwanted body movements and habits such as swaying, pacing, jangling keys.
5. Do not use closed-up body language such as crossed arms or hand over the mouth.
6. Sweep the room constantly to make eye contact with everyone in the audience.
7. Be aware of any phrases or words you are using repeatedly.
8. Speak clearly and use intonation in your voice.
9. Smile and use encouraging gestures to the audience, especially if you want their participation.
10. Use people's names (but make sure they are correct!).
11. Address audience members' concerns and questions honestly.
12. Pace yourself and the presentation – keep your eye on the clock. Leave enough time for the conclusions and recommendations.
13. Before you start, work out some appropriate words for concluding the presentation.

SUMMARY

Reporting market research findings provides an opportunity to make a strong impact on an audience. Clients are increasingly opting for reports that are based on presentation slides rather than a separate narrative report. These presentation style reports must communicate the findings clearly and lead to firm conclusions and recommendations.

Clear reporting comes from a logical structure that incorporates the different stages of the research. Time spent on developing a clear structure before the report writing begins will be well rewarded. It is to be expected that the structure and the content will change as the report is checked and edited many times.

Reporting requires a balance of text, tables, charts, diagrams and graphics to communicate the different data.

Most reports are presented orally and this can be nerve-racking to a junior researcher. Audiences attending presentations may have mixed needs, and the researcher should know what these are and bear them in mind.

Good presenters make good presentations and they are supported by good slides. Presentation skills can be honed by diligent preparation and practice.

Appendix: The Market Research Society Code of Conduct

INTRODUCTION

The Market Research Society

With over 8,000 members in more than 50 countries, The Market Research Society (MRS) is the world's largest international membership organisation for professional researchers and others engaged in (or interested in) marketing, social or opinion research.

It has a diverse membership of individual researchers within agencies, independent consultancies, client-side organisations, and the academic community, and from all levels of seniority and job functions.

All members agree to comply with the MRS Code of Conduct, which is supported by the Codeline advisory service and a range of specialist guidelines on best practice.

MRS offers various qualifications and membership grades, as well as training and professional development resources to support these. It is the official awarding body in the UK for vocational qualifications in market research.

MRS is a major supplier of publications and information services, conferences and seminars and many other meeting and networking opportunities for researchers.

MRS is 'the voice of the profession' in its media relations and public affairs activities on behalf of professional research practitioners, and aims to achieve the most favourable climate of opinions and legislative environment for research.

The purpose of the 'Code of Conduct'

This edition of the Code of Conduct was agreed by The Market Research Society to be operative from July 1999. It is a fully revised version of a self-regulatory code which has been in existence since 1954. This Code is based upon and fully compatible with the ICC/ESOMAR International Code of Marketing and Social Research Practice. The Code of Conduct is designed to support all those engaged in marketing or social research in maintaining professional standards. It applies to all members of The Market Research Society, whether they are engaged in consumer, business to business, social, opinion or any other type of confidential survey research. It applies to all quantitative and qualitative methods for data gathering. Assurance that research is conducted in an ethical manner is needed to create confidence in, and to encourage co-operation among, the business community, the general public, regulators and others.

The Code of Conduct does not take precedence over national law. Members responsible for international research shall take its provisions as a minimum requirement and fulfil any other responsibilities set down in law or by nationally agreed standards.

The purpose of guidelines

MRS Guidelines exist or are being developed in many of these areas in order to provide a more comprehensive framework of interpretation. These guidelines have been written in recognition of the increasingly diverse activities of the Society's members, some of which are not covered in detail by the Code of Conduct. A full list of guidelines appears on the Society's website, and is also available from the Society's Standards Manager.

One particular guideline covers the use of databases containing personal details of respondents or potential respondents, both for purposes associated with confidential survey research and in cases where respondent details are passed to a third party for marketing or other purposes. This guideline has been formally accepted by the Society, following extensive consultation with members and with the Data Protection Registrar/Commissioner.

Relationship with data protection legislation

Adherence to the Code of Conduct and the database Guidelines will help to ensure that research is conducted in accordance with the principles of data protection legislation. In the UK this is encompassed by the Data Protection Act 1998.

Data protection definitions

Personal Data means data which relates to a living individual who can be identified

- from the data, or
- from the data and other information in the possession of, or likely to come into the possession of, the data controller

and includes any expression of opinion about the individual and any indication of the intentions of the data controller or any other person in respect of the individual.

Processing means obtaining, recording or holding the information or data or carrying out any operation or set of operations on the information or data, including

- organisation, adaptation or alteration
- retrieval, consultation or use
- disclosure by transmission, dissemination or otherwise making available
- alignment, combination, blocking, erasure or destruction.

It is a requirement of membership that researchers must ensure that their conduct follows the letter and spirit of the principles of Data Protection legislation from the Act. In the UK the eight data protection principles are.

- **The First Principle**
  Personal data shall be processed fairly and lawfully.[1]

- **The Second Principle**

  Personal data shall be obtained only for one or more specified and lawful purposes, and shall not be further processed in any manner incompatible with that purpose or those purposes.

- **The Third Principle**

  Personal data shall be adequate, relevant and not excessive in relation to the purpose or purposes for which they are processed.

- **The Fourth Principle**

  Personal data shall be accurate and, where necessary, kept up to date.

- **The Fifth Principle**

  Personal data processed for any purpose or purposes shall not be kept longer than is necessary for that purpose or those purposes.

- **The Sixth Principle**

  Personal data shall be processed in accordance with the rights of data subjects under this Act.

- **The Seventh Principle**

  Appropriate technical and organisational measures shall be taken against unauthorised or unlawful processing of personal data and against accidental loss or destruction of, or damage to, personal data.

- **The Eighth Principle**

  Personal data shall not be transferred to a country or territory outside the European Economic Area, unless that country or territory ensures an adequate level of protection for the rights and freedoms of data subjects in relation to the processing of personal data.

Exemption for research purposes

Where personal data processed for research, statistical or historical purposes are not processed to support decisions affecting particular individuals, or in such a way as likely to cause substantial damage or distress to any data subject, such processing will not breach the Second Principle and the data may be retained indefinitely despite the Fifth Principle.

As long as the results of the research are not published in a form, which identifies any data subject, there is no right of subject access to the data.

Code definitions

- **Research**

  Research is the collection and analysis of data from a sample of individuals or organisations relating to their characteristics, behaviour, attitudes, opinions or possessions. It includes all forms of marketing and social research such as consumer and industrial surveys, psychological investigations, observational and panel studies.

■ **Respondent**

A respondent is any individual or organisation from whom any information is sought by the researcher for the purpose of a marketing or social research project. The term covers cases where information is to be obtained by verbal interviewing techniques, postal and other self-completion questionnaires, mechanical or electronic equipment, observation and any other method where the identity of the provider of the information may be recorded or otherwise traceable. This includes those approached for research purposes whether or not substantive information is obtained from them and includes those who decline to participate or withdraw at any stage from the research.

■ **Interview**

An interview is any form of contact intended to provide information from a respondent.

■ **Identity**

The identity of a respondent includes, as well as his/her name and/or address, any other information which offers a reasonable chance that he/she can be identified by any of the recipients of the information.

■ **Children**

For the Purpose of the Code, children and young people are defined as those aged under 18. The intention of the provisions regarding age is to protect potentially vulnerable members of society, whatever the source of their vulnerability, and to strengthen the principle of public trust. Consent of a parent or responsible adult should be obtained for interviews with children under 16. Consent must be obtained under the following circumstances:

■ In home/at home (face-to-face and telephone interviewing)
■ Group discussions/depth interviews
■ Where interviewer and child are alone together.

Interviews being conducted in public places, such as in-street/in-store/central locations, with 14 and 15 years olds may take place without consent if a parent or responsible adult is not accompanying the child. In these situations an explanatory thank you note must be given to the child.

Under special circumstances, a survey may waive parental consent but only with the prior approval of the Professional Standards Committee.

- **Records**

  The term records includes anything containing information relating to a research project and covers all data collection and data processing documents, audio and visual recordings. Primary records are the most comprehensive record of information on which a project is based; they include not only the original data records themselves, but also anything needed to evaluate those records, such as quality control documents. Secondary records are any other records about the Respondent.

- **Client**

  Client includes any individual, organisation, department or division, including any belonging to the same organisation as the research agency which is responsible for commissioning a research project.

- **Agency**

  Agency includes any individual, organisation, department or division, including any belonging to the same organisation as the client which is responsible for, or acts as, a supplier on all or part of a research project.

- **Professional Body**

  Professional body refers to The Market Research Society.

- **Public Place**

  A 'public place' is one to which the public has access (where admission has been gained with or without a charge) and where an individual could reasonably expect to be observed and/or overheard by other people, for example in a shop, in the street or in a place of entertainment.

PRINCIPLES

Research is founded upon the willing co-operation of the public and of business organisations. It depends upon their confidence that it is conducted honestly, objectively, without unwelcome intrusion and without harm to respondents. Its purpose is to collect and analyse information, and not directly to create sales nor to influence the opinions of anyone participating in it. It is in this spirit that the Code of Conduct has been devised.

The general public and other interested parties shall be entitled to complete assurance that every research project is carried out strictly in accordance with this Code, and that their rights of privacy are respected. In particular, they must be assured that no information which could be used to identify them will be made available without their agreement to anyone outside the agency responsible for conducting the research. They must also be assured that the information they supply will not be used for any purposes other than research and that they will not be adversely affected or embarrassed as a direct result of their participation in a research project.

Wherever possible respondents must be informed as to the purpose of the research and the likely length of time necessary for the collection of the information. Finally, the research findings themselves must always be reported accurately and never used to mislead anyone, in any way.

RULES

A. Conditions of Membership and Professional Responsibilities

A.1 Membership of the professional body is granted to individuals who are believed, on the basis of the information they have given, to have such qualifications as are specified from time to time by the professional body and who have undertaken to accept this Code of Conduct. Membership may be withdrawn if this information is found to be inaccurate.

General responsibilities

A.2 Members shall at all times act honestly in dealings with respondents, clients (actual or potential), employers, employees, subcontractors and the general public.

A.3 Members shall at all times seek to avoid conflicts of interest with clients or employers and shall make prior voluntary and full disclosure to all parties concerned of all matters that might give rise to such conflict.

A.4 The use of letters after an individual's name to indicate membership of The Market Research Society is permitted in the case of Fellows (FMRS) and Full Members (MMRS). All members may point out, where relevant, that they belong to the appropriate category of the professional body.

A.5 Members shall not imply in any statement that they are speaking on behalf of the professional body unless they have the written authority of Council or of some duly delegated individual or committee.

Working practices

A.6 Members shall ensure that the people (including clients, colleagues and sub-contractors) with whom they work are sufficiently familiar with this Code of Conduct and that working arrangements are such that the Code is unlikely to be breached through ignorance of its provisions.

A.7 Members shall not knowingly take advantage, without permission, of the unpublished work of a fellow member which is the property of that member. Specifically, members shall not carry out or commission work based on proposals prepared by a member in another organisation unless permission has been obtained from that organisation.

A.8 All written or oral assurances made by anyone involved in commissioning of conducting projects must be factually correct and honoured.

Responsibilities to other members

A.9 Members shall not place other members in a position in which they might unwittingly breach any part of this Code of Conduct.

Responsibilities of clients to agencies

A.10 Clients should not normally invite more than four agencies to tender in writing for a project. If they do so, they should disclose how many invitations to tender they are seeking.

A.11 Unless paid for by the client, a specification for a project drawn up by one research agency is the property of that agency and may not be passed on to another agency without the permission of the originating research agency.

Confidential survey research and other activities

(apply B.15 and Notes to B.15)

A.12 Members shall only use the term *confidential survey research* to describe research projects which are based upon respondent anonymity and do not involve the divulgence of identities or personal details of respondents to others except for research purposes.

A.13 If any of the following activities are involved in, or form part of, a project then the project lies outside the scope of confidential survey research and must not be described or presented as such:

(a) enquiries whose objectives include obtaining personal information about private individuals per se, whether for legal, political, supervisory (e.g. job performance), private or other purposes:

(b) the acquisition of information for use by credit-rating or similar purposes;

(c) the compilation, updating or enhancement of lists, registers or databases which are not exclusively for research purpose (e.g. which will be used for direct or relationship marketing);

(d) industrial, commercial or any other form of espionage;

(e) sales or promotional responses to individual respondents;

(f) the collection of debts;

(g) fund raising;

(h) direct or indirect attempts, including the framing of questions, to influence a respondent's opinions or attitudes on any issue other than for experimental purposes which are identified in any report or publication of the results.

A.14 Where any such activities referred to by paragraph A.13 are carried out by a member, the member must clearly differentiate such activities by:

(a) not describing them to anyone as confidential survey research and

(b) making it clear to respondents at the start of any data collection exercise what the purposes of the activity are and that the activity is not confidential survey research.

Scope of code

A.15 When undertaking confidential survey research based on respondent anonymity, members shall abide by the ICC/ESOMAR

International Code of Conduct which constitutes Section B of this Code.

A.16 MRS Guidelines issued, other than those published as consultative drafts, are binding on members where they indicate that actions or procedures *shall* or *must* be adhered to by members. Breaches of these conditions will be treated as breaches of the Code and may be subject to disciplinary action.

A.17 Recommendations within such guidelines that members should behave in certain ways are advisory only.

A.18 It is the responsibility of members to keep themselves updated on changes or amendments to any part of this Code which are published from time to time and announced in publications and on the web pages of the Society. If in doubt about the interpretation of the Code, members may consult the Professional Standards Committee or its Codeline Service set up to deal with Code enquiries.

Disciplinary action

A.19 Complaints regarding breaches of the Code of Conduct by those in membership of the MRS must be made to The Market Research Society.

A.20 Membership may be withdrawn, or other disciplinary action taken, if, on investigation of a complaint, it is found that in the opinion of the professional body, any part of the member's research work or behaviour breaches this Code of Conduct.

A.21 Members must make available the necessary information as and when requested by the Professional Standards Committee and Disciplinary Committee in the course of an enquiry.

A.22 Membership may be withdrawn, or other disciplinary action taken, if a member is deemed guilty of unprofessional conduct. This is defined as a member:

(a) being guilty of any act or conduct which in the opinion of a body appointed by Council might bring discredit on the profession, the professional body or its members;

(b) being guilty of any breach of the Code of Conduct set out in this document;

(c) knowingly being in breach of any other regulations laid down from time to time by the Council of the professional body;

(d) failing without good reason to assist the professional body in the investigation of a complaint;

(e) having a receiving order made against him/her or making any arrangement or composition with his/her creditors;

(f) being found to be in breach of the Data Protection Act by the Data Protection Registrar.

A.23 No member will have his/her membership withdrawn, demoted or suspended under this Code without an opportunity of a hearing before a tribunal, of which s/he will have at least one month's notice.

A.24 Normally, the MRS will publish the names of members who have their membership withdrawn, demoted or are suspended or have other disciplinary action taken with the reasons for the decision.

A.25 If a member subject to a complaint resigns his/her membership of the Society whilst the case is unresolved, then such resignation shall be published and in the event of re-admission to membership the member shall be required to co-operate in the completion of any outstanding disciplinary process.

B. ICC/ESOMAR Code of Marketing and Social Research Practice

General

B.1 Marketing research must always be carried out objectively and in accordance with established scientific principles.

B.2 Marketing research must always conform to the national and international legislation which applies in those countries involved in a given research project.

The rights of respondents

B.3 Respondents' co-operation in a marketing research project is entirely voluntary at all stages. They must not be misled when being asked for co-operation.

B.4 Respondents' anonymity must be strictly preserved. If the respondent on request from the Researcher has given permission for data to be passed on in a form which allows that respondent to identified personally:

(a) the Respondent must first have been told to whom the information would be supplied and the purposes for which it will be used, and also

(b) the Respondent must ensure that the information will not be used for any non-research purpose and that the recipient of the information has agreed to conform to the requirements of the Code.

B.5 The Researcher must take all reasonable precautions to ensure that Respondents are in no way directly harmed or adversely affected as a result of their participation in a marketing research project.

B.6 The Researcher must take special care when interviewing children and young people. The informed consent of the parent or responsible adult must first be obtained for interviews with children.

B.7 Respondents must be told (normally at the beginning of the interview) if observation techniques or recording equipment are used, except where these are used in a public place. If a respondent so wishes, the record or relevant section of it must be destroyed or deleted. Respondents' anonymity must not be infringed by the use of such methods.

B.8 Respondents must be enabled to check without difficulty the identity and bona fides of the Researcher.

The professional responsibilities of researchers

B.9 Researchers must not, whether knowingly or negligently, act in any way which could bring discredit on the marketing research profession or lead to a loss of public confidence in it.

B.10 Researchers must not make false claims about their skills and experience or about those of their organisation.

B.11 Researchers must not unjustifiably criticise or disparage other Researchers.

B.12 Researchers must always strive to design research which is cost-efficient and of adequate quality, and then to carry this out to the specification agreed with the Client.

B.13 Researchers must ensure the security of all research records in their possession.

B.14 Researchers must not knowingly allow the dissemination of conclusions from a marketing research project which are not adequately supported by the data. They must always be prepared to make available the technical information necessary to assess the validity of any published findings.

B.15 When acting in their capacity as Researchers the latter must not undertake any non-research activities, for example database marketing involving data about individuals which will be used for direct marketing and promotional activities. Any such non-research activities must always, in the way they are organised and carried out, be clearly differentiated from marketing research activities.

Mutual rights and responsibilities of researchers and clients

B.16 These rights and responsibilities will normally be governed by a written Contract between the Researcher and the Client. The parties may amend the provisions of rules B.19 – B.23 below if they have agreed this in writing beforehand; but the other requirements of this Code may not be altered in this way. Marketing research must also always be conducted according to the principles of fair competition, as generally understood and accepted.

B.17 The Researcher must inform the Client if the work to be carried out for that Client is to be combined or syndicated in the same project with work for other Clients but must not disclose the identity of such clients without their permission.

B.18 The Researcher must inform the Client as soon as possible in advance when any part of the work for that Client is to be subcontracted outside the Researcher's own organisation (including the use of any outside consultants). On request the Client must be told the identity of any such subcontractor.

B.19 The Client does not have the right, without prior agreement between the parties involved, to exclusive use of the Researcher's services or those of his organisation, whether in whole or in part. In carrying out work for different clients, however, the Researcher must endeavour to avoid possible clashes of interest between the services provided to those clients.

B.20 The following Records remain the property of the Client and must not be disclosed by the Researcher to any third party without the Client's permission:

  (a) marketing research briefs, specifications and other information provided by the Client;
  (b) the research data and findings from a marketing research project

(except in the case of syndicated or multi-client projects or services where the same data are available to more than one client).

The Client has, however, no right to know the names or addresses of Respondents unless the latter's explicit permission for this has first been obtained by the Researcher (this particular requirement cannot be altered under Rule B-16).

B.21 Unless it is specifically agreed to the contrary, the following Records remain the property of the Researcher:

(a) marketing research proposals and cost quotations (unless these have been paid for by the Client). They must not be disclosed by the Client to any third party, other than to a consultant working for the Client on that project (with the exception of any consultant working also for a competitor of the Researcher). In particular, they must not be used by the Client to influence research proposals or cost quotations from other Researchers.

(b) the contents of a report in the case of syndicated research and/or multi-client projects or services when the same data are available to more than one client and where it is clearly understood that the resulting reports are available for general purchase or subscription. The Client may not disclose the findings of such research to any third party (other than his own consultants and advisors for use in connection with his business) without the permission of the Researcher.

(c) all other research Records prepared by the Researcher (with the exception in the case of non-syndicated projects of the report to the Client, and also the research design and questionnaire where the costs of developing these are covered by the charges paid by the Client).

B.22 The Researcher must conform to current agreed professional practice relating to the keeping of such records for an appropriate period of time after the end of the project. On request the Researcher must supply the Client with duplicate copies of such records provided that such duplicates do not breach anonymity and confidentiality requirements (Rule B.4); that the request is made within the agreed time limit for keeping the Records; and that the Client pays the reasonable costs of providing the duplicates.

B.23 The Researcher must not disclose the identity of the Client (provided there is no legal obligation to do so) or any confidential information about the latter's business, to any third party without the Client's permission.

B.24 The Researcher must, on request, allow the Client to arrange for checks on the quality of fieldwork and data preparation provided that the Client pays any additional costs involved in this. Any such checks must conform to the requirements of Rule B.4.

B.25 The Researcher must provide the Client with all appropriate technical details of any research project carried out for that Client.

B.26 When reporting on the results of a marketing research project the Researcher must make a clear distinction between the findings as such, the Researcher's interpretation of these and any recommendations based on them.

B.27 Where any of the findings of a research project are published by the Client, the latter has a responsibility to ensure that these are not misleading. The Researcher must be consulted and agree in advance the form and content of publication, and must take action to correct any misleading statements about the research and its findings.

B.28 Researchers must not allow their names to be used in connection with any research project as an assurance that the latter has been carried out in conformity with this Code unless they are confident that the project has in all respects met the Code's requirements.

B.29 Researchers must ensure that Clients are aware of the existence of this Code and of the need to comply with its requirements.

NOTES

How the ICC/ESOMAR International Code of Marketing and Social Research Practice should be Applied

These general notes published by ICC/ESOMAR apply to the interpretation of Section B of this Code in the absence of any specific interpretation which may be found in the MRS Definitions, in Part A of the MRS Code or in Guidelines published by the MRS. MRS members who are also members of ESOMAR will in addition be subject to requirements of the guidelines published by ESOMAR.

These Notes are intended to help users of the Code to interpret and apply it in practice.

The Notes, and the Guidelines referred to in them, will be reviewed and reissued from time to time. Any query or problem about how to apply the Code in a specific situation should be addressed to the Secretariat of MRS.

The rights of respondents

All Respondents entitled to be sure that when they agree to co-operate in any marketing research project they are fully protected by the provisions of this Code and that the Researcher will conform to its requirements. This applies equally to Respondents interviewed as private individuals and to those interviewed as representatives of organisations of different kinds.

Note on Rule B.3

Researcher and those working on their behalf (e.g. interviewers) must not, in order to secure Respondents' co-operation, make statements or promises which are knowingly misleading or incorrect – for example, about the likely length of the interview or about the possibilities of being re-interviewed on a later occasion. Any such statements and assurances given to Respondents must be fully honoured.

Respondents are entitled to withdraw from an interview at any stage and to refuse to co-operate further in the research project. Any or all of the information collected from or about them must be destroyed without delay if the Respondents so request.

Note on Rule B.4

All indications of the identity of Respondents should be physically separated from the records of the information they have provided as soon as possible after the completion of any necessary fieldwork quality checks. The Researcher must ensure that any information which might identify Respondents is stored securely, and separately from the other information they have provided; and that access to such material is restricted to authorised research personnel within the Researcher's own organisation for specific research purposes (e.g. field administration, data processing, panel or 'longitudinal' studies or other forms of research involving recall interviews).

To preserve Respondents' anonymity not only their names and addresses but also any other information provided by or about them which could in practice identify them (e.g. their Company and job title) must be safeguarded.

These anonymity requirements may be relaxed only under the following safeguards:

(a) Where the Respondent has given explicit permission for this under the conditions of 'informed consent' summarised in Rule 4 (a) and (b).
(b) where disclosure of names to a third party (e.g. a Subcontractor) is essential for any research purpose such as data processing or further interview (e.g. an independent fieldwork quality check) or for further follow-up research. The original Researcher is responsible for ensuring that any such third party agrees to observe the requirements of this Code, in writing, if the third party has not already formally subscribed to the Code.

It must be noted that even these limited relaxations may not be permissible in certain countries. The definition of 'non-research activity', referred to in Rule 4(b), is dealt with in connection with Rule 15.

Note on Rule B.5

The Researcher must explicitly agree with the Client arrangements regarding the responsibilities for product safety and for dealing with any complaints or damage arising from faulty products or product misuse. Such responsibilities will normally rest with the Client, but the Researcher must ensure that products are correctly stored and handled while in the Researcher's charge and that Respondents are given appropriate instructions for their use. More generally, Researchers should avoid interviewing at inappropriate or inconvenient times. They should also avoid the use of unnecessarily long interviews; and the asking of personal questions which may worry or annoy Respondents, unless the information is essential to the purposes of the study and the reasons for needing it are explained to the Respondent.

Note on Rule B.6

The definitions of 'children' and 'young people' may vary by country but if not otherwise specified locally should be taken as 'under 14 years' and '14 – 17 years' (under 16, and 16 – 17 respectively in the UK).

Note on Rule B.7

The Respondent should be told at the beginning of the interview that recording techniques are to be used unless this knowledge might bias the Respondent's subsequent behaviour: in such cases the Respondent must be told about the recording at the end of the interview and be given the opportunity to see or hear the relevant section of the record and, if they so wish, to have this destroyed. A 'public place' is defined as one to which the public has free access and where an individual could reasonably expect to be observed and/or overheard by other people present, for example in a shop or in the street.

Note on Rule B.8

The name and address/telephone number of the Researcher must normally be made available to the Respondent at the time of interview. In cases where an accommodation address or 'cover name' are used for data collection purposes arrangements must be made to enable Respondents subsequently to find without difficulty or avoidable expense the name and address of the Researcher. Wherever possible 'Freephone' or similar facilities should be provided so that Respondents can check the Researcher's bona fides without cost to themselves.

The professional responsibilities of researchers

This Code is not intended to restrict the rights of Researchers to undertake any legitimate marketing research activity and to operate competitively in so doing. However, it is essential that in pursuing these objectives the general public's confidence in the integrity of marketing research is not undermined in any way. This Section sets out the responsibilities which the Researcher has towards the public at large and towards the marketing research profession and other members of this.

Note on Rule B.14

The kinds of technical information which should on request be made available include those listed in the Notes to Rule B.25. The Researcher must not however disclose information which is confidential to the Client's business, nor need he/she disclose information relating to parts of the survey which were not published.

Note on Rule B.15

The kinds of non-research activity which must not be associated in any way with the carrying out of marketing research include: enquiries whose objectives are to obtain personal information about private individuals *per se*, whether for legal, political, supervisory (e.g. job performance), private or other purposes; the acquisition of information for use for credit-rating or similar purposes; the compilation, updating or enhancement of lists, registers or databases which are not exclusively for research purposes (e.g. which will be used for direct marketing); industrial, commercial or any other form of espionage; sales or promotional attempts to individual Respondents; the collection of debts; fund-raising; direct or indirect attempts, including by the design of the questionnaire, to influence a Respondent's opinions, attitudes or behaviour on any issue.

Certain of these activities – in particular the collection of information for databases for subsequent use in direct marketing and similar operations – are legitimate marketing activities in their own right. Researchers (especially those working within a client company) may often be involved with such activities, directly or indirectly. In such cases it is essential that a clear distinction is made between these activities and marketing research since by definition marketing research anonymity rules cannot be applied to them.

Situations may arise where a Researcher wishes, quite legitimately, to become involved with marketing database work for direct marketing (as distinct from marketing research) purposes: such work must not be carried out under the name of marketing research or of a marketing research Organisation as such.

The mutual rights and responsibilities of researchers and clients

This Code is not intended to regulate the details of business relationships between Researchers and Clients except in so far as these may involve principles of general interest and concern. Most such matters should be regulated by the individual business. It is clearly vital that such Contracts are based on an adequate understanding and consideration of the issues involved.

Note on Rule B.18

Although it is usually known in advance what subcontractors will be used, occasions do arise during the project where subcontractors need to be brought in, or changed, at very short notice. In such cases, rather than cause delays to the project in order to inform the Client it will usually be sensible and acceptable to let the Client know as quickly as possible after the decision has been taken.

Note on Rule B.22

The period of time for which research Records should be kept by the Researcher will vary with the nature of the project (e.g. ad hoc, panel, repetitive) and the possible requirements for follow-up research or further analysis. It will normally be longer for the stored research data resulting from a survey (tabulations, discs, tapes etc.) than for primary field records (the original completed questionnaires and similar basic records). The period must be disclosed to, and agreed by, the Client in advance. In default of any agreement to the contrary, in the case of ad hoc surveys the normal period for which the primary field records should be retained is one year after completion of the fieldwork while the research data should be stored for possible further analysis for at least two years. The Researcher should take suitable precautions to guard against any accidental loss of the information, whether stored physically or electronically, during the agreed storage period.

Note on Rule B.24

On request the Client, or his mutually acceptable representative, may observe a limited number of interviews for this purpose. In certain cases, such as panels or in situations where a Respondent might be known to (or be in subsequent contact with) the Client, this may require the previous agreement of the Respondent. Any such observer must agree to be bound by the provisions of this Code, especially Rule B.4.

The Researcher is entitled to be recompensed for any delays and increased fieldwork costs which may result from such a request. The Client must be informed if the observation of interviews may mean that the results of such interviews will need to be excluded from the overall survey analysis because they are no longer methodologically comparable.

In the case of multi-client studies the Researcher may require that any such observer is independent of any of the Clients.

Where an independent check on the quality of the fieldwork is to be carried out by a different research agency the latter must conform in all respects to the requirements of this Code. In particular, the anonymity of the original Respondents must be fully safeguarded and their names and addresses used exclusively for the purposes of back-checks, not being disclosed to the Client. Similar considerations apply where the Client wishes to carry out checks on the quality of data preparation work.

Notes on Rule B.25

The Client is entitled to the following information about any marketing research project to which he has subscribed:

(1) **Background**

- for whom the study was conducted
- the purpose of the study
- names of subcontractors and consultants performing any substantial part of the work

(2) **Sample**

- a description of the intended and actual universe covered
- the size, nature and geographical distribution of the sample (both planned and achieved); and where relevant, the extent to which any of the data collected were obtained from only part of the sample
- details of the sampling method and any weighting methods used
- where technically relevant, a statement of response rates and a discussion of any possible bias due to non-response

(3) **Data collection**

- a description of the method by which the information was collected
- a description of the field staff, briefing and field quality control methods used
- the method of recruiting Respondents; and the general nature of any incentives offered to secure their co-operation
- when the fieldwork was carried out
- (in the case of 'desk research') a clear statement of the sources of the information and their likely reliability

(4) **Presentation of results**

- the relevant factual findings obtained
- bases of percentages (both weighted and unweighted)
- general indications of the probable statistical margins of error to be attached to the main findings, and the levels of statistical significance of differences between key figures
- the questionnaire and other relevant documents and materials used (or, in the case of a shared project, that portion relating to the matter reported on).

The Report on a project should normally cover the above points or provide a reference to a readily available document which contains the information.

Note on Rule B.27

If the Client does not consult and agree in advance the form of publication with the Researcher the latter is entitled to:

(a) refuse permission for his name to be used in connection with the published findings and
(b) publish the appropriate technical details of the project (as listed in the Notes to B.25).

Note on Rule B.29

It is recommended that Researchers specify in their research proposals that they follow the requirements of this Code and that they make a copy available to the Client if the latter does not already have one.

CODELINE

Codeline is a free, confidential answer service to Market Research Society Code of Conduct related queries raised by market researchers, clients, respondents and other interested parties. The aim of Codeline is to provide an immediate, personal and practical interpretation and advice service.

Codeline is directly responsible to the MRS Professional Standards Committee (PSC) to which each query and its response is reported at PSC's next meeting. Queries from enquirers are handled by an individual member of the Codeline panel, drawn from past members of the PSC. As long as contact can be made with the enquirer, queries will be dealt with by Codeline generally within 24 hours. Where necessary, the responding Codeline member can seek further specialist advice.

Codeline's response to enquirers is not intended to be definitive but is the personal interpretation of the individual Codeline member, based on personal Code-related experience. PSC and Codeline panellists may highlight some of the queries and responses for examination and ratification by the PSC, the ultimate arbiter of the Code, at its next meeting. In the event that an individual Codeline response is not accepted by the PSC the enquirer will be notified immediately.

Enquirer details are treated as totally confidential outside the PSC but should 'Research' or any other MRS journal wish to refer to a particularly interesting or relevant query in 'Problem Page' or similar, permission is sought and obtained from the enquirer before anonymous publication and after that query's examination by PSC.

Codeline operates in the firm belief that a wide discussion of the issues arising from queries or anomalies in applying the Code and its associated guidelines within the profession will lead both to better understanding, awareness and application of the Code among members and to a better public appreciation of the ethical standards the market research industry professes and to which it aspires.

How to use Codeline

Codeline deals with any market research ethical issues. To contact Codeline please phone or fax the MRS Secretariat who will then allocate your query to a Codeline panellist.

If you choose to contact MRS by phone, the MRS Secretariat will ask you to confirm by fax the nature of your query, whether or not the caller is an MRS member or works for an organisation which employs an MRS member and a phone number at which you can be contacted. This fax will then be sent to the allocated panellist who will discuss your query directly with you by phone as soon as possible after receipt of your enquiry.

Please forward any queries about the MRS Code of Conduct and Guidelines, in writing to the:

MRS Secretariat, 15 Northburgh Street, London EC1V OJR
Tel: 020 7490 4911 Fax: 020 7490 0608

Notes

CHAPTER 1

1 Market research is now more or less recognized as a distinct profession. It is based on evolving theory and is carried out to recognized codes of practice. However, it is an unregulated profession with no restrictions on entry.

CHAPTER 2

1 If a sample of 500 is statistically likely to be accurate to plus or minus 5 per cent, what size of sample will be needed to increase the accuracy to plus or minus 2.5 per cent? It is not 1,000 but nearer 2,000 and the costs involved are possibly more than twice as high. Diminishing returns very much apply.

CHAPTER 6

1 Referred to as hall tests in Europe.
2 A hall test (a term used mainly in Europe) is a product test carried out in a rented room close to a busy shopping precinct (the room often being a church hall). Over a period of a couple of days shoppers are recruited by a team of interviewers to visit the hall and observe, taste and answer questions on a specific subject. In a couple

of days, up to 100 people could carry out the test. It is usually repeated in at least a couple of different cities. In the United States the test is usually carried out in rooms in a shopping mall and hence is known as a mall intercept test.

A clinic is a term mostly associated with researching new cars. A suitably large venue such as an exhibition centre or hotel is used to accommodate the cars, and target customers are recruited to observe and answer questions in a similar way to the hall test. The clinic is not the unique preserve of car manufacturers, and has been used by manufacturers of forklift trucks, cement mixers and mixer showers.

CHAPTER 7

1   Social grade or social class is a term used mainly in the United Kingdom, where the occupation of the respondent is used to position that person in terms of income, education and to some extent, life style.

CHAPTER 12

1   A visit to www.perseus.com is well worthwhile as the site contains sample questionnaires and tips for carrying out Web-based surveys.

CHAPTER 13

1   In the example the total mean score is calculated:
$(2 \times 25 + 1 \times 40) - (1 \times 18 + 2 \times 3) \div 100$
The neither likely nor unlikely response has been given a zero value.
2   The weighting factor is calculated by dividing the percentage of the population who are owner-occupiers by the percentage amongst the sample: $75 \div 50 = 1.50$. For tenants the corresponding calculation is $25 \div 50 = 0.50$.
3   The interval of US $340 – 345 could be further broken down – it accounts for half of all responses. However, it may be that this range is considered narrow enough within the context of the particular project.

4   To facilitate the analysis the data commonly needs collecting in a particular way, and therefore multivariate analysis of this (and any other) type must usually be planned at the questionnaire design stage.

APPENDIX

1   In particular shall not be processed unless at least one of the conditions in Schedule 2 is met, and in the case of sensitive data, at least one of the conditions of Schedule 3 is also met. (These schedules provide that in determining whether personal data has been processed fairly, consideration must be given to the basis on which it was obtained.)

Bibliography

CHAPTER 1: INTRODUCTION

Aaker, D A, Kumar, V and Day, G S (2000) *Market Research*, 7th edn, John Wiley, Chichester

Achenbaum, A A (1993) The future challenge to market research, *Marketing Research*, **5**(2), pp 12–18

Baines, P and Chanarker, B (2002) *Introducing Marketing Research*, John Wiley, Chichester

Baker, M J (1993) Look before you leap, in *Research for Marketing*, pp 1–40, Macmillan, London

Birn, R (ed) (2002) *The International Handbook of Market Research Techniques*, 2nd edn, Kogan Page, London

Bowles, T (1991) Issues facing the UK research industry, *Journal of the Market Research Society*, **33**, pp 71–81

Chisnall, P (1992) Role and development of marketing research, in *Marketing Research*, 4th edn, pp 3–22, McGraw-Hill, London

Cowan, D (1993) Understanding in market research, *Marketing Intelligence & Planning*, **11**(11), pp 9–15

Cowan, D (1994) Good information, *Journal of the Market Research Society*, **36**(2), pp 105–14

Crimp, M and Wright, L T (1995) An introduction to the marketing research process, in *The Marketing Research Process*, 4th edn, pp 1–19, Prentice-Hall, London

Demby, E H (1987) The future holds everything from better sampling to brain research, *Marketing News*, **12**(18), pp 19–20

Elliott, R and Jobber, D (1995) Expanding the market for market research, *Journal of the Market Research Society*, **37**(1), pp 143–58

Freeling, A (1994) Marketing is in crisis – can market research help?, *Journal of the Market Research Society*, **36**, pp 97–104

Gates, R H and Jarboe, G R (1987) Changing trends in data acquisition for marketing research, *Journal of Data Collection*, **27**(1), pp 25–29

Gill, J and Johnson, P (1997) *Research Methods for Managers*, Paul Chapman, London

Goodyear, J (1989) The structure of the British market research industry, *Journal of the Market Research Society*, **31**, pp 427–37

Goodyear, M (1996) Guest editorial, *Journal of the Market Research Society*, **38**(1), pp 1–6

Hague, P (2002) *Marketing Research*, 3rd edn, Kogan Page, London

Hague, P and Jackson, P (1992) *Marketing Research In Practice*, Kogan Page, London

Hooley, G J and West, C J (1984) The untapped markets for marketing research, *Journal of the Market Research Society*, **26**(4)

Jackson, P (1994) *Buying Market Research*, Kogan Page, London

Jackson, P (1997) *Quality in Market Research*, Kogan Page, London

Kent, R (1993) Perspectives on marketing research, in *Marketing Research in Action*, pp 1–21, Routledge, London

Laborie, J L (1990) Marketing research in the decade ahead, *Marketing and Research Today*, **18**(4), pp 221–26

Laitin, J A and Klaperman, B A (1994) The brave new world of marketing research, *Medical Marketing and Media*, **29**(7), pp 44–51

Lazier, W (1974) Marketing research: past accomplishments and potential future developments, *Journal of the Market Research Society*, **16**(3)

McDonald, C and Vangelder, P (eds) (1998) *ESOMAR Handbook of Market and Opinion Research*, 4th edn, ESOMAR, London

McGivern, Y (2002) *The Practice of Market and Social Research: an Introduction*, FT Prentice-Hall, London

Morello, G (1993) The hidden dimensions of marketing, *Journal of the Market Research Society*, **35**, pp 293–313

Oostveen, J and Wouters, J (1991) The ESOMAR annual market study: the state of the art of marketing research, *Marketing and Research Today*, **19**(4), pp 214–18

Proctor, T (2000) *Essentials of Market Research*, Pearson Education, Essex

Schafer, M (1990) Data collection in the UK and how it differs from the US, *Applied Marketing Research*, **30**(2), pp 30–35

Smith, D V L and Fletcher, J H (2001) *Inside Information: Making use of marketing data*, John Wiley, Chichester

CHAPTER 2: MARKET RESEARCH DESIGN

Brewer, T (1986) Don't make a move without doing research, *ABA Banking Journal*, **78**(11), pp 76–85

Butler, P (1994) Marketing problems: from analysis to decision, *Marketing Intelligence and Planning*, **12**(2), pp 4–13

Chapman, R G (1989) Problem-definition in marketing research studies, *Journal of Services Marketing*, **3**(3), pp 51–59

Chisnall, P M (2001) *Marketing Research*, McGraw-Hill Education, Europe

Czinkota, M R and Pronkinen, I A (1994) Market research for your export operations: Part I – using secondary sources of research, *International Trade Forum*, **3**, pp 22–33

Goodyear, M J (1990) Qualitative research, in *A Handbook of Market Research Techniques*, ed R Birn, P Hague and P Vangelder, Kogan Page, London

Hair, J, Bush, R and Ortinau, D (2002) *Marketing Research*, McGraw-Hill Education, Europe

McDonald, M (1992) *Marketing Plans: How to prepare them, how to use them*, Butterworth Heinemann, Oxford

Shingleton, J (1994) Black Rhino to leaping gazelle – how an integrated research programme helped rejuvenate Lex Vehicle Leasing Limited, *Journal of the Market Research Society*, **36**, pp 205–16

Smith, D and Dexter, A (1994) Quality in market research: hard frameworks for soft problems, *Journal of the Market Research Society*, **36**, pp 115–33

Stephen, E H and Soldo, B J (1990) How to judge the quality of a survey, *American Demographics*, **12**(4), pp 42–43

Weinman, C (1991) It's not 'art', but marketing research can be creative, *Marketing News*, **25**(8), pp 9–24

Yuspeh, S (1989) Dracula and Frankenstein revisited: two research ogres in need of restraint, *Journal of Advertising Research*, **29**(1), pp 53–59

CHAPTER 3: DESK RESEARCH

BECTA (1997) Information sheet on Internet searching [Online] http://www.becta.org.uk

Clausen, H (1996) Web information quality as seen from libraries, *New Library World*, **97**(1130), pp 4–8

Dale, A, Arber, S and Procter, M (1988) *Doing Secondary Research*, Unwin Hyman, London

Jackson, P (1994) *Desk Research*, Kogan Page, London

Newson-Smith, N (1986) Desk research, in *Consumer Market Research Handbook*, 3rd edn, ed R Worcester and J Downham, pp 7–27, ESOMAR, McGraw-Hill, London

Powell, T (1991) Despite myths, secondary research is a valuable tool, *Marketing News*, **25**(18), pp 28–33

Saunders, M N K and Lewis, P (1997) Great ideas and blind alleys? A review of the literature on starting research, *Management Learning*, **28**(3), pp 341–53

Stewart, D W and Kamins, M A (1993) *Secondary Research: Information sources and methods*, 2nd edn, Sage, Newbury Park, California

CHAPTER 4: FOCUS GROUPS

Bhaduri, M, de Souza, M and Sweeney, T (1993) International qualitative research: a critical review of different approaches, *Marketing and Research Today*, **2**(3), pp 171–8

Bristol, T and Fern, E (2003) The effects of interaction on consumers' attitudes in focus groups, *Psychology and Marketing*, **20**(5), pp 433–54

Budden, M (1999) Focus groups: theory and practice, *Psychology and Marketing*, **16**(4)

Byers, P Y and Wilcox, J R (1991) Focus groups: a qualitative opportunity for researchers, *Journal of Business Communication*, **28**(1), pp 63–78

Collins, L (1991) Everything is true, but in a different sense: a new perspective on qualitative research, *Journal of the Market Research Society*, **33**, pp 31–38

Colwell, J (1990) Qualitative market research: a conceptual analysis and review of practitioner criteria, *Journal of the Market Research Society*, **32**

Cooper, P (1989) Comparison between the UK and US: the qualitative dimension, *Journal of the Market Research Society*, **31**(4), pp 509–20

de Groot, G (1986) Qualitative research: deep, dangerous, or just plain dotty?, *European Research*, **14**(3), pp 136–41

Edmunds, H (1999) *The Focus Group Research Handbook*, NTC, Lincolnwood, Illinois

Ereaut, G, Imms, M and Callingham, M (eds) (2002) *Qualitative Market Research: Principle and practice*, (7 vols), Sage, London

Esser, W (1995) From the 'triad' to a 'quadriga': a systematic qualitative marketing research programme for the Far East, *Marketing and Research Today*, **23**(1), pp 20–24

Gabriel, C (1990) The validity of qualitative market research, *Journal of the Market Research Society*, **32**, pp 507–20

Glen, R (1998) New skills now, *Research*, **384**, pp 46–48

Goldman A E and MacDonald, S S (1987) *The Group Depth Interview*, Prentice-Hall, Englewood Cliffs, New Jersey

Goodyear, M (1990) Qualitative research, in *A Handbook of Market Research Techniques*, ed R Birn, P Hague and P Vangelder, p 229, Kogan Page, London

Greenbaum, T L (2000) *Moderating Focus Groups: A practical guide for group facilitation*, Sage, London

Griggs, S (1987) Analysing qualitative data, *Journal of the Market Research Society*, **29**(1), pp 15–34

Hague, P (2002) *Market Research*, 3rd edn, Kogan Page, London

Hall, J (2000) Moderators must motivate focus groups, *Marketing News*, **34**(19)

Hayward, W and Rose, J (1990) We'll meet again ... repeat attendance at group discussions – does it matter?, *Journal of the Market Research Society*, **32**, pp 377–408

Henderson, N R (1990) Focus groups for the last decade of the twentieth century, *Applied Marketing Research*, **30**(2), pp 20–22

Johnson, B C (1990) Focus group positioning and analysis: a commentary on adjuncts for enhancing the design of health care research, *Health Marketing Quarterly*, **7**(1), pp 153–68

Kaushik, M and Sen, A (1990) Semiotics and qualitative research, *Journal of the Market Research Society*, **32**, pp 227–43

Kreugar, R A (1998) *Developing Questions for Focus Groups (Focus Group Kit 3)*, Sage, Thousand Oaks, California

Kreugar, R A (1998) *Moderating Focus Groups (Focus Group Kit 4)*, Sage, Thousand Oaks, California

Kreugar, R A (1998) *Analyzing and Reporting Focus Group Results (Focus Group Kit 6)*, Sage, Thousand Oaks, California

Kreugar, R A and Casey, M A (2000) *Focus Groups: A practical guide for applied research*, 3rd edn, Sage,Thousand Oaks, California

Langer, J (2000) 'On' and 'offline' focus groups, *Marketing News*, **34**(12)

Langer, J (2001) Get more out of focus group research, *Marketing News*, **35**(20)

Lazarsfeld, P (1972) *Qualitative Analysis: Historical and critical essays*, Allyn & Bacon, Boston

Lazarsfeld, P (1986) *The Art of Asking Why*, Advertising Research Foundation, New York, (original work produced in 1934 in the *National Marketing Review*)

Lesley, Y (2001) Focus group results rule changes, *Marketing Magazine*, **106**(9)

Lonnie, K (2001) Combine phone, Web for focus groups, *Marketing News*, **35**(24)

Marks, L (1998) New horizons of qualitative research, *Research*, **384**, pp 44–45

McQuarrie, E F (1996) *The Market Research Toolbox: A concise guide for beginners*, Sage, Thousand Oaks, California

Merton, R K (1987) The focused interview and focus groups: continuities and discontinuities, *Public Opinion Quarterly*, **51**(4), pp 550–66

Merton, R K, Fiske, M and Kendall, P L (1956) *The Focused Interview*, Free Press, Glencoe, Illinois

Merton, R K and Kendall, P L (1946) The focused interview, *American Journal of Sociology*, **51**, pp 541–57

Morgan, D L (1998) *The Focus Group Guidebook (Focus Group Kit 1)*, Sage, Thousand Oaks, California

Morgan, D L (1998) *Planning Focus Groups (Focus Group Kit 2)*, Sage, Thousand Oaks, California

Morgan, D L (1997) *Focus Groups: A qualitative research*, Sage, Thousand Oaks, California

Morgan, D L (1993) *Successful Focus Groups: Advancing the state of the art*, Sage, Thousand Oaks, California

Robson, S and Hedges, A (1993) Analysis and interpretation of qualitative findings, Report of the MRS Qualitative Interest Group, *Journal of the Market Research Society*, **35**, pp 23–35

Rowan, M M (1991) Bankers beware! Focus groups can steer you wrong, *Bottomline*, **8**(4), pp 37–41

Rust, R T and Cooil, B (1994) Reliability measures for qualitative data: theory and implications, *Journal of Marketing Research*, **31**(1), pp 1–14

Ruyter, K de (1996) Focus versus nominal group interviews: a comparative analysis, *Marketing Intelligence and Planning*, **14**(6)

Sampson, P M J (1967) Commonsense in qualitative research, *Journal of the Market Research Society*, **9**(1)

Spiggle, S (1994) Analysis and interpretation of qualitative data in consumer research, *Journal of Consumer Research*, **21**(3), pp 491–503

Sweeney, J C *et al* (1997) Collecting information from groups, a comparison of methods, *Journal of the Market Research Society*, **39**(2), pp 397–411

Sykes, W (1990) Validity and reliability in qualitative market research: a review of the literature, *Journal of the Market Research Society*, **32**, pp 289–328

Sykes, W (1991) Taking stock: issues from the literature on validity and reliability in qualitative research, *Journal of the Market Research Society*, **33**, pp 3–12

Wagner, M and D'Onofrio, M (1999) How to conduct online focus groups, *Advertising Age's Business Marketing*, **84**(10)

Warren, M (1991) Another day, another debrief: the use and assessment of qualitative research, *Journal of the Market Research Society*, **33**, pp 13–18

Warren, M and Craig, A (1991) Qualitative research product and policy, *Marketing and Research Today*, **19**(1), pp 43–49

Wells, S (1991) Wet towels and whetted appetites or a wet blanket? The role of analysis in qualitative research, *Journal of the Market Research Society*, **33**, pp 39–44

Yelland, F and Varty, C (1997) DIY: consumer driven research, *Journal of the Market Research Society*, **39**(2), pp 297–315

CHAPTER 5: DEPTH INTERVIEWS

Chirban, J T (1996) *Interviewing in Depth: The interactive-relational approach*, Sage, London

Goldman, A E (1987) *The Group Depth Interview: Principles and practice*, Prentice-Hall International, London

Gummesson, E (2000) *Qualitative Methods in Management Research*, 2nd edn, Sage, Thousand Oaks, California

Gummitt, J (1980) *Interviewing Skills*, Industrial Society, London

Healey, M J (1991) Obtaining information from businesses, in *Economic Activity and Land Use*, ed M J Healey, pp 193–251, Longman, Harlow

Kahn, R and Cannel, C (1957) *The Dynamics of Interviewing*, John Wiley, New York and Chichester

Robson, C (2001) *Real World Research*, Blackwell, Oxford

Silverman, D (1998) *Qualitative Research, Theory, Method and Practice*, Sage, London

Strauss, A and Corbin, J (1990) *Basics of Qualitative Research*, Sage, Newbury Park, California

CHAPTER 6: OBSERVATION

Ackroyd, S and Hughes, J (1992) *Data Collection in Context*, 2nd edn, Longman, London

Boote, J and Mathews, A (1999) Saying is one thing; doing is another: the role of observation in marketing research, *Qualitative Market Research*, 2(1), pp 15–21

Buck, S (1990) Peoplemeters, in *A Handbook of Market Research Techniques*, ed R Birn, P Hague and P Vangelder, Kogan Page, London

Delbridge, R and Kirkpatrick, I (1994) Theory and practice of participant observation, in *Principles and Practice in Business and Management Research*, pp 35–62, Dartmouth, Aldershot

Jack, S (1996) *The Compleat observer? A field research guide to observation*, Falmer Press, London and Washington, DC

Punch, M (1993) Observation and the police the research experience, in *Social Research Philosophy Politics and Practice*, ed M Hammersley, pp 181–99, Sage, London

CHAPTER 7: SAMPLING AND STATISTICS

Baker, K (1989) Using geodemographics in market research, *Journal of the Market Research Society*, **31**, pp 37–44

Baker, M J (1991) Sampling, in *Research for Marketing*, pp 100–31, Macmillan, London

Bolton, R N (1994) Covering the market, *Marketing Research* 6(3), pp 30–35

Brown, P J B (1991) 'Exploring geodemographics', in *Handling Geographical Information*, ed I Masser and M Blakemore, pp 221–59, Longman Scientific & Technical, London

Cornish, P (1989) Geodemographic sampling in readership surveys, *Journal of the Market Research Society*, **31**, pp 45–51

Cowan, C D (1991) Using multiple sample frames to improve survey coverage, quality, and costs, *Marketing Research*, **3**(4), pp 66–69

Crimp, M and Wright, L T (1995) Sampling in survey research, in *The Marketing Research Process*, 4th edn, pp 107–31, Prentice-Hall, London

Dent, T (1992) How to design for a more reliable customer sample, *Business Marketing*, **17**(2), pp 73–77

Evans, N and Webber, R (1995) Geodemographic profiling: MOSAIC and EuroMOSAIC, in *The Market Research Process*, 4th edn, ed M Crimp and L T Wright, Prentice-Hall, London

Fish, K E, Barnes, J H and Banahan, B F (1994) Convenience or calamity? Pharmaceutical study explores the effects of sample frame error on research results, *Journal of Health Care Marketing*, **14**(1), pp 45–49

Frankel, M R (1989) Current research practices: general population sampling including geodemographics, *Journal of the Market Research Society*, **31**(4), pp 447–55

Geurts, M, Whitlark, D, Christensen, H and Lawrence, K (1994) Calculating sample sizes for population with multinominal proportions, *Marketing and Research Today*, **22**(3), pp 214–19

Gy, P M (1998) *Sampling For Analytical Purposes*, (trans A G Royle), John Wiley, Chichester

Hague, P and Harris, P (1993) *Sampling and Statistics*, Kogan Page, London

Hahlo, G (1992) Examining the validity of re-interviewing respondents for quantitative surveys, *Journal of the Market Research Society*, **34**, pp 99–118

Harris, P (1977) The effect of clustering on cost and sampling errors of random samples, *Journal of the Market Research Society*, **19**(3)

Leventhal, B (1990) Geodemographics, in *A Handbook of Market Research Techniques*, ed R Birn, P Hague and P Vangelder, Kogan Page, London

Marsh, C and Scarborough, E (1990) Testing nine hypothesis about quota sampling, *Journal of the Market Research Society*, **32**, pp 485–506

Mitchell, V W (1992) The future of geodemographic information handling, *Logistics Information Management*, **5**(3), pp 23–29

Noble, I *et al* (1998) Bringing it all back home, *Journal of the Market Research Society*, **49**(2), pp 43–120

Semon, T T (1994a) A good sample of accounts may not always be a good sample of your customers, *Marketing News*, **28**(9), pp 8–11

Semon, T T (1994b) Save a few bucks on sample size, risk millions in opportunity loss, *Marketing News*, **28**(1), p 19

Shiffler, R E and Adams, A J (1987) A correction for biasing effects of pilot sample size on sample size determination, *Journal of Marketing Research*, **24**(3), pp 319–21

Sleight, P (1993) *Targeting Customers: How to use geodemographics and lifestyle data in your business*, NTC Publications, Henley-on-Thames

Sleight, P and Leventhal, B (1989) Applications of geodemographics to research and marketing, *Journal of the Market Research Society*, **31**, pp 75–101

Swan, J E, O'Connor, S J and Seung, D L (1991) A framework for testing sampling bias and methods of bias reduction in a telephone survey, *Marketing Research*, **3**(4), pp 23–34

Watson, M A (1992) Researching minorities, *Journal of the Market Research Society*, **34**(4), pp 337–44

Whitlark, D, Geurts, M D, Christensen, H B, Kays, M A and Lawrence, K D (1993) Selecting sample sizes for marketing research surveys: advantages of using the coefficient of variation, *Marketing and Research Today*, **21**(1), pp 50–54

CHAPTER 8: QUESTIONNAIRE DESIGN

Bolton, R (1993) Pretesting questionnaires: content analyses of respondents' concurrent verbal protocols, *Marketing Science*, **12**(3), pp 280–303

Carroll, S (1994) Questionnaire design affects response rate, *Marketing News*, **28**(1), pp 14–23

Crimp, M and Wright, L T (1995) Questionnaire design, in *The Marketing Research Process*, 4th edn, pp 132–62, Prentice-Hall, London

Diamontopoulos, A, Reynolds, N and Schlegelmilch, B (1994) Pretesting in questionnaire design: the impact of respondent characteristics on error detection, *Journal of the Market Research Society*, **36**, pp 295–313

Douglas, V (1995) Questionnaire too long? Try variable, *Marketing News*, **29**(5), p 38

Fink, A (1995a) *How To Ask Survey Questions*, Sage, Thousand Oaks, California

Fink, A (1995b) *The Survey Handbook*, Sage, Thousand Oaks, California

Foddy, W (1994) *Constructing Questions for Interviews and Questionnaires*, Cambridge University Press, Cambridge

Frazer, L (2000), *Questionnaire Design and Administration: A practical guide*, John Wiley, Brisbane

Hague, P (1987) Good and bad in questionnaire design, *Industrial Marketing Digest*, **12**(3), pp 161–170

Hague, P (1993) *Questionnaire Design*, Kogan Page, London

Martin-Williams, J (1986) Questionnaire design, in *Consumer Market Research Handbook*, 3rd edn, ed R Worcester and J Downham, pp 111–45, ESOMAR, McGraw-Hill, London

Oppenheim, A (1970), *Questionnaire Design and Attitude Measurement*, Heinemann Educational, London

Payne, S (1951) *The Art of Asking Questions*, Princeton University Press, Princeton, New Jersey

Peterson, Robert (2000) *Constructing Effective Questionnaires*, Sage, London

Prunk, T (1994) The value of questionnaires, *Target Marketing*, **17**(10), pp 37–40

Reynolds, N, Diamontopoulos, A and Schlegemilch, B (1993) Pretesting in questionnaire design: a review of the literature and suggestions for further research, *Journal of the Market Research Society*, **35**, pp 171–82

Sawyer, C (1990) The art of the question: it can make or break your research effort, *Sales and Marketing in Canada*, **31**(10), pp 16–17

Sudman, S and Bradburn, N M (1982) *Asking Questions: A practical guide to questionnaire design*, Jossey-Bass, Chichester

Vittles, P (1994) Question time, *Health Service Journal* (May), pp 34–34

Wilson, N (1994) *Questionnaire Design: A practical introduction*, University of Ulster, Newtown Abbey

CHAPTER 9: FACE-TO-FACE INTERVIEWING

Guengel, P C, Berchman, T R, and Cannell, C E (1983) *General Interviewing Techniques: A self instructional workbook for telephone and personal interviewer training*, Survey Research Centre, University of Michigan, Ann Arbor

Holbrook, A L and Green, M C (2003) Telephone vs. face-to-face interviewing of national probability samples with long questionnaires: comparisons of respondent satisficing and social desirability response bias, *Public Opinion Quarterly*, **67**, pp 79–125

Torrington, D (1991) *Management Face to Face*, Prentice-Hall, London

CHAPTER 10: TELEPHONE INTERVIEWING

Anonymous (1996) Forum focuses on future of telephone interviewing, *Marketing News*, **30**(11), p 34

Collins, M, Sykes, W, Wilson, P and Blackshaw, N (1988) Non-response: the UK experience, in *Telephone Survey Methodology*, ed R M Groves *et al*, John Wiley, New York

Curry, J (1990) Interviewing by PC: what we could not do before, *Applied Marketing Research*, **30**(1), pp 30–37

Czaja, R, Blair, J and Sebestik, J P (1982) Respondent selection in a telephone survey: a comparison of three techniques, *Journal of Marketing Research*, **19**, pp 381–85

DePaulo, P and Weitzer, R (1994) Interactive phone technology delivers survey data quickly, *Marketing News*, **28**(1), p 15

Dickson, J R, Faria, A J and Frieson, D (1994) Live v automated telephone interviewing, *Marketing Research*, **6**(1), pp 28–35

Dillman, D A (1978) *Mail and Telephone Surveys: The total design method*, John Wiley, New York

Gershowitz (1990) Entering the 1990s – the state of data collection – telephone data collection, *Applied Marketing Research*, **30**(2), pp 16–19

Groves, R M (1979) *Surveys by Telephone: A national comparison with personal interviews*, Academic Press, New York and London

Havice, M J and Banks, M J (1991) Live and automated telephone surveys: a comparison of human interviews and an automated technique, *Journal of the Market Research Society*, **33**, pp 91–102

O'Rourke, D and Blair, J (1983) Improving random respondent selection in telephone interviews, *Journal of Marketing Research*, **20**, pp 428–32

Perkins, W S and Roundy, J (1993) Discrete choice surveys by telephone, *Journal of the Academy of Marketing Science*, **21**(1), pp 33–38

CHAPTER 11: SELF-COMPLETION QUESTIONNAIRES

Albaum, G (1987) Do source and anonymity affect mail survey results?, *Journal of the Academy of Marketing Science*, **15**(3), pp 74–81

Appel, V and Baim, J (1992) Predicting and correcting response rate problems using geodemography, *Marketing Research*, **4**(1), pp 22–28

Blyth, W (1990) Panels and diaries, in *A Handbook of Market Research Techniques*, ed R Birn, P Hague and P Vangelder, Kogan Page, London

Blyth, B and Piper, H (1994) Speech recognition – a new dimension in survey research, *Journal of the Market Research Society*, **36**, pp 183–203

Brehm, J (1994) Stubbing our toes for a foot in the door? Incentives and survey response, *International Journal of Public Opinion Research*, **6**(1), pp 45–64

Brennan, M, Hoek, J and Astridge (1991) The effects of monetary incentives on the response rate and cost-effectiveness of a mail survey, *Journal of the Market Research Society*, **33**, pp 229–42

Brown, M (1994) What price response?, *Journal of the Market Research Society*, **36**, pp 227–44

Faria, A J, Dickinson, J R and Filipic, T V (1990) The effect of telephone versus letter prenotification on mail survey response rate, speed, quality and cost, *Journal of the Market Research Society*, **32**, pp 551–69

Farrel, B and Elken, T (1994) Adjust five variables for better mail surveys, *Marketing News*, **28**(18), p 20

Gajari, A M, Faria, A J and Dickinson, J R (1990) A comparison of the effect of promised and provided lotteries, monetary and gift incentives on mail survey response rate, speed and cost, *Journal of the Market Research Society*, **32**, pp 141–63

Gaynor, J (1994) An experiment with cash incentives on a personal interview survey, *Journal of the Market Research Society*, **36**, pp 360–65

Helgeson, J G (1994) Receiving and responding to a mail survey: a phenomenological examination, *Journal of the Market Research Society*, **36**, pp 339–47

Kamins, M A (1989) The enhancement of response rates to a mail survey through a labelled probe foot-in-the-door approach, *Journal of the Market Research Society*, **31**(2), pp 273–83

Martin, C L (1994) The impact of topic interest on mail survey response behaviour, *Journal of the Market Research Society*, **36**, pp 327–38

Martin, W S, Duncan, W J, Powers, T L and Sawyer, J C (1989) Costs and benefits of selected response inducement techniques in mail survey research, *Journal of Business Research*, **19**(1), pp 67–79

Mason, N (1990) EPOS, in *A Handbook of Market Research Techniques*, ed R Birn, P Hague and P Vangelder, Kogan Page, London

McCarthy, T (1990) Retail audits, in *A Handbook of Market Research Techniques*, ed R Birn, P Hague, P Vangelder, Kogan Page, London

McKee, D O (1992) The effect of using a questionnaire identification code and message about non-response follow-up plans on mail survey response characteristics, *Journal of the Market Research Society*, **34**, pp 179–91

Meier, E (1991) Response rate trends in Britain, *Admap*, **26**(11), pp 41–44

Nebenzahl, I D and Jaffe, E D (1995) Fascimile transmission versus mail delivery of self-administered questionnaires in industrial surveys, *Industrial Marketing Management*, **24**(3), pp 167–75

Ratneshwar, S and Stewart, D W (1989) Nonresponse in mail surveys: an integrative review, *Applied Marketing Research*, **29**(3), pp 37–46

Schlegelmilch, B and Diamontopoulos, A (1991) Prenotification and mail survey response rates: a quantitative integration of the literature, *Journal of the Market Research Society*, **33**, pp 243–56

Schuldt, B A and Totten, J W (1994) Electronic mail v. mail survey response rates, *Marketing Research*, **6**(1), pp 36–40

Semon, T T (1994) Projecting survey results is always a problem, *Marketing News*, **28**(15), pp 17–18

Steele, T J, Schwendig, W L and Kilpatrick, J A (1992) Duplicate responses to multiple survey mailings: a problem?, *Journal of Advertising Research*, **32**(2), pp 26–33

Swires-Hennessy, E and Drake, M (1992) The optimum time at which to conduct survey interviews, *Journal of the Market Research Society*, **34**(1), pp 61–78

Tse, A, Ching, R, Ding, Y, Fong, R, Yeung, E and Au, A (1994) A comparison of the effectiveness of mail and facsimile as a survey media on response rate, speed and quality, *Journal of the Market Research Society*, **36**, pp 349–55

CHAPTER 12: E-SURVEYS

Alan, W, and Nial, L (2003) Internet based marketing research: a serious alternative to traditional research methods?, *Marketing Intelligence & Planning*, **21**(2)

Coomber, R (1997) Using the internet for survey research, *Sociological Research Online*, **2**(2) [Online] http://www.socresonline.org.uk/socresonline/2/2/2.html

De Ville, B (1995) Internet for marketing research, *Marketing Research*, **7**(3), pp 36–38

Dillman, D A and Andrew, D (1999) *Mail and Internet Surveys: The tailored design method*, 2nd edn, John Wiley, New York and Chichester

Dodd, J (1998) Market research on the Internet: threat or opportunity?, *Marketing and Research Today*, (February), pp 60–66

Neffendorf, H (1993) Survey computing in the 1990s: a technology update, *Journal of the Market Research Society*, **35**, pp 205–10

Schon, N, Mulders, S, and Dren, R (2002) On-line qualitative market research: interviewing the world at a fingertip, *Qualitative Market Research*, **5**(3)

Schonlau, M (2002) *Conducting Research Surveys via E-Mail and the Web*, Rand, Santa Monica, California

Witmer, D F, Coleman, R W and Katzman, S L (1999) From paper and pen to screen and keyboard: towards a methodology for survey research on the Internet, in *Doing Internet Research*, ed S Jones, pp 145–62, Sage, Thousand Oaks, California

CHAPTER 13: DATA ANALYSIS

Alt, M (1990) *Exploring Hyperspace: A non-mathematical explanation of multivariate analysis*, McGraw-Hill, London

Baker, K (1991) *Research for Marketing* (ch 9), Macmillan, London

Balnaves, M and Caputi, P (2001) *Introduction to Quantitative Research Methods: An investigative approach*, Sage, London

Blamires, C (1990) Segmentation, in *A Handbook of Market Research Techniques*, ed R Birn, P Hague and P Vangelder, Kogan Page, London

Byrne, D (2002) *Interpreting Quantitative Data*, Sage, London

Catterall, M and Maclaren, P (1998) Using computer software for the analysis of qualitative market research data, *Journal of the Market Research Society*, **40**(3), pp 207–22

Davies, R (1993) Statistical modelling for survey analysis, *Journal of the Market Research Society*, **35**(3), pp 235–47

Dey, I (1993) *Qualitative Data Analysis*, Routledge, London

Diamantopoulos, A (1997), *Taking the Fear out of Data Analysis: A step-by-step approach*, Dryden Press, London

Fox, J, and Long, J S (eds) (1990) *Modern Methods of Data Analysis*, Sage, Newbury Park, California

Freeman, P (1991) Using computers to extend analysis and reduce data, *Journal of the Market Research Society*, **33**(2), pp 127–36

Freeman, P and Rennolls, K (1994) Modelling methodology. Basics to neural nets – a return to ignorance?, *Journal of the Market Research Society*, **36**, pp 69–77

Funkhouser, G R, Chatterjee, A and Parker, R (1994) Segmenting samples, *Marketing Research*, **6**(1), pp 40–46

Gatty, R (1966) Multivariate analysis for marketing research: an evaluation, *Applied Statistics* (Series C), **15**(3)

Hague, P and Harris, P (1993) *Sampling and Statistics*, Kogan Page, London

Holmes, C (1986) Multivariate analysis of market research data, in *Consumer Market Research Handbook*, ed R Worcester and J Downham, pp 351–75, McGraw-Hill, London

Hooley, G (1980) A guide to the use of quantitative techniques in marketing, *European Journal of Marketing*, **14**(7)

Jackling, P (1990) Analysing data-tabulations, in *A Handbook of Market Research Techniques*, ed R Birn, P Hague and P Vangelder, Kogan Page, London

Kent, R (1993) *Marketing Research in Action*, (ch 6), Routledge, London

Michell, V W (1994) How to identify psychographic segments: part 1 & 2, *Marketing Intelligence & Planning*, **12**(7), pp 4–16

Miles, M B and Huberman, A M (1994) *Qualitative Data Analysis*, Sage, Thousand Oaks, California

Moore, K, Burbach, R and Heeler, R (1995) Using neural nets to analyze qualitative data, *Marketing Research*, **7**(1), pp 34–39

Morgan, R (1990) Modelling: conjoint analysis, in *A Handbook of Market Research Techniques*, ed R Birn, P Hague and P Vangelder, Kogan Page, London

Nichisato, S and Gaul, W (1988) Marketing data analysis by dual scaling, *International Journal of Research in Marketing*, **5**(3), pp 151–70

Owen, D (1991) Every decoding is another encoding, *Journal of the Market Research Society*, **33**(4), pp 321–33

Punj, G and Stewart, D W (1983) Cluster analysis in market research: review and suggestions for application, *Journal of Marketing Research*, **20**

Robson, S (1993) Analysis and interpretation of qualitative findings, *Journal of the Market Research Society*, **35**(1), pp 23–35

Schwoerer, J and Frappa, J P (1986) Artificial intelligence and expert systems:

any applications for marketing and marketing research?, *European Research*, **14**(4), pp 10–24

Venugopal, V and Bates, W (1994) Neural networks and statistical techniques in marketing research: a conceptual comparison, *Marketing Intelligence and Planning*, **12**(7), pp 30–38

Wells, S (1991) Wet towels and whetted appetites or a wet blanket, *Journal of the Market Research Society*, **33**(1), pp 39–44

Westwood, D *et al* (1974) The trade-off model and its extensions, *Journal of the Market Research Society*, **18**(3)

CHAPTER 14: REPORTING

Britt, S H (1971) The writing of readable research reports, *Journal of Marketing* (May)

Joseph, A (1998), *Put it in Writing: Learn how to write clearly, quickly, and persuasively*, McGraw-Hill, New York and London

Hague, P and Roberts, C (1994) *Presentations and Report Writing*, Kogan Page, London

Lane, J (1999) *Writing Clearly: An editing guide*, 2nd edn, Heinle & Heinle, Pacific Grove, California

Leigh, A (1997) *Persuasive Reports and Proposals*, Institute of Personnel and Development, London

Mohn, N C (1989) How to present marketing research results effectively, *Marketing and Research Today*, **17**(2), pp 115–18

Roman, K and Raphaelson, J (1985) *Writing That Works*, HarperCollins, New York

Sussmans, J (1991) *How to Write Effective Reports*, Gower, Aldershot

Tufte, E R (1983) *The Visual Display of Quantitative Information*, CT Graphics Press, Cheshire

Van Embden, J (1987) *Report Writing*, McGraw-Hill, London

Zwlazny, G (1991) *Say It With Charts*, Business One Irwin, Holmwood, Illinois

Index